If you have a home computer with Internet access you may:
- request an item to be placed on hold.
- renew an item that is not overdue or on hold.
- view titles and due dates checked out on your card.
- view and/or pay your outstanding fines online (over $5).

To view your patron record from your home computer click on Patchogue-Medford Library's homepage: **www.pmlib.org**

Method and Metaphysics in Maimonides'
Guide for the Perplexed

REFLECTION AND THEORY IN THE STUDY OF RELIGION SERIES
SERIES EDITOR
Theodore M. Vial, Jr., Illiff School of Theology
A Publication Series of
The American Academy of Religion
and
Oxford University Press

WORKING EMPTINESS
Toward a Third Reading of Emptiness in Buddhism and Postmodern Thought
Newman Robert Glass

WITTGENSTEIN AND THE MYSTICAL
Philosophy as an Ascetic Practice
Frederick Sontag

AN ESSAY ON THEOLOGICAL METHOD
Third Edition
Gordon D. Kaufman

BETTER THAN WINE
Love, Poetry, and Prayer in the Thought of Franz Rosenzweig
Yudit Kornberg Greenberg

HEALING DECONSTRUCTION
Postmodern Thought in Buddhism and Christianity
Edited by David Loy

ROOTS OF RELATIONAL ETHICS
Responsibility in Origin and Maturity in H. Richard Niebuhr
Melvin Keiser

HEGEL'S SPECULATIVE GOOD FRIDAY
The Death of God in Philosophical Perspective
Deland S. Anderson

NEWMAN AND GADAMER
Toward a Hermeneutics of Religious Knowledge
Thomas K. Carr

GOD, PHILOSOPHY, AND ACADEMIC CULTURE
A Discussion between Scholars in the AAR and APA
Edited by William J. Wainwright

LIVING WORDS
Studies in Dialogues about Religion
Terence J. Martin

LIKE AND UNLIKE GOD
Religious Imaginations in Modern and Contemporary Fiction
John Neary

CONVERGING ON CULTURE
Theologians in Dialogue with Cultural Analysis and Criticism
Edited by Delwin Brown, Sheila Greeve Davaney, and Kathryn Tanner

BEYOND THE NECESSARY GOD
Trinitarian Faith and Philosophy in the Thought of Eberhard Jüngel
Paul DeHart

LESSING'S PHILOSOPHY OF RELIGION AND THE GERMAN ENLIGHTENMENT
Toshimasa Yasukata

AMERICAN PRAGMATISM
A Religious Genealogy
M. Gail Hamner

OPTING FOR THE MARGINS
Postmodernity and Liberation in Christian Theology
Edited by Joerg Rieger

MAKING MAGIC
Religion, Magic, and Science in the Modern World
Randall Styers

THE METAPHYSICS OF DANTE'S COMEDY
Christian Moevs

PILGRIMAGE OF LOVE
Moltmann on the Trinity and Christian Life
Joy Ann McDougall

MORAL CREATIVITY
Paul Ricoeur and the Poetics of Moral Life
John Wall

MELANCHOLIC FREEDOM
Agency and the Spirit of Politics
David Kyuman Kim

FEMINIST THEOLOGY AND THE CHALLENGE OF DIFFERENCE
Margaret D. Kamitsuka

PLATO'S GHOST
Spiritualism in the American Renaissance
Cathy Gutierrez

TOWARD A GENEROUS ORTHODOXY
Prospects for Hans Frei's Postliberal Theology
Jason A. Springs

CAVELL, COMPANIONSHIP, AND CHRISTIAN THEOLOGY
Peter Dula
Comparative Theology and the Problem of Religious Rivalry
Hugh Nicholson

FORTUNATE FALLIBILITY
Kierkegaard and the Power of Sin
Jason A. Mahn

SECULARISM AND RELIGION-MAKING
Arvind Mandair and Markus Dressler

METHOD AND METAPHYSICS IN MAIMONIDES'
Guide for the Perplexed
Daniel Davies

Method and Metaphysics in Maimonides' *Guide for the Perplexed*

Daniel Davies

OXFORD
UNIVERSITY PRESS

OXFORD
UNIVERSITY PRESS

Oxford University Press, Inc., publishes works that further
Oxford University's objective of excellence
in research, scholarship, and education.

Oxford   New York
Auckland   Cape Town   Dar es Salaam   Hong Kong   Karachi
Kuala Lumpur   Madrid   Melbourne   Mexico City   Nairobi
New Delhi   Shanghai   Taipei   Toronto

With offices in
Argentina   Austria   Brazil   Chile   Czech Republic   France   Greece
Guatemala   Hungary   Italy   Japan   Poland   Portugal   Singapore
South Korea   Switzerland   Thailand   Turkey   Ukraine   Vietnam

Published by Oxford University Press, Inc.
198 Madison Avenue, New York, New York 10016

www.oup.com

Oxford is a registered trademark of Oxford University Press.

Library of Congress Cataloging-in-Publication Data
Davies, Daniel, 1977–
Method and metaphysics in Maimonides' Guide for the perplexed / Daniel Davies.
p. cm.
Includes bibliographical references and index.
ISBN 978-0-19-976873-8
1. Maimonides, Moses, 1135–1204. Dalalat al-ha'irin.   2. Mysticism—Judaism.
3. Jewish philosophy.   4. Philosophy, Medieval.   I. Title.
BM545.D35D38 2011
181'.06—dc22   2010044085

9 8 7 6 5 4 3 2 1

Printed in the United States of America
on acid-free paper

CONTENTS

Acknowledgments   *vii*

Introduction   *1*

1. Interpreting Maimonides in His Multiple Contexts   *5*

2. A Dialectical Topic: Creation   *26*

3. Necessity and the Law   *43*

4. Religious Language (A):
   Negative Theology and Divine Perfections   *54*

5. Religious Language (B):
   Perfections and Simplicity   *68*

6. Religious Language (C):
   God's Knowledge as a Divine Perfection   *85*

7. "Secrets of the Torah": Ezekiel's Vision of the Chariot   *106*

8. The Scope and Accuracy of Ezekiel's Prophecy   *134*

9. "A Kind of Conclusion"   *155*

Note on References   *161*
Notes   *163*
Bibliography   *199*
Index   *211*

ACKNOWLEDGMENTS

In my life of learning so far, I have been fortunate to come across wonderful teachers who have in some way influenced this book. Avraham Stein introduced me to the world of Jewish philosophy and taught me that it is possible to strive for intellectual honesty within the tradition. My undergraduate tutor at the University of Birmingham, Gerard Norton, played an important role in encouraging my academic career. I was also fortunate to be taught by Karen Kilby, whose continuing advice has been welcome. Denys Turner was an inspirational teacher then and continued to be an influence during my time in Cambridge.

The present work grew out of my doctoral thesis, which was funded by the Arts and Humanities Research Board. I thank my supervisor, Tony Street, for the role he played in helping me bring that to fruition. His suggestions almost always proved fruitful and pushed me just enough to stimulate me without making me feel too overwhelmed. His positive attitude and patient reassurance and encouragement were no less important than his willingness to read closely everything I presented him with and also to offer insightful comments, no matter what the standard. I would also like to acknowledge Nicholas de Lange's help. I was able to rework much of the thesis while holding a Spalding Visiting Fellowship at Clare Hall, Cambridge, and I thank the staff and fellowship there for a wonderful experience. Between thesis and book, a number of people have helped out. Peter Adamson and George Wilkes both offered some helpful criticisms and advice. Kenneth Seeskin reviewed the manuscript, and his suggestions were extremely useful. An anonymous reviewer saved me from some errors. I am particularly grateful to David Burrell for all of his support, both personal and professional, and for encouraging my project. Thanks also to Ted Vial for accepting the manuscript into his series.

So many people have touched my personal life over the course of this book's creation. They have taught me things, often unwittingly, either about myself or about others, or have helped contribute in some way to the work, as well as broadening my horizons. I cannot note them all, but some deserve particular mention. I would particularly like to thank Ben Outhwaite and all of the members of the Taylor-Schechter Genizah Research Unit, who provided me with the ideal first "postdoc" position and a wonderful working environment. Omar Alí-de-Unzaga's help and friendship were also invaluable. The entire Shocket family deserves a special mention, especially Gloria and Stuart for their incredible hospitality over the years.

My family as a whole has always been supportive and understanding. I thank Aunty Reeva and Uncle Leslie for their comforting, constant presence, Adam and Shlomit for their hospitality and attitude, Emma and Daniel for their kindness and care, and, of course, Josh, Ari, Noam, Miri, and Eitan, who are always such fun.

Mere acknowledgment seems to belittle my parents' contribution. They are more loving and generous than any of their children have a right to expect. At times, their giving natures seem inexhaustible, and it is often difficult to know how to show thanks. I do not need to articulate my appreciation of them, although it is far too rarely expressed. I dedicate this book to the memory of my darling mum, who passed away while I was reviewing the edited files.

Introduction

Moses Maimonides' *Guide for the Perplexed* is often considered the high point of medieval Jewish Aristotelianism. Its influence was so great that post-Maimonidean medieval Jewish philosophy was almost always written with reference to the "Master of the *Guide*," whether the later author supported or opposed his views. Ever since the *Guide* appeared toward the end of the twelfth century, there have been competing interpretations of its meaning. The work abounds with unnamed references and allusions, inchoate ideas, and laconic explanations. Apparent or real contradictions confront the reader in numerous places, and solutions to the many difficulties in interpreting the work are still debated today. Such debates are apparent in the scholarly discussions of Maimonides' true metaphysical opinions. Metaphysics encompasses several themes that are central to the *Guide*, but there is no consensus about what Maimonides' real beliefs about them were or about how he expressed them. The overarching theme of this book is Maimonides' multiple methods of communication, which I consider through novel readings of key issues in the *Guide*: creation, God's existence, God's attributes, divine knowledge, biblical exegesis. In studies of Maimonides, these topics are often considered in isolation from one another. I argue that they are interrelated and that in order to understand Maimonides' arguments, we must consider them together, within the context of the *Guide* as a whole. Doing so throws light on the way in which Maimonides wrote the *Guide* and on the arguments he advances.

One of the terms commonly used to refer to metaphysics is "divine science" (*'ilm al-ilāhi*), a name that reflects its perceived exalted status among the different branches of philosophy. Rational thought builds toward metaphysics and there reaches its peak. For various reasons, though, it is not the subject that Maimonides, or, indeed, other medieval thinkers, would have used to introduce philosophy. There are preparatory sciences that train the prospective metaphysician's mind, such as mathematics, logic, and astronomy. Only after mastering these disciplines was a student considered qualified to progress to more difficult subjects. The same point is made by the rabbinic tradition of which Maimonides is a part: there are matters that can only be understood by those who undertake the requisite training.

For someone who is trying to provide a commentary on the most important teachings of the rabbinic tradition, particularly if he considers such teachings to be those taught by metaphysics, this didactic program causes problems. An author needs to take into account both the proper interpretations of the texts, as he sees them, and the appropriate way to display those interpretations to the public, some members of which will be on different rungs of the educational ladder from others. This is the situation Maimonides finds himself in when setting out to write the *Guide*. He states that his aim is to comment on texts that are written in parables. But he thinks that they are written in parables for a reason. In his commentary, then, he needs to explain the deeper meaning of scripture in a way that opens it out to the kinds of people who in earlier times would have been able to uncover it without his help. However, he needs to do so in a way that does not reveal too much to those unprepared and to whom the parabolic nature of scripture is intended to communicate a surface meaning only. Effectively, he tries to imitate the Torah and the rabbinic tradition by communicating through this one book to people of numerous different levels. If he succeeds, what he takes to be the message of the Torah and the rabbinic tradition is transformed into an idiom that is useful in Maimonides' own age. As he writes in his introduction, "my goal is that the truth should flash out and then be concealed so as not to oppose the divine goal, which one cannot possibly oppose, which placed those truths particular to knowledge of God, beyond the general populace, as is said 'the Lord's secret is for the Godfearing.'"[1]

Part of the aim of this book is to explain how Maimonides goes about achieving his goal. The *Guide* is a multilayered commentary on a multilayered text. It is written with multiple levels of meaning and using a variety of registers of discourse, because Maimonides thinks that both the Bible and rabbinic literature are also written in such a way. He attempts to duplicate the different levels in his own work, because he thinks that scripture is written with all of those meanings in mind. After all, the sages teach that "there are seventy aspects to the Torah."[2] From the point of view of the aims of the *Guide*, what is important is less the inner meaning of the *Guide* than the inner meaning of scripture, and Maimonides attempts to express to the worthy what he takes that inner meaning to be.

Perhaps inevitably, there are many competing interpretations of the *Guide*, a variety of which are often called esoteric. Much of the impetus for the different esoteric readings of the *Guide* stems from the work itself and from this attempt to imitate the rabbinic tradition. A number of statements appear to support the view that Maimonides has something to hide. Furthermore, at the end of the introduction to part one, he states that he intends to contradict himself in two different ways and that the contradictions should not be easy to detect. These contradictions and the way in which Maimonides intends his treatise to be used as a companion and teacher to the tradition, rather than a summation of knowledge found in it, will be explained in greater detail in chapter 1 of this book. In this context, I will also consider the different ways in which the *Guide* has been read and the various messages it is said to possess. Because the secondary literature on Maimonides is vast, the writings about individual metaphysical doctrines will be considered along with the doctrines themselves, rather than in the first chapter.

Over the course of recent decades, scholars have come to a greater appreciation of the role that dialectic plays in the *Guide*. Nevertheless, disagreements over how exactly it is used and what the consequences are for Maimonides' position remain. It is clear that some of the discussions in the *Guide* proceed in dialectical fashion, but how much that recognition explains is debated. In the first chapter, besides discussing the different ways in which Maimonides has been interpreted, I pay attention to the ways in which dialectic has been said to play a role in the *Guide*. I argue that it accounts for some of the perceived esotericism. Maimonides places strict limits on the ability of reason to demonstrate that certain beliefs are true or false. In these situations, he uses dialectic to support a particular position. In chapter 2, I show how such an aspect of dialectic is apparent in the discussion of creation. In this case, contradictions can be explained as results of dialectical methods of writing and arguments, rather than evidence that the author holds an esoteric view opposed to his apparent view. Chapter 3 expands on some of the issues raised and addresses the dialectical evidence that Maimonides offers for his position.

But that is not the only reason for perceived inconsistencies. Another is the pedagogical way of writing that Maimonides uses in order to prod his students into progressing at an appropriate pace. From discussions in which this is apparent, some have concluded that Maimonides holds some positions that are opposed to others that he also holds. In opposition to these interpreters, I think that Maimonides would have considered coherence to be a necessary condition of truth, although on its own, it would not be a sufficient condition. Indeed, this is what allows him to assert the truth of the law's view regarding a number of issues. The position that Maimonides advances is in itself coherent, although sometimes it is difficult to see how. The student is left to think the matter through on the basis of Maimonides' hints and pointers. This accounts for some apparent contradictions and aids Maimonides' effort to imitate the tradition by teaching according to the needs of a student. Chapters 4, 5, and 6 consider an issue in which Maimonides leaves much work for the reader to do. Specifically, when he discusses the divine nature, he does not go into as much detail as he might. I suggest a way to reconcile supposed contradictions so that the apparent meaning of the *Guide* can be preserved. The positions that Maimonides puts forward are interconnected and implied by his arguments for creation. They are therefore connected to the discussion in chapters 2 and 3.

The philosophical positions that Maimonides espouses are his own. He ought to be taken at face value when he says that he believes in doctrines such as creation. However, he ought also to be taken at face value when he says that there are matters he wishes to hide and ways in which he contradicts himself. It seems, then, that to take Maimonides at his word would entail a rejection of his word, and that is something that requires some explanation. Some scholars have emphasized that the *Guide* is first and foremost a commentary on scripture. The discussions mentioned so far do not obviously fit into this mold. In chapters 7 and 8, I explain how Maimonides interpreted the "account of the chariot" (*ma'aseh merkabah*) at the beginning of Ezekiel. Ezekiel's narrative is crucial, since it is traditionally taken to be the deepest of all "secrets of the Torah." Furthermore, *ma'aseh merkabah* is a term that Maimonides uses to refer to metaphysical speculation. These chapters also illustrate the way in which Maimonides uses hints and pointers to interpret parts of scripture. Recognizing that in explanations of passages like this Maimonides employs one of the contradictions mentioned in his introduction facilitates a new reading of the *Guide*. The *Guide* is a book with a number of different "inner" meanings, reflecting the multiple "inner" meanings of scripture itself. There are contradictions between different explanations of scripture because the messages of those parts of scripture are not all equal.

The overall message I wish to present concerns the way in which Maimonides' *Guide* should be read. My reading argues that a coherent metaphysical view emerges from the pages of the *Guide* and that all of the various doctrines treated need to be considered together as a whole. Independent study is necessary because Maimonides considers it important that students work through the issues he discusses on their own. Only then can they be considered worthy of the knowledge he imparts. That is one reason the *Guide* is written in a manner that makes it difficult to understand, but the presence of dialectical and pedagogical techniques is not the only way in which the *Guide* is esoteric. Maimonides also states that there are times when discussions proceed on the basis of different premises. I wish to show that these discussions reflect the different views present in scripture according to Maimonides' interpretation of the sacred texts. Scripture contains a variety of worldviews, which begin from different starting points, although each one might be coherent in itself. In order to reflect the different views of scripture, Maimonides' own explanations will be varied.

CHAPTER 1

Interpreting Maimonides in His Multiple Contexts

1.1 MAIMONIDES' LIFE

Moses Maimonides was born in Córdoba in the Hebrew year 4898 (1137/1138). For the most part, "Sefarad" was a place in which Jews lived comfortably among the Muslim and Christian majorities and produced many important works. There was an increase in Hebrew literature, including the development of great poetry, and contact with the Arabic tradition facilitated philosophical activity. Córdoba had been under Almoravid rule since 1085. They afforded the Jews some security and toleration, though less than previous dynasties had granted. In 1148, both their rule and the toleration came to an end when the city was conquered by the more fanatical Almohad group from Morocco. Maimonides then left Córdoba and fled with his family to Fez, after a period wandering around Andalusia. Eventually, Maimonides settled in Egypt, where he spent most of his life. There he became an important figure, revered through much of the Jewish world and influential outside it, too, an influence apparent in the role he played in helping free captives held in Jerusalem by the Crusaders. From the corpus of medical works he wrote, it is clear that Maimonides was an important doctor. He was the royal physician in Saladin's court and also taught medicine. Maimonides remained in Egypt, where he served as "head of the Jews," until his death in 1204.[1]

1.2 THE MAJOR RELIGIOUS WORKS

Maimonides' literary output was substantial. In 1168, he completed his first major work, a running commentary on the Mishnah (CM) designed to open up the discussions of the Tannaim to the wider Jewish population by explaining their meaning in Judeo-Arabic.[2] Although it is chiefly concerned with *halaḳic* matters, CM contains explicitly philosophical sections, including the "Eight Chapters on Ethics," which is Maimonides' introduction to Ethics of the Fathers, and the famous thirteen principles which were influential on later Jewish doctrines and an abridged version of which are now included in the prayer book.[3]

Within the Jewish community, the most famous and influential of Maimonides' works is the Mishneh Torah (MT), a compendium of *halaḳah* comprising fourteen books. This work was innovative in a number of ways. Maimonides attempted to encompass the entire *halaḳah* within it in clear Hebrew, thereby making laws previously available only to Talmudic scholars accessible to all and allowing people to learn them more easily.[4] MT also includes occasional brief philosophical sections, most notably the very first section, "Laws of the Foundations of the Torah."[5]

Maimonides also wrote the *Guide for the Perplexed* (*Dalālat al-Ḥā'irīn*), completed around 1190, during this period. The *Guide* is often considered his major philosophical work, and it is the book for which he is best known outside the Jewish community.[6] Since its publication, the *Guide* has been the subject of much controversy. This can partially be explained by the author's reputation, indicated by the famous elegy "From Moses until Moses there were none like Moses," as a result of which he is often quoted approvingly by thinkers with very different beliefs, thinkers as diverse as the ḥasid Shneur Zalman of Liadi on the one hand and Moses Mendelssohn on the other.[7] Later strands of Judaism often want to claim Maimonides the philosopher as their own hero and interpret him in the necessary manner.[8] When a thinker perceives opinions with which he or she disagrees in the *Guide*, explanations are offered.[9] Reluctance to accept that such an authoritative figure adopted a stance contrary to that which the interpreter adheres to gave rise to differing interpretations. For example, in order to explain Maimonides' writing the *Guide*, many kabbalists say that he changed his mind after its completion.[10] Alternatively, it may be asserted that similarities between the Zohar and Maimonides' own works indicate that he was familiar with kabbalah. If the traditional date of the Zohar's origin, which places it in the second century, is accepted, such evidence may be considered persuasive. However, scholars consider the Zohar to be post-Maimonidean, and in that case, the influence would have occurred in the other direction.[11] Maimonides was aware of earlier protokabbalistic ideas that would have influenced the Zohar and often opposed them.[12]

Nevertheless, reaction to the "great eagle" has not always been positive. During his lifetime, Maimonides was forced to defend himself from a charge that he did not hold a belief that was considered by some, including, at least ostensibly, Maimonides himself, to be an essential dogma of Judaism: the resurrection of the dead.[13] Resurrection is the last of the thirteen principles of faith outlined in CM. However, it is the one principle that he does not explain in detail when he lists them; he simply states that it has already been explained. Earlier, he says that resurrection is for the righteous alone, who, even when dead, are called living. By contrast, the wicked are considered dead even when alive. The only other time Maimonides repeats this idea is when he explains the term *life* in the *Guide*, where it is given an allegorical interpretation, and he uses the same rabbinic prooftext. Some draw the conclusion that resurrection is to be understood allegorically.[14] This particular problem exploded in the 1230s, around the same time as the *Guide* was burned in Montpellier.[15] Ever since, his views have aroused controversy at one time or another. At one point, it seems that a rumor circulated alleging that he was reincarnated in the body of a worm as punishment for his rationalism.[16] In the nineteenth century, Luzzato went as far as questioning whether Maimonides had indeed written the *Guide*.[17] Clearly, interpretations of Maimonides often depend on the religious stance of the interpreter.

1.2.1 Relationship between the *Guide* and Maimonides' Earlier Works

One of the issues that has puzzled commentators is the relationship between the *Guide* and the previous works. Some have argued that the *Guide* presents a philosophical system so opposed to the *halakic* Judaism contained in MT that the views Maimonides presents in the respective works must be distinguished from one another. Different impressions given by those works of what his philosophical views are have sometimes been partially explained by discriminating between the aims of his early, popular works, intended for all, and the later, "esoteric" *Guide*, aimed at the elite.

Following Leo Strauss, a number of interpreters assert that there is an unbridgeable gap between Judaism and philosophy.[18] According to this view, each represents a coherent system, but they cannot be honestly reconciled. It is then argued that Maimonides could not have tried to reconcile the two, since he was a great philosopher and must have realized that such a task was impossible. Consequently, an interpreter may construct different positions from different parts of the *Guide*, characterize one as religious and another as philosophical, and assert the presence of inconsistencies and contradictions.[19] Maimonides is then presumed to have affirmed only one of the two contradictory positions, usually that which the scholar deems more radical and therefore more in need of concealment. It is tempting to put the sharp division between religion and philosophy down to a modern enlightenment ideology, which was a reaction against religious authority and obscurantism in favor of rational thought and empirical investigation, and argue that it is read back into Maimonides.[20] However, a similar way of reading the *Guide* has a long history among Hebrew commentators, which predates the enlightenment and stretches back to the thirteenth century.[21]

There is no simple division between MT and the *Guide* along these lines, though, so the perceived conflict does not explain the differences between them, at least not immediately. On the contrary, there is evidence that Maimonides presents his philosophical views in MT, though without explaining them fully. Furthermore, the philosophical notions in MT are presented in such a way as to be acceptable to a number of different audiences. Despite the apparent radical nature of some of the doctrines presented, traditional believers would consider those doctrines traditional because of the vocabulary and style in which Maimonides expresses them in MT. The wise, however, would understand the true meaning of the doctrines.[22] Nevertheless, it is worth dwelling briefly on the relationship between the philosophy in the earlier and later works as an introduction to consideration of the *Guide* itself.[23]

The continuity between Maimonides' works has led scholars to use CM and MT as hermeneutic tools to interpret the *Guide*, an approach that holds immediate attraction, since the earlier works are clearer than the *Guide* on philosophical issues, even if their explanations are brief. However, contrasting conclusions are drawn from the attempt to interpret the *Guide* in the light of CM and MT. Neither of those conclusions considers the plain meaning of both Maimonides' early and later works to reflect his entire meaning. One argues that the position stated clearly in MT should be taken as Maimonides' true opinion. The other argues that it represents what Maimonides wished to teach the masses, rather than a full explanation of his own position, which is to be found in the *Guide*. On the one hand, then, Maimonides has been taken to present his own opinions in open fashion in his earlier works, while disguising them in the *Guide*. For example, there are times when Maimonides' openly stated positions in MT appear to be closer to those positions he associates with Aristotle in the *Guide* but which he himself rejects. According to Shlomo Pines, Maimonides reveals his true opinion in the *Guide* but only to those capable of understanding it, while he reveals that opinion openly in MT.[24] Pines uses the example of Maimonides' proof for God's existence. In MT, Maimonides offers the statement that "the sphere rotates eternally" (*ha-galgal soḇeḇ tamid*) as a premise for his proof that there must be a Prime Mover. From this, Pines concludes that Maimonides presents Aristotle's version of the eternity of the world as his own. In the *Guide*, on the other hand, that view seems to be rejected, but in truth, according to Pines, it is accepted.[25] On the other hand, it has been argued that the earlier works represent a less sophisticated position that must be ultimately rejected, as becomes apparent to the student of the *Guide*. For example, Heidi Ravven applies this principle to show that Maimonides' presentation of the prophetic phenomenon in the *Guide* would be more difficult, and perhaps harmful, for the average believer than the position in MT.[26] This is so even though the position of CM and MT is closer to Aristotle's, as presented in the *Guide*, than it is to Maimonides' own position.

1.2.2 Differences between *Fiqh* and *Kalām*

The sparse character of Maimonides' explanations in MT and the contrasting sophistication of the *Guide* may be explained by the diverse natures of the two works. Lawrence Berman argues that the differences between the *Guide* and MT should be understood against the background of Alfarabi's account of religious work.[27] According to Berman, who elaborates on one of Strauss's observations, the *Guide* is a work of dialectical theology (*kalām*), while MT is a work of jurisprudence (*fiqh*). Both of these are examples of religious writings, which, in Alfarabi's system, are inferior to works of demonstrative philosophy. Philosophical knowledge represents truth as it is, and religious knowledge is part of a progression toward that truth. Because of the different functions that jurisprudence and theology play in a religious community, there are differences between the two works. It is therefore to be expected that the theological doctrines appearing in the *Guide* should be more sophisticated than those in MT. Berman successfully establishes that the *Guide* is a work of *kalām* and explains the meaning of such a statement within the context of Alfarabi's understanding of religion in general and of Maimonides' application of that to Judaism. Even so, when the idea is used as a key to understanding Maimonides' doctrines, the assertion has been interpreted in a number of ways, drawing various meanings from the *Guide*.

1.2.3 The *Guide* as *Kalām* and Esoteric Readings

One way that Berman's insight has been employed is in favor of the view that Maimonides applies Alfarabi's system because he accepts Alfarabi's thought as a whole. Some evidence for this approach may be taken from the fact that Maimonides wrote a letter to his translator, ibn Tibbon, in which he praises Alfarabi's works, saying that they are "faultlessly excellent."[28] This has been taken as an affirmation by Maimonides of Alfarabi's doctrines in general, as if Maimonides agrees with Alfarabi on all issues.[29] According to such a line of argument, because the *Guide* aims at strengthening adherence to religion, it must be written in a way that serves such a purpose. In this context, the distinction often made between two coherent overall positions, one of which is a traditional religious position while the other is closer to Aristotle's, is said to be present in the *Guide*. It is presumed that the hidden doctrine would be the position closer to the philosophers and farther from the sensibilities of average religious believers.[30] The writer needs to hide such positions in order to protect himself from charges of heresy and also in order to protect the simplistic belief of the masses.

A reader who is aware of how demonstrations work will be able to understand that demonstrative philosophy is true and that the dialectical arguments are inferior. On this account, while the *Guide* may use dialectical arguments, the educated reader will know that they are not meant to replace demonstrations. Therefore, the doctrines advanced in the *Guide* would then be representative of a certain level of truth but not of the ultimate level, and Maimonides' real position may then be seen to be in accord with that of Alfarabi. When he appears to adopt positions contrary to those adopted with certainty (*yaqīn*) by Alfarabi, the reason is to be found in the nature and aim of a work of *kalām*. Maimonides' true position would then accord with that represented by the higher level of knowledge gained through demonstrations.[31] However, the evidence from the letter to ibn Tibbon is not unequivocal, and his comment there does not necessitate such a view. Even though Maimonides praises Alfarabi's work with such a glowing reference, his own arguments, and the positions he adopts, should not be ignored. Maimonides must be allowed to speak for himself.[32]

In light of the description of the *Guide* as a work of *kalām,* some interpreters attempt to allow Maimonides to do exactly that, while preserving his "true" affinity with the views of the *falāsifa*. This way of interpretation could accept that the *Guide* exhibits many dialectical traits while identifying hints, which show that Maimonides accepts a view closer to demonstrative philosophy.[33] Given that *kalām* is supposed to lead to increasingly certain knowledge, Maimonides would have written a book that intends not only to represent the dialectical position but also to lead the reader to a greater philosophical understanding, ultimately in agreement with demonstration. In order to detect what is behind the explicit "exoteric" opinion and penetrate toward the perceived inner, philosophical depths of the *Guide*, a number of sophisticated literary methods of identifying hints toward such deeper positions are expounded. For example, sometimes Maimonides is said to have distinguished between a "we" position, which is what he attributed to the community as a whole, and a more sophisticated "I" position. In this case, they may both be different from the "philosopher's" position, but Maimonides' own opinion still remains obscure unless the reader pays close attention to the author's style.[34]

Another popular approach is to focus on the lists in the *Guide*. For example, Leonard Kravitz argues that the list of seven contradictions that Maimonides outlines in his introduction hints at the importance of lists in the *Guide* in general.[35] Maimonides presents the contradictions as a method of explaining things that should not be explained to everyone. Because there are things that must remain hidden, the contradictions cannot exhaust the instruction that is revealed to the careful reader, since Maimonides openly states to all his readers that they are a key. Kravitz concludes that their presence in a list is what Maimonides reveals. Furthermore, he argues, the fact that the relevant contradictions are the antepenultimate and the final members of the list indicates that the reader should pay special attention to the antepenultimate and the final members of all lists in the *Guide*.[36] Kravitz uses other types of hints, which, he believes, facilitates a reading of the *Guide* that portrays Maimonides as an adherent of positions he ostensibly rejects.

A similar, influential, literary method of reading the *Guide* is advanced by Abraham Nuriel. He focuses on the individual words that Maimonides uses, considers the context in which certain key words appear, and argues that the use and context of such words reveal Maimonides' true opinion. This opinion is often contrary to that which is openly stated.[37] In Maimonides' instruction to pay careful attention to every word used in the *Guide* and his statement that no word appears out of place, Nuriel's method may find clear support from within the *Guide* itself.[38] Nuriel points out the importance of paying attention to Maimonides' terminology. However, such attention should not compromise that given to understanding the arguments involved. In response, one may focus instead on the coherence of the positions that Maimonides advances, and attention should be paid to the arguments and how they are made.[39] In this vein, much recent work has explained Maimonides' use of *kalām* in such a way that it explains perceived inconsistencies rather than generating them.

If an interpreter propounds an esoteric reading of the *Guide*, the attitude that must be taken toward the claim that it is *kalām* is expressed by Warren Zev Harvey: "In Berman's view the *Guide* is kalamic with regard to the vulgar reader, but philosophic with regard to the elite reader. If this is Berman's view, I have no quarrel with it."[40] Nevertheless, Harvey seems to presume that Maimonides thought that philosophy is capable of reaching demonstrations regarding every important metaphysical issue. Harvey's assertion is too bold, since he divorces *kalām* from philosophy rather than seeing it as a part of philosophical discourse. In response to such assertions as this, scholars have explained that greater understanding of the role of dialectical theology in Maimonides' work explains the issues that are raised by esoteric readings. A feature of *kalām* works is that they use dialectic (*jadalīya*), which is less certain than demonstrative philosophy (*burhānīya*). Harvey's opposition of *kalām* and philosophy presumably distinguishes between dialectic and demonstrative philosophy. While he is right to say that dialectic is considered inferior to demonstration, his account diminishes the important role dialectic plays in philosophical discourse, particularly in the *Guide*. Maimonides was happy to use dialectic, although he took the dialectical theologians (*mutakallimūn*) to task for misusing it.[41]

1.2.4 The *Guide* as *Kalām:* A Response to Esotericism

This book supports the opinion that recognizing that dialectic is used extensively in the *Guide* does not entail the view that Maimonides hides an esoteric doctrine but, on the contrary, explains some problems in Maimonides scholarship that may otherwise be seen to indicate the presence of such a doctrine. Such a view has been argued by a number of scholars, though with different emphases. In opposition to esoteric readings, Joel Kraemer argues that lack of appreciation of the nature of Aristotelian dialectic has led scholars to raise "false issues" concerning Maimonides' "true" opinion.[42] Dialectic is not the exclusive property of the theologians. The reasons any thinker may use it need to be considered.

Dialectical examination of arguments helps assess the worth of the arguments. Nevertheless, dialectical argument is inferior to demonstration. When dialectical arguments are used in the *Guide*, the positions that Maimonides argues for are often supported by evidence that has a dialectical level of certainty. In these cases, Maimonides does not assent to the position in question with as much certainty as when he thinks that a demonstration is available. A dialectical argument may be distinguished from a demonstrative argument according to the type of premises it employs. Whereas a demonstration is based on apodictic premises, a dialectical argument is based on acceptable premises.[43] In Maimonides' opinion, such premises are available either as generally accepted opinions (*mašhūrāt*) or as premises based on the authority of tradition (*taqlīd*), so they are beliefs based on the consensus of the wise or the wider community, or beliefs received from trusted sources.[44] When he openly states that no demonstration is available, he uses evidence based on acceptable premises. In some discussions, he begins by clarifying the different possibilities and considering their conclusions. He then offers evidence from other doctrines to support one of them.

In Maimonides' scheme, as with those of other medieval Arabic philosophers, dialectical arguments perform an important philosophical role. He explicitly uses dialectical manners of argument on a number of occasions. One of the ways in which a dialectical discussion may proceed is by examining different positions in order to establish what follows from their premises. The premises can then be judged according to what they necessarily entail. Furthermore, if the truth value of the premises is unknown, different positions can be compared according to their conclusions and their consistency with other positions. This is particularly useful when there is a reason to accept or reject those other positions, since it provides a criterion for accepting or rejecting the premises being considered.

A feature of the *Guide* that indicates its dialectical nature is the presence of discussions that proceed in dialectical fashion. During these discussions, the different options are presented and then examined. Maimonides then assents to one of the positions on the basis of evidence that possesses a dialectical level of certainty. Although he does not present his conclusions as being as certain as those based on demonstrative premises, he accepts the positions that are supported by the most important dialectical evidence.[45] Since there are areas in which no demonstration is available, dialectical evidence has an important role to play in deciding what is accepted as true.[46]

The reason Maimonides uses dialectical methods is disputed. Even among those who do not believe that Maimonides hides a metaphysical doctrine from the masses, different explanations are given for the presence of dialectic and its consequences for understanding the *Guide*. Different positions will be discussed in greater detail during the course of this book. I will argue that Maimonides uses dialectical methods of expressing his opinions for a number of reasons. In addition to the need to use dialectical premises when no demonstration is available, then, Maimonides employs dialectic for further reasons. An examination of the introduction to the *Guide* will help to clarify them.

1.3   THE INTRODUCTION TO THE *GUIDE FOR THE PERPLEXED*

I noted above that Maimonides' status has contributed to the proliferation of different explanations of his meaning. Lack of understanding of dialectical writing has also caused confusion. The *Guide* lends itself to diverse interpretations because of the way it is written. Esoteric accounts such as those outlined above often take their cue from Maimonides' introduction, so I now turn to an examination of the introduction itself.

1.3.1   Imitating Oral Discussion: Teaching and Withholding

The *Guide* begins with a personal address to a student, Joseph ibn Judah.[47] Maimonides writes that he intends the work as a whole to be a continuation of the study that Joseph has already begun, indicating that it is supposed to replace personal instruction. As Kraemer points out, the "literary genre and rhetorical style" of the work are indications of its dialectical character and indicate a reason that Maimonides employs a dialectical writing style.[48] Specifically, one of the advantages oral teaching has over written instruction, particularly when it is directed toward an individual student, is that the teacher may choose what to tell the student and in how much detail. Given the choice, Maimonides would prefer to adopt such a method, but he is aware that it is impossible. His student is no longer in close proximity, nor are others whom the *Guide* may help. Nevertheless, he attempts to write the *Guide* in a way that imitates oral instruction by explaining its contents to each reader according to the reader's own ability. Accordingly, Maimonides states that he does not intend to explain the full contents of the work to all of its readers: "It is not the purpose of this treatise to make its totality intelligible to the vulgar or to beginners in speculation, nor to teach those who have not engaged in any study other than the science of the law [*'ilm al-šarī'a*]—I mean the legalistic study of the law [*fiqh*]."[49] The reason for this is that it deals with subject matter that is inappropriate for such people to learn: "the purpose of this treatise and of all those like it is the science of the law in its true sense [*'ilm al-šarī'a 'ala al-ḥaqīqa*]."[50] Although Maimonides never explicitly states what the "science of the law in its true sense" is, that it is physics and metaphysics is the "almost inescapable conclusion."[51]

Despite the constraints, Maimonides feels it is necessary to address those who are worthy of learning, even with the risks of putting his instruction in writing:

> I am the man who when the concern pressed him and his way was straitened and he could find no other device by which to teach a demonstrated truth other than by giving satisfaction to a single virtuous man while displeasing ten thousand ignoramuses—I am he who prefers to address that single man by himself, and I do not heed the blame of those many creatures. For I claim to liberate that virtuous one from that into which he has sunk, and I shall *Guide* him in his perplexity until he becomes perfect and he finds rest.[52]

However, Maimonides is careful enough to write in a certain level of code in order to ensure that only those who are worthy succeed in understanding the full message of the *Guide*. He offers instruction concerning how to understand the meaning of the treatise to the few for whom he writes: "If you wish to grasp the entirety of this treatise so that none of its details escape you, you must connect its chapters with each other."[53] Reading an individual chapter will never be sufficient to understand the entire intention behind that chapter. Furthermore, reading the entire *Guide* is also insufficient to understand the intention behind the treatise as a whole: "You ought rather to learn everything that ought to be learned and constantly study this Treatise. For it will then elucidate for you most of the obscurities of the law."[54] The *Guide* provides pointers to a correct understanding of the law but also assumes knowledge on the part of the reader. In order for it to "elucidate most of the obscurities of the law," the pupil "ought to learn everything that ought to be learned." Furthermore, the reader is expected to continue to "constantly study this treatise" so that mentions of, or allusions toward, knowledge that is gained elsewhere may be identified and applied to an understanding of Maimonides' meaning. Maimonides is indicating that he explains his teaching using dialectic and maieutic. The *Guide* thus adopts certain premises that a pupil familiar with philosophy would identify more easily and uses arguments that such a student understands from previous studies.[55]

Dialectic is practiced during arguments between two opponents. One of the methods of a dialectician is to draw out the conclusions of an adversary's stated premises. By doing so, the dialectician is able to show that an opponent holds inconsistent views about the matter under discussion and thereby try to persuade the adversary that his premises are false. As Aristotle explains, "the job of the questioner is to lead the argument so as to make the answerer state the most unacceptable of the consequences made necessary as a result of the thesis."[56] The *Guide* is not a dispute taking place between two people. Nevertheless, since Maimonides intends to replicate oral teaching, this aspect of dialectical discourse is present. As mentioned above, there are a number of occasions in which Maimonides adopts his opponent's premises and considers their consequences. Often he does this openly by setting out different opinions on a particular issue and proceeding to examine them. Through a dialectical examination of the positions, he considers the validity and consequences of the views in question. Their consequences may then be assessed in order to decide which of them is most acceptable. Furthermore, the practice of adopting an adversary's opinion and showing what it should lead to is present even in discussions in which Maimonides claims to demonstrate what he attempts to show.[57] Sometimes it is necessary to identify those positions that Maimonides does not present as his own, but rather adopts and explains, in order to understand his position as a whole.

1.3.2 Dialectic and the *Guide*'s Obscurity: Methods of Withholding Knowledge

At the end of his introduction, Maimonides outlines seven possible causes of contradictions (*tanāquḍ*) or contradictory statements (*taḍādd*). He states that he intentionally uses the fifth and seventh in the *Guide*.[58] This has been taken as an explanation of how Maimonides intends to keep information from the masses. Maimonides states that the fifth type of contradiction is also used in the books of many who "know the truth."[59] It is therefore not indicative of a kind of esotericism found only in the *Guide*. The fifth type of contradiction is a feature of the way in which difficult subject matters must be taught. It occurs when a teacher explains something to a pupil that seems to contradict an earlier teaching. The reason for its presence is that at an earlier stage of development, a pupil requires a simple explanation. Since the full explanation is more complicated, it may appear to contradict the early, simpler explanation.[60] Because this kind of contradiction occurs in the *Guide*, Maimonides may explain the same topic in both a simple and a more detailed way. A simpler explanation would be preparatory for a more accurate, sophisticated explanation.[61]

The presence of the fifth contradiction need not imply that Maimonides hides a secret doctrine. The *Guide* is a letter of instruction. Its purpose is to teach individuals with a specific requirement. It is also designed to teach the pupil according to the pupil's capabilities. In order to teach only those who are worthy and also make sure that they are taught according to their own capabilities, Maimonides makes full use of dialectical methods of writing. There are features of dialectical writing that are appropriate for teaching, since they force the reader to work in order to understand them fully. Maimonides is thereby able to simulate, to a certain extent, oral discussion, in which the pupil is told as much as is appropriate but no more. So dialectical writing enables Maimonides to withhold knowledge from any readers who are unworthy of it but also to encourage them to progress to a level at which they will be worthy.[62] The fifth type of contradiction can therefore be explained by the presence of the kind of dialectical discussion explained above and by the method of teaching employed in the *Guide*. However, the seventh must be accounted for in a different way.

1.3.3   The Seventh Contradiction: What Kind of Esotericism?

The necessity when discussing very obscure matters [*umūr ǧāmiḍa ǧiddan*] [of which] it is proper to conceal [*iḫfā'*] some parts and to disclose [*iẓhār*] others. Sometimes in the case of certain dicta it is necessary for the discussion to proceed on the basis of a certain premise, whereas in another place it is necessary that it proceed on the basis of another premise contradicting the first one. In such cases the vulgar should not perceive the contradiction; the author accordingly uses some device to conceal it by all means.[63]

The seventh type of contradiction occurs when different discussions proceed on the basis of different and contradictory premises. Maimonides states that the contradiction between the two sets of premises ought not to be perceived by the masses.[64] This kind of contradiction fuels the claim that Maimonides hides an esoteric doctrine since, in his introduction, he states that he does not intend his *Guide* to be intelligible to all and also that he is contradicting himself.

While the fifth contradiction may be explained by the dialectical nature of the *Guide* and, perhaps, the need to reveal knowledge only to those who are capable of thinking the issues through while educating the masses, the seventh seems to imply that there is something that must, at all costs, be hidden from the masses. That is, Maimonides seems to be stating that the masses should be unaware of a genuine problem that is being presented. Nevertheless, some have appealed to the dialectical nature of certain premises in order to explain the presence of this contradiction as well. Yair Lorberbaum argues that the "very obscure matters" that must be treated in this way "are undoubtedly matters of metaphysics and topics in physics that border on them."[65] In a valuable close reading of the text of the seventh contradiction, Lorberbaum states that in these discussions, part must be revealed and part concealed. He points out that the question of contradiction is only raised subsequent to that point, and Maimonides states that it is sometimes necessary "with respect to a certain dicta." That dicta is, says Lorberbaum, "a given philosophical matter (a view or outlook) the discussion of which is multifarious, leading to different conclusions that are considered at different points and in different contexts."[66] Because of the nature of the subject under discussion, it is necessary to "treat those matters on the basis of differing, contradictory premises."[67] Lorberbaum accurately describes the nature of a dialectical discussion, but he is wrong to identify it with the seventh cause for contradictions.

On Lorberbaum's reading, the seventh contradiction is used when Maimonides pursues discussions for which he has no demonstration. He then appeals to premises with dialectical rather than demonstrative levels of certainty. Lorberbaum follows Kenneth Seeskin in taking the seventh contradiction to apply when Maimonides' discussions lead to aporia. However, he departs from Seeskin by arguing that pursuing a metaphysical topic in such a way enables Maimonides to apprehend truths that cannot be perceived through the use of discursive reason.[68] In such a discussion, on this view there can be no absolute certainty, and the inconsistency and contradiction are the result of lack of such certainty. Since the masses require dogma and certainty, the fact of inconsistency is what must be kept from them. Lorberbaum concludes that what Maimonides is trying to hide from the masses is the very fact that there are matters about which he is uncertain.[69] While it is true that the fact of contradiction is what Maimonides says is to be hidden, and it is also true that contradictions are not always obvious in the dialectical discussions, Lorberbaum's conclusions are countered by the fact that Maimonides openly states on a number of occasions that the human intellect cannot be certain of some matters. The following statement is an example: "there are existents and matters that, according to the human intellect's nature, it is not capable of apprehending in any way or through any cause."[70] In these, he appeals to acceptable rather than demonstrable premises.

Part of Maimonides' dialectical method of writing is illustrated in chapter 2 of this book, in which I consider what Maimonides has to say about the world's creation, an area concerning which there has been disagreement throughout the centuries. Many have argued that Maimonides holds a secret, esoteric position that is opposed to his profession of creation ex nihilo. He presents the available positions and then examines them to see which should be accepted. Besides illustrating Maimonides' dialectical method of writing, in which seemingly inconsistent statements are explained by their different contexts, this chapter introduces the idea that Maimonides assents to topics on the basis of dialectical evidence when he does not think that a demonstration is possible. The position he presents as that of the law is supported by such evidence. Dialectical evidence is used to argue for and assent to a position that would be intelligible but unsupported without such evidence. The reason dialectic is used is not to perceive something that cannot be understood by reason. Rather, it is used because, without it, there would be no grounds for assenting to one position rather than another. Chapter 3 considers further issues arising from Maimonides' account. There I show that he uses dialectical methods even when proving God's existence, which he thinks is demonstrable. As mentioned above, a feature of dialectical discourse consists in adopting premises that are considered false. Besides demonstrating God's existence, these proofs are meant to show that God is incorporeal and simple. Therefore, the demonstrations are important bases for Maimonides' interpretation of

God and the divine attributes. Despite the demonstrative level of the conclusions Maimonides presents, the dialectical nature of the work is apparent even in this chapter, since at times Maimonides adopts his opponents' premises in order to make his point. The premise Maimonides uses in order to prove God's existence, but with which he disagrees, is that of the eternity *a parte ante* of the world.

Together, chapters 2 and 3 show that the seventh type of contradiction cannot be explained solely by the need to hide uncertainty from the masses. Maimonides makes no effort to hide the fact that there are crucial metaphysical issues concerning which he is uncertain because he has no demonstration for them and that, in those areas, he uses dialectical evidence. Nor does he make any effort to conceal the fact that there are times when he adopts premises with which he disagrees. The question arises concerning what Maimonides' position is when he does not claim to possess demonstrative knowledge. As stated above, he affirms what he takes to be the position of the law.

A number of scholars have argued that Maimonides uses dialectic to present different positions at different times. In common with Lorberbaum, some have then argued that these positions may be inconsistent. Marvin Fox argues that when treating inconsistencies that are not contradictions in which one side has been demonstrated, Maimonides illustrates how to balance two "divergent" positions in tension: "To know how to keep them in balance and to live with the tension is precisely what is required of the religious man who seeks and discovers philosophical truth."[71] As a religious man, "Maimonides asks us to accept the claim that he has demonstrated inconsistent propositions about God."[72] "There are times, as in the case of providence and divine causality, when we may even have to affirm inconsistent propositions, simply because we can neither refute them nor give them up."[73] David Blumenthal goes further, arguing that in using the seventh kind of contradiction, Maimonides intends to draw attention to a postphilosophical kind of knowledge that reaches beyond discursive reason.[74] To be sure, Blumenthal is right to point out that there was an important tradition of interpreting Maimonides as a philosopher with mystical leanings, particularly in Yemen, and that this tradition has been neglected in Western scholarship. However, Blumenthal's description of "intellectual mysticism" does not satisfy Maimonides' account of the seventh cause of contradiction. Furthermore, Tzvi Langermann explains that Yemenite Maimonideans did not view "Maimonides as the teacher of a specific doctrine which must be accepted in its narrower sense."[75] They may not have been concerned by Maimonides' "true position" and might not have been trying to explain it.[76]

Against these readings, I will argue that there is a coherent position presented in the name of the law. When Maimonides adopts different, contradictory premises in dialectical discussions, he does so not because he assents to all of those positions but because he wishes to test them, as is common in dialectical procedures. Were Maimonides trying to affirm genuinely contradictory or incoherent beliefs, he would certainly be affirming something false, even though he may be advancing an opinion he could not otherwise have had. Eventually, he does opt for one of the positions in question but not until after examining them using dialectic. The position Maimonides eventually adopts is coherent, even if it is not assented to with the same certainty that would be given to arguments based on demonstrations. Scholars who have emphasized that Maimonides uses dialectic in order to reach beyond demonstrations are correct in pointing out that he draws attention to the limits of intellect and uses dialectical arguments in such instances. However, lack of certainty does not entail self-contradiction, and Maimonides does not use contradictions in order to transcend the bounds of human intellect. Nor does it mean that there is a mystical and experiential element to Maimonides' teaching that is available only after the intellect has been transcended. It is important that intellectual limits are recognized and that people do not think they are capable of knowing more than is humanly possible. Additionally, there are beliefs about which Maimonides does not think it possible to reach demonstrative conclusions. In the absence of demonstrative arguments, he uses dialectical evidence in order to support his opinions. Maimonides presents a coherent worldview on the basis of such evidence, rather than an inconsistent set of positions. There are times when he accepts positions on the basis of other doctrines he holds, and this is only possible if the overall position coheres.

One of the beliefs accompanying the law's position on creation, which is the nexus of the law's worldview, is belief in God's knowledge of particulars. For this reason, I then turn to the issue of God's knowledge. It is considered in the context of God's attributes as a whole. Chapters 4 and 5 address Maimonides' religious language and his famous "doctrine of negative attributes." I argue that despite his reluctance to predicate words of God, Maimonides does accept that "absolute perfections" exist in God. This is a point that has often been overlooked, since readers have failed to notice that much of the discussion, as with that of creation, is presented in dialectical fashion. If the manner of writing is not recognized, then Maimonides' meaning is easy to misconstrue. Recent writers have argued that there is an inconsistency between Maimonides' negative theology and his claim that knowledge and intellect should be predicated of God. The conclusions an interpreter draws from such an inconsistency depend on the reasons inconsistencies are thought to exist in the *Guide*. Some argue for a hidden doctrine. Therefore, the question addressed in chapter 6 is whether the position Maimonides presents openly is coherent. I argue that there is no inconsistency between Maimonides' negative theology and his statements concerning God's knowledge and intellect, since both of those should be seen as "absolute perfections" in God, which I argue are admissible in chapter 5. Chapter 6 therefore further explains the position of the law on God's knowledge and argues that God's knowledge of particulars is implied by the law's view as a whole. Maimonides presents his own positions in the name of the law and asserts a number of them on the law's authority.

To sum up, dialectical considerations lead Maimonides to a worldview that cannot be asserted with absolute certainty. These considerations are used when there is no possibility of such certainty. However, they do not lead to a worldview that is incoherent in itself. The law's position is coherent but indemonstrable. Attention to this fact explains many perceived contradictions in the *Guide*. It also accounts for a certain type of esoteric writing, since Maimonides expects his readers to be familiar with philosophical arguments that are alluded to, rather than explicit, in the *Guide* and to be able to think the issues through for themselves if they are to understand his meaning.

If Maimonides presents his opinion concerning the matters dealt with in the five chapters outlined above in an esoteric fashion, that esotericism is the result of the difficulty of the subject matter and the fact that it needs to be explained in a particular way. However, it does not mean that he hides a true opinion that is in accord with the view that he professes openly to oppose. It also does not follow from this examination that Maimonides affirms contradictory premises or that he thinks that metaphysical truths that the intellect cannot grasp can be grasped by a mysterious faculty of intuition. Nevertheless, it is important to take into account the question of esotericism, and further investigation shows that there are matters that Maimonides does intend to hide, rather than simply explain in different degrees of detail to different audiences. If such contradictions are to be found at all in the *Guide,* they are not the result of the kind of dialectical writing explained above.

The seventh cause of contradiction suggests the presence of an esoteric doctrine, and although it is taken in a variety of different ways, esotericism of some kind is widely held to be present in the *Guide*. Not all agree that the *Guide* is esoteric, however, since it is difficult to discover the contradictions, so difficult that Herbert Davidson recently wrote, "I have not been able to identify a single contradiction in the *Guide* which fits the specifications for deliberate contradictions of the seventh type laid out by Maimonides in his introduction to the book."[77] I agree with Davidson inasmuch as those apparent or real contradictions that have so far been taken by scholars to be of the seventh type do not fit Maimonides' description. However, I disagree with him inasmuch as I think that there are such contradictions in the *Guide*.

A possible location of contradictions of the seventh type is suggested by a comment appearing when Maimonides explains where different types of contradictions are used. There he writes that the third and fourth are used in prophetic books. He then states that he wrote the introduction to the *Guide* for this reason,[78] a comment reminding the reader of the aim of the *Guide*: scriptural exegesis.[79] Consideration of Maimonides' proclaimed purpose in writing the *Guide* goes some way toward explaining why it is written in the manner it is and why he chooses to use the literary techniques he outlines in the introduction to the work. The seventh type of contradiction, if it is to be found at all in the *Guide*, is therefore probably to be found in connection with scriptural exegesis. If this is correct, the "very obscure" matters mentioned at the beginning of the seventh cause for contradictions are not obscure philosophical matters but "obscure" parables of scripture that have philosophical matters as their deeper meanings. In the *Guide*, Maimonides tries to explain them to those who are capable of understanding, while not making the entirety of his exegesis accessible to everyone. This brings to mind Maimonides' aims in writing the *Guide*. It is one of the methods he uses to imitate the rabbinic commentaries, and he attributes it to the midrashic authors or other biblical commentators as well.

1.3.4 The Purpose of the *Guide*

The introduction begins with Maimonides outlining two aims he has in writing the *Guide*: explaining terms in scripture and explaining the difficult parables of scripture. "The first purpose of this treatise is to explain the meanings of certain terms occurring in the books of prophecy."[80] The primary aim of the *Guide* is exegesis. This exegesis is targeted at those who are confused by the inconsistencies between philosophical truth, which they have begun to learn, and the apparent meaning of scripture. Such a person is unsure whether to follow the external sense of scripture or to accept the intellect's conclusions.

> Hence he would remain in a state of perplexity [*ḥaira*] and confusion [*dahiša*] as to whether he should follow his intellect, renounce what he knew concerning the terms in question, and consequently consider that he has renounced the foundations of the law. Or he should hold fast to his understanding of these terms and not let himself be drawn on together with his intellect, rather turning his back on it and moving away from it, while at the same time perceiving that he had brought loss to himself and harm to his religion.[81]

They must be taught to read the sacred texts correctly in order to see that there is a deeper truth beneath the surface of the text and that the intellect does not conflict with its true intention. The exegesis also helps point them toward greater understanding of the truth.

> This treatise also has a second purpose: namely, the explanation of very obscure parables [*amṯāl ḥafiya ǧiddan*] occurring in the books of the prophets, but not explicitly identified there as such.[82]

Maimonides specifies the target of the secondary goal as "one who truly possesses knowledge." This person is aware of philosophical truth but needs to be pointed toward the correct interpretations of certain parables:

> if we explain these parables to him or if we draw his attention to their being parables, he will take the right road and be delivered from this perplexity.[83]

Scripture is written using parables so that it may address people on different levels, since the inner meanings of those parables ought not to be explained fully to everyone. The surface meaning is suitable for the vulgar, and the deeper meaning should be perceived by the wise. However, if he is to explain the parables, Maimonides needs to invent a way of doing so that allows those worthy of the true explanation to understand it while simultaneously withholding it from the masses.

> If we should adhere to parables [*tamṯīl*] and to concealment of what ought to be concealed . . . we would, as it were, have replaced one individual by another of the same species. If, on the other hand, we explained what ought to be explained, it would be unsuitable for the vulgar among the people.[84]

Maimonides must explain the parables without explaining them to everyone and thereby practicing an exegesis that destroys the boundaries between the different registers of discourse used by scripture.[85] However, simply explaining through use of parables would be insufficient, since that would not help those to whom Maimonides attempts to communicate truths. Ideally, Maimonides' exegesis should reveal the correct interpretation of a parable while leaving the vulgar with the impression that "one individual is being replaced by another of the same species." With this in mind I return to the beginning of the seventh contradiction:

> In speaking about very obscure matters it is necessary to conceal some parts and to disclose others.

In order to explain the parables of scripture without explaining them fully to everyone, Maimonides discloses part of the meaning and conceals part of the meaning. This is an aspect of his exegetical strategy when he explains the "very obscure" parables. In chapters dedicated to them, he points toward the deeper meaning of scripture with revealing comments. However, the comments alone never amount to a complete explanation but rather amount to a pointer toward the full explanation. In this context, then, "very obscure matters" may be understood as the "secrets of the Torah" as they are expressed in scripture. This reading explains why Maimonides writes the entire introduction in order to explain the contradictions occurring in scripture that derive from the third and fourth causes. It also connects the seventh cause of contradictions with the exegetical purpose of the *Guide* as a whole.

An apparent problem arises from this explanation. As stated above, Maimonides proclaims that the purpose of the *Guide* is the "science of the law in the true sense" and that this science is physics and metaphysics. But that seems to oppose the assertion that the *Guide* is primarily exegesis. However, there is no conflict once Maimonides' methods of presentation are considered further: he refers to certain scriptural passages as "secrets of the Torah"; he also states that deep philosophical and theological issues constitute those secrets in truth. The secrets of the Torah can be both scriptural passages and their deeper meanings. Maimonides presents philosophical arguments that require training and dedication, as well as sharp understanding. He presents interpretations of biblical passages as puzzles that presuppose a certain level of knowledge. Maimonides expresses some of that knowledge clearly but not all of it, and he does not always explicitly relate it to the passage in question. The science of the law in its true sense is to be found in scripture when correctly interpreted.

> As for the discussion concerning attributes, and the way they should be negated with regard to him; and as for the meaning of the attributes that may be ascribed to him, as well as the discussion concerning his creation of that which he created, the character of his governance of the world, the "how" of his providence with respect to what is other than he, the notion of his will, his apprehension, and his knowledge of all that he knows; and likewise for the notion of prophecy and the "how" of its various degrees, and the notion of his names, though they are many, being indicative of one and the same thing—it should be considered that all these are obscure [*ġamaḍ*] matters. In fact, they are truly the mysteries of the Torah and the secrets constantly mentioned in the books of the prophets and in the dicta of the sages.[86]

Maimonides uses allusions (*tanbīh*), but in order to provide a complete explanation, he also has to explain the meaning of the allusions. When he is discussing very obscure parables of scripture explicitly, he limits the explanations to the use of hints. However, the deeper meaning of the parable in question is often discussed more extensively in other sections of the *Guide*. Many of the hints, therefore, point toward other sections of the *Guide*, and it is the reader's task to "connect its chapters with one another" in order to grasp the meaning of Maimonides' exegesis and the full force of the *Guide*. Sometimes he also hints at matters of natural science that he does not explain elsewhere in the *Guide*. In these cases also, the reader's task is to complete Maimonides' hints through personal study. Maimonides expects a competent reader to be versed in philosophy and science independently of the instruction imparted in the *Guide* and to apply that to the exegesis. "The science of the law in its true sense" is the purpose of the *Guide* because it is also the purpose of scripture. Maimonides explains physics and metaphysics in order to explain scripture.

The final section of this book turns to the exegetical purpose of the *Guide*. I examine the vision at the beginning of Ezekiel, which is known as the "account of the chariot." As I mentioned in the introduction, the account of the chariot is also the way Maimonides names metaphysics. It is traditionally considered the deepest secret of the Torah. To this end, chapter 7 explains Maimonides' exegesis of the passage and shows that he presents it in a way that reveals some things and conceals others by hinting at its meaning. He does not intend to reveal its meaning to those who are unworthy, either because they are incapable of understanding Maimonides' hints or because they are not prepared to put sufficient effort into doing so. The masses would read the chapters explicitly devoted to the chariot and believe that he has "replaced one individual with another of the same species."

Hints are often indications toward another part of the *Guide* that must be identified by the reader and applied to the scriptural passage. The philosophical parts of the *Guide* are therefore accounted for within the context of its exegetical goal. Maimonides' exegesis requires at least two elements. First, he needs to point out which parts of scripture should be interpreted, and second, he needs to explain the hermeneutical tool by which they are to be understood. The second element involves explaining what the law's position is in order to explain to his readers what the intention of the law is, even if scripture seems to advocate a position contrary to the law.[87] Therefore, there are explicitly exegetical sections of the *Guide* and also sections that focus on the true intention of the law, the "science of the law according to its true sense."

Maimonides is faced with the same task even when different prophetic texts teach different things according to the "inner" meaning. For that reason, there are at least two different cosmological systems present in the *Guide*, both of which Maimonides appears to consider acceptable. One seems to be Maimonides' own position and is probably also that of the law, while the other is one with which he disagrees. That both cannot be assented to simultaneously should not be announced to the masses.[88] As Maimonides states, "the vulgar should not perceive the contradiction." One of these positions may be used to interpret the true meaning of part of scripture, and the other may be used to interpret the true meaning of another part of scripture. The seventh cause of contradictions is applied in this context. Maimonides states that on occasion, it is necessary for different discussions to proceed on the basis of contradictory premises. In Maimonides' view, the deeper meanings of scriptural parables are not all the same.[89] In order to explain parables that have different meanings in parts of the Guide not obviously aimed at explaining those parables, without explicitly stating that the purpose of those parts is exegesis, it is necessary for the discussion to proceed along contradictory premises. The fact that there is a contradiction must be hidden from the masses.

The account of the chariot is a case in which Maimonides needs to adopt a premise, or perhaps premises, contradictory to those that are used to explain the true intention of the law. The reason is that on Maimonides' account, Ezekiel's meaning is different from that of the law. Chapter 8 proceeds to a discussion and interpretation of some matters implied by Maimonides' interpretation, namely Ezekiel's mistakes. These are revealed through a careful reading of the *Guide*. That there is a contradiction between Maimonides' explanations of Ezekiel and his explanations of the true position of the law is never explicitly stated. Furthermore, Maimonides hides it from the masses. He does this first by using the method of revealing and concealing. He then demands of the reader the ability to identify the explanations of those hints within the *Guide* and also the ability to apply knowledge that can only be gained from sources other than the *Guide* in order to understand what the importance of the mistakes is. That understanding of "very obscure" scriptural passages is what ought to be hidden from the masses. They accordingly should not be aware of the contradiction between the inner meanings of the two different passages, since that would awaken them to the idea that parts of scripture contain false teachings.

CHAPTER 2

A Dialectical Topic: Creation

The world's creation is a good place to begin an investigation into Maimonides' metaphysical ideas. It is a central preoccupation of the *Guide*, taking up fourteen chapters in the middle of the work, and in Maimonides' view, it bears upon other questions of God's nature and relationship to the world. Creation also makes for a good entry point into the discussions of Maimonides' esotericism, because so much of the literature dealing with creation in the *Guide* focuses on his supposedly hidden position. Whereas he discusses three possible positions, which he attributes to Aristotle, Plato, and the law, and presents arguments purporting, at least, to support one of them, there have been centuries of disagreement over which, if any, he really believed to be true. I will offer a reading of the *Guide* that preserves its apparent position on creation. Distinguishing among different purposes of apparently conflicting accounts indicates that the worth of the three positions can be classified: two are acceptable philosophically; two are acceptable from the point of view of revelation; only one of them satisfies the criteria of both. Aristotle's is philosophically sound. Plato's is acceptable to revelation. The only position that Maimonides deems to uphold both reason and revelation is that of Moses. On a plain reading of the *Guide,* this is why he repeatedly asserts its truth. Conflicting attitudes that Maimonides takes to Plato are not contradictory at all. They merely stem from the different aspects addressed in different parts of the *Guide*. Apparent contradictions do not point to a hidden position.

But why, if it is philosophically unacceptable, does Maimonides even bother discussing Plato's view? He does so because there are people who believe it to be true. Recall the things for which Aristotle writes that dialectic is useful or necessary. These include examining the positions that people hold in order to work out what follows from them. A dialectician is then able to change the mind of the person holding a particular opinion by showing the person that such a belief entails other beliefs that are either in conflict with the initial premise, and therefore incoherent, or unacceptable on other grounds.

> It is useful in relation to encounters because, once we have reckoned up the opinions of the public, we shall speak to them, not from the beliefs of others, but from their own beliefs, changing their minds about anything they may seem to us not to have stated well.[1]

So dialectic examines the positions that people hold in order to check whether they need to change their minds. This activity would work only if consistency is a criterion used to judge whether an opinion can be correct. On that basis, if someone holds a belief that conflicts with another view that he also holds, there is a need to find a solution to the inconsistency or to stop believing in one of those positions.

> It is useful in relation to the philosophical sciences because if we have the ability to go through the difficulties on either side we shall more readily discern the true as well as the false in any subject.

Although the fact that Maimonides' discussion of creation follows a dialectical pattern has been noted, the ramifications have yet to be drawn out. Elaborating them will go some way toward explaining features that have previously been taken to indicate that he hides an esoteric position.[2] In part, the confusion arises as a result of apparent inconsistencies in Maimonides' stance toward creation. However, while there may be inconsistencies, they do not stem from Maimonides' esoteric rejection of the position he professes to espouse. Once it is recognized that Maimonides only professes to assert his opinion with dialectical support in this area and treats the matter with a dialectical method of writing, these inconsistencies can be explained, and there is no reason to conclude that he is hiding his true opinion. The plain meaning of the *Guide* can then be seen to make sense.

So, besides illustrating the way in which Maimonides employs dialectic in his chapters on creation, this chapter defends a nonesoteric reading of Maimonides' view of creation. He assents to creation ex nihilo for two reasons. First, unlike the Platonic position, it is philosophically sound. Second, unlike the Aristotelian position, it is in accord with beliefs taught by the law. He argues backward from positions that the law espouses, which I will consider in chapter 3 below. I will have more to say about the doctrine's importance in Maimonides' thought and whether he could have adopted alternative accounts of creation that preserve the world's everlastingness there, and I will also argue that there are good reasons to accept that this reading reflects Maimonides' true opinion. For now, it is sufficient to say that, at least prima facie, he adopts the position he presents as that of the law, that the world is created from nothing and has existed for a finite time: he adheres to creation ex nihilo and de novo.

2.1 THE THREE ALTERNATIVES

There is, first, a need to address the three opinions that Maimonides discusses: Mosaic, Platonic, Aristotelian. Each of them, he says, is espoused by a group or groups of theists. The first is described as "the opinion of all who believe in the law of Moses" and is presented as a basis of the law.[3] The opinion of the law is that the whole world was brought into existence by God "after having been purely and absolutely nonexistent": the law teaches creation ex nihilo.[4] The second opinion is that of Plato and others. They claim that it is logically impossible that God should create something out of nothing, so they posit the eternal existence of matter out of which God forms different things at different times.[5] On this account, the heavens are subject to generation and corruption just like the beings existing in the sublunar world. Those adhering to this position can be divided into smaller sects of those who accept variations of the opinion, but Maimonides does not see fit to discuss any more than the basic principle of the position here.[6] The third opinion is described as that of Aristotle and his followers. They hold that the world has existed eternally in its present state. The heavens are not subject to generation and corruption, and the sublunar world as a whole is not susceptible to nonbeing.[7] The created world therefore exists necessarily.[8]

Before considering what Maimonides' refutation of Aristotle amounts to, it is worth explaining that Maimonides does not think that any of these opinions can be demonstrated to be true. He argues that Aristotle himself considered the eternity thesis not to have been demonstrated but, rather, to be the position most likely to be correct. Aristotle could not have made the mistake of believing himself to possess a demonstration over the question addressed here, as he is too aware of the difference between demonstrative and dialectical arguments to fall into that trap.[9] There are two relevant aspects of dialectic. First, in order to deal with the lack of such a demonstration, Maimonides presents the questions concerning creation in dialectical fashion. Each position is explained and examined in turn. Such a style is the appropriate way to examine an idea concerning which there can be no demonstration but in which acceptable evidence must be used. In this way, he is able to decide which position to adopt on the basis of acceptable considerations. This is the second relevant aspect of dialectic. He decides what should be assented to on the basis of acceptable, rather than demonstrable, evidence. Maimonides assesses the acceptability of the positions on the basis of their implications. After taking the positions to their conclusions, he is able to see the whole picture and claim that one position is more likely to be true on the basis of which set of implications is more likely to be true. His strategy is to outline each of the possible alternatives and consider them according to their consequences. Maimonides does not attempt to demonstrate anything in response to Aristotle but instead argues that the position of the law is philosophically acceptable. Since no demonstration is possible, any position that Maimonides adopts he can only adopt on the authority either of tradition or of generally accepted opinions. As mentioned above, acceptable premises can be either generally accepted opinions or beliefs received from one deemed trustworthy.[10] Since Maimonides says that none of the proponents of the different positions can lay claim to possessing demonstrations, assent must be either derived from acceptable premises or suspended.

> It is preferable that a point for which there is no demonstration remain a problem or that one of the two contradictory propositions simply be accepted.[11]

Maimonides explicitly states that he is also relying on the evidence of Abraham and Moses, which gives greater dialectical weight to the position of the law.[12] Although he does not believe that there can be any demonstrations for creation, Maimonides certainly claims to assent to the proposition that the world is created.

2.2 AN ARISTOTELIAN ARGUMENT FOR THE ETERNITY OF THE WORLD

A number of arguments for Aristotle's view are summarized in one chapter of the *Guide*. Maimonides states that three of them were advanced by followers of Aristotle and begin from God. They are the "metaphysical" proofs. Aristotle's own methods, which were elaborated by his followers, are "physical" and begin from the world. My present concern is with the physical proofs, as I will take my cue for my own particular reading of Maimonides' arguments from his explanation of why he does not feel compelled to accept these physical proofs. More precisely, I begin from a comment he makes after finishing his explanation, as will become clear below.

Maimonides describes the fourth of the physical methods as "a very powerful method for establishing the eternity of the world."[13] He presents it in the following way. Aristotle pointed out that the existence of everything is preceded by the possibility of its existence. His followers applied this principle to the question of creation using the following dilemmatic argument. If creation is posited, one of three possibilities must be true: before the world existed, its existence must have been either necessary, impossible, or possible. It could not have been necessary. Had it been necessary, there would not have been a time at which it did not exist, but the basis of the present argument is that there was. So the world's existence must have been either impossible or possible. If it were impossible, it could not exist now. It does exist now; therefore, its existence was not impossible. Rather, it must have been possible. However, if it were possible, there must have been something existing bearing the possibility to become the world. In that case, there would have been something existing before the world was created. Maimonides does not explicitly say so, but this would amount to an acceptance of the eternity of matter or something similar, since matter is that which contains possibility. Hence none of the three alternatives results in anything other than eternity. Therefore, the world has always existed.

2.2.1 Maimonides' Refutation

Maimonides now proceeds to explain how he casts doubt on Aristotle's claim. In the section tackling the physical arguments, he says that those arguments that Aristotle offers cannot be demonstrative, since they do not satisfy his own criteria for demonstration. The reason for this, Maimonides says, is that Aristotle bases his arguments on observation of how the world is in its present state. According to Maimonides, such an argument cannot lead to demonstrative knowledge of the particular question being dealt with here, because Aristotle attempts to extrapolate from observation of the way things exist now to the way they would exist in a situation in which they did not possess their present stable nature. Things currently have a stable nature, but one cannot argue, based on this observation, that they always had such a nature.

> A being's state of perfection and completion furnishes no indication of the state of that being preceding its perfection.[14]

In response to the Aristotelian argument outlined above, Maimonides is now able to say that although a thing's existence must be preceded by its potentiality in the current, stable state of existence, it is invalid to draw the same conclusions regarding God's creation of the world. "In the case of a thing created from nothing, neither the senses nor the intellect point to something that must be preceded by its possibility."[15] While the Aristotelian argument would hold for a demonstration of the way things are in the world at present, and perhaps for the way they will remain in the future, it cannot be a demonstration about creation.[16] The argument holds for things that can be examined but not for creation ex nihilo, as creation is an act different from anything within the bounds of experience.

> No inference can be drawn in any respect from the nature of a thing after it has been generated, has attained its final state, and has achieved stability in its most

perfect state, to the state of that thing while it moved toward being generated. Nor can an inference be drawn from the state of a thing when it moves toward being generated to its state before it begins to move thus.[17]

Since Maimonides takes this principle to prove that the Aristotelian position is no more certain than an opinion, he believes that there is no obligation to affirm Aristotle's position. In fact, as Maimonides goes on to explain, Aristotle's position leads to certain problems that show it to be inadequate. By contrast, the opinion of the law is able to explain all of these difficulties. So Maimonides advises not to affirm Aristotle's position but, rather, to side with the opinion of the law.

2.2.2 The "Disclaimer"

But here Maimonides makes a comment that seems to indicate that he is hiding something, that he holds an esoteric view alongside his explicit position on creation. Immediately after arguing that Aristotle's physical arguments for the eternity of the world are not demonstrative, that they only have dialectical force, he writes:

هَذَا كُلُّهُ ايضًا يُحتَاجُ اِلَيهِ اِنْ أُخِذَ النَصُّ عَلَى ظَاهِرِهِ وَاِنْ كَانَ لَيسَ الأَمْرُ كَذَلِك كَمَا سَيَبَيَّنَ اذَا امْعَنَّا فِى القَوَلِ[18]

Pines translates this statement as follows:

> All these assertions are necessary if the text of Scripture is taken in its external sense, even though it must not be so taken, as shall be explained when we shall speak of it at length.

With this translation, the statement may be read as a disclaimer. Accordingly, it disposes of the need for a critique of Aristotle. If the "disclaimer" is accepted, all criticisms that Maimonides makes of Aristotle's reasoning are only necessary if the literal sense of scripture is accepted. But here Maimonides clearly instructs the reader not to do so. It follows that there is no need for the critique. Since there is no need to critique Aristotle's opinion, there is, presumably, no need to reject it. Maimonides appears to be backtracking and indicating, through an aside, that he does not reject Aristotle in favor of the law at all, even though he writes as if he does. Jonathan Malino argues that the disclaimer is firm evidence that Maimonides accepted Aristotle's opinion concerning creation, and that his critique is only apparent: "Here Maimonides seems to be saying that his principle (especially as he has phrased it in the very temporal summary which prefaces his remark) is necessary in order to interpret scripture externally, which, however, should not be done."[19]

It is difficult to see how Maimonides' statement can be taken any other way. He appears to be expressing reservations about his own refutation of Aristotle. However, what he is actually saying here is slightly more subtle, and closer attention to the Arabic wording reveals that there are more than two positions involved. Maimonides does not distinguish between the literal sense of scripture, which is to be rejected, and the Aristotelian view, which, by a process of elimination, must now be accepted. Rather, he has all three of the positions outlined in this part of the *Guide* in mind. The important word that the Pines translation elides is the third word of this sentence, *aydan,* meaning "also." A more exact translation of the disclaimer would read as follows:

> All these assertions are also necessary if the text of Scripture is taken literally, even though it should not be so taken, as shall be explained when we shall speak of it at length.[20]

Now the statement can no longer be read as indicating Maimonides' reservations about the position of scripture and the law, both of which teach the same thing. It impels a more complex reading of the *Guide* and of Maimonides' arguments. Maimonides is not saying that the critique of Aristotle is necessary only if scripture is taken literally and that, because it should not be taken literally, there is no need to criticize Aristotle at all. Rather, he is stating that there are two opinions for which these particular refutations of Aristotle are required, one of which is the view of the law and the other of which is implied by the literal sense of scripture. The view of the law is that which Maimonides is trying to defend by using this principle, and it is presumably, at least on a prima facie reading of the *Guide*, the true inner meaning of scripture, even if not its surface meaning. By refuting Aristotle, the way is cleared to take scripture literally as well. However, although the scriptural account appears to be validated by this critique, Maimonides warns the reader not to accept it. The surface scriptural view needs to be refuted, and in order to refute it, one must employ the arguments against Aristotle's view. Maimonides is not equating the contextual sense with the Mosaic view; it teaches something else.

In the disclaimer, then, Maimonides is still discussing three positions: Aristotle, the law, and the plain meaning of scripture. This is a clear indication that the opinion of the law and the opinion implied by the literal sense of scripture are two different positions, both of which are opposed to Aristotle.[21] Since they both disagree with Aristotle, it is necessary to refute Aristotle's position in order to accept either of them.

2.3   AMBIGUITIES AND INCONSISTENCIES: SCRIPTURE AND PLATO

The disclaimer implies that Maimonides distinguishes creation ex nihilo from the literal teaching of scripture and that both are distinguished from the opinion of Aristotle. There are thus at least three positions considered. By opposing the literal sense of scripture to Aristotle's view, as if they were the only two options, some scholars have been led to identify the literal sense with the opinion of the law, and the external scriptural view is then taken to be that of creation ex nihilo.[22] However, it is now clear that no such opposition is warranted.

What, then, is taught by the literal sense of scripture, and why is it problematic? Pines notes that Maimonides explicitly explains the literal sense of scripture in chapter 2:30, in which Maimonides disagrees with some of the sages of the Midrash who teach that time did not have a beginning.[23] Here is the relevant passage from that chapter:

> The statement, which you find formulated by some of the sages that time existed before the creation of the world is very difficult, for that is the opinion of Aristotle, which I have explained to you: he holds that time cannot be conceived to have a beginning, which is incongruous. Those who made this statement were conducted to it by their finding in scripture the terms: "one day", "a second day". He who made this statement construed these terms according to their external sense and as follows: inasmuch as a rotating sphere and a sun did not yet exist, whereby was the first day measured? They express their opinion in the following text: "the first day—Rabbi Judah, son of Rabbi Simon, said: hence [we learn] that there existed before that an order of time. Rabbi Abahu said: hence [we learn] that the Holy One, may his name be blessed, used to create worlds and destroy them again." This second opinion is even more incongruous than the first. Consider what was the difficulty for these two [sages]. It was the notion that time existed prior to the existence of this sun.[24]

Here Maimonides once again states that the literal sense of scripture is not to be accepted. However, on this occasion, his reason for rejecting it is quite surprising; perhaps it is even opposed to the implications of the statement in the earlier chapter. Above he distinguished the scriptural view from Aristotle's and rejected both; here they are grouped together and rejected because they teach the same thing. Maimonides clearly states that some sages adopted the plain meaning of scripture and, consequently, believed in the eternity *a parte ante* of time, as Aristotle did. So scripture, when taken literally, teaches the eternity of the world.

However, it was shown above that Maimonides distinguishes the literal sense of scripture from the opinion of Aristotle. So if 2:17 is taken into account, and the sages accept the literal meaning of scripture, they cannot be said to accept the opinion of Aristotle in its entirety. Therefore, Maimonides' point seems to be that these sages accepted the opinion of Aristotle because they argue that time existed before the creation of the world. They agree with Aristotle only inasmuch as they agree that "time cannot be conceived to have a beginning," not necessarily in other aspects as well. If Maimonides is to be taken at his word, these two comments need to be squared. Whereas here Maimonides states that Aristotle teaches the same thing as scripture, above he wrote that in order to accept scripture, Aristotle's view must be refuted. The implication above is that the literal sense of scripture does not accord with Aristotle. The literal sense of scripture affirms that time is without beginning, but perhaps scripture can be distinguished from Aristotle along other lines. That is the implication of what Maimonides says in the earlier chapter.

The picture is yet more puzzling when another chapter is brought into the equation, showing that there is a further complication to Maimonides' attitude toward scripture. Aside from the fact that the reason he wants to take scripture in a nonliteral sense is ambiguous, his advice on whether or not one ought to interpret scripture on creation at all appears to be ambivalent. Twice he has indicated quite clearly that the scriptural account of creation is not to be taken literally. His reservations about the literal sense of the scriptural creation account and his clear instruction not to accept it indicate that he does not advocate accepting that sense. He goes on, however, to say the opposite in a different chapter. He says that because there is no demonstration available in the area of creation, it is necessary to consider the literal sense of scripture to be true.[25] The literal sense of scripture, it seems, is the evidence that should be accepted in the face of a lack of demonstrative evidence.

However, it remains the case that the external sense of the scriptural account of creation must be distinguished both from the position of the law and from that of Aristotle. The remaining position is either the Platonic position or one that does not represent any of the three involved in this discussion.[26] There is a similar, or even identical, inconsistency in Maimonides' attitude toward the Platonic account as well. In Maimonides' explanation, this inconsistency shows Plato's position to be equivalent to the literal sense of the passage of scripture under discussion. Both scripture and Plato include two elements, and these account for Maimonides' apparently inconsistent attitudes toward them. They are both described with the same ambiguity, and in each case for the same reason. Both positions are presented as acceptable from one point of view and unacceptable from another. I will return to the question of taking scripture literally below, but first consider the third position that Maimonides says is adopted by believers, Plato's belief in creation from preexistent matter.

It is striking that the same inconsistency appears in Maimonides' various presentations of Plato. That he appears to adopt inconsistent stances toward Plato's understanding of creation has already been noted.[27] When explaining what the three positions are, he claims that the Platonic position is unacceptable:

> It is useless for us to wish to prove as true the assertion of the people holding the
> second opinion, I mean that according to which the heaven is subject to

generation and passing-away. For they believe in eternity; and there is, in our opinion, no difference between those who believe that heaven must of necessity be generated from a thing and pass away into a thing or the belief of Aristotle who believed that it is not subject to generation and corruption.[28]

This criticism of Plato echoes the above criticism of the sages who took scripture literally. Plato teaches the eternity of the world, and his opinion must therefore be rejected. If the plain meaning of scripture implies Plato's position, it would make sense to interpret scripture, since Plato is to be rejected along with Aristotle. It is clear, then, that inasmuch as both the literal sense of scripture and Plato teach eternity, they are to be grouped together with Aristotle's position and must be rejected.

However, later on in the *Guide,* Maimonides seems to consider Plato's position admissible. On that occasion, as with the scriptural position, the issue concerns the implications that an understanding of creation has for the acceptability of certain other doctrines. Maimonides says that Aristotle's opinion is ruled out, since it entails necessity, thereby making miracles impossible. Furthermore, it makes prophecy and the entire Torah impossible:

[Aristotle's view] destroys the law in its principle, necessarily gives the lie to every miracle, and reduces to inanity all the hopes and threats that the law has held out.[29]

By contrast, since Plato's belief does not destroy the foundations of the law, scripture may be interpreted in line with his position. It is clear, then, that Maimonides adopts different attitudes toward the Platonic opinion at different places in the *Guide.* Furthermore, his presentations of the Platonic and scriptural accounts contain the very same inconsistency and, at least apparently, for the same reasons. Since Maimonides claims that those three positions account for all of the opinions that have been adopted by any who believe in God, I do not believe that there is any need to posit four different positions here: the law's, Aristotle's, Plato's, and Scripture's. The inconsistencies are intelligible if scripture and Plato are identical.

2.4 AN EXPLANATION OF THE AMBIGUITY IN MAIMONIDES' PRESENTATION

In this instance, the important point to note is that Maimonides rejects the belief in the eternity of time *a parte ante* which is common to both scripture and Plato, as well as Aristotle. Such a belief implies necessity and ought to be rejected. However, there is an element of Plato's position that is taught by the law and is also implied by the literal sense of scripture. That aspect of scripture and Plato must be retained. So Maimonides is discussing different aspects of the doctrine in the different places. The difficulty for readers arises because he does not spell out the entire meaning in either place. On each occasion, he writes only about the question with which he is concerned in that place. As Maimonides advises in the introduction to the *Guide*, the reader needs to take into account more than that which is being dealt with in a particular chapter in order to understand all of the chapter's ramifications.[30]

So far, it has emerged that since Plato teaches eternity, his position is to be rejected. Since scripture appears to teach eternity, it is to be interpreted. However, both positions are also considered acceptable.[31] Despite these apparent inconsistencies, Maimonides does not change his mind or hide a secret opinion. Rather, he is making different points regarding his attitude to the Platonic account on the two different occasions.[32] The reason Maimonides appears to affirm the Platonic-scriptural view in one place and reject it in another is that he is considering that position from different points of view on the two different occasions. That position contains two elements. First, it affirms the eternity of time, and second, it allows for God's use of purpose in creation. Considered from one point of view, the question of the eternity of time, Plato's opinion is unacceptable. For that reason, when Maimonides discusses Plato's opinion in the context of beginningless time, he rejects it. Considered from another, the question of God's creating with purpose, it is acceptable. Therefore, when he discusses it in the context of divine freedom, he accepts it. The same attitudes emerge in Maimonides' examination of the literal sense of scripture, and so this also explains the different attitudes he has toward scripture. The contexts of his discussions influence his comments.

To take stock, this is what I have tried to show so far in this chapter. There are three alternative positions available to Maimonides as a theist: the law's, Plato's, and Aristotle's. Maimonides contrasts the position of the law with that of Aristotle, both of which are coherent in themselves. He argues that Aristotle's position is no more viable than that of the law. He even goes further and claims that the law seems more likely than Aristotle to accord with reality. Nevertheless, rational speculation is not decisive. Since Maimonides argues that no demonstration is possible in the matter of creation, he is forced either to suspend judgment or to turn to other considerations to make a decision. Assent is given to the position of the law on the basis of dialectical authority. Maimonides bases his decision on the evidence of Abraham and Moses.

At this point, I would like to introduce the issue of coherence. I believe that Maimonides considered coherence to be a basic requirement for a philosophical position to be true. Coherence is a necessary but insufficient condition of truth.[33] I believe, therefore, that Maimonides considered his own views to be coherent. If he did not, he would not have needed to explain inconsistencies and, perhaps more tellingly, would have had no need to reject Aristotle. He would have been able simply to accept Aristotle's view and deny that it is opposed to the law. This approach is not an option, because the law contains a number of ideas that are connected with one another. That is why the question of creation is so important. In order to accept the law's view of other matters, it is necessary to accept the law's view of creation. Which view of creation one adopts will depend on one's view of other crucial topics. Specifically, as I will argue in later chapters, it has ramifications for what can be said about God's knowledge. It must be the case that the law's position as a whole is coherent if Maimonides is to use it as evidence in favor of creation by taking into account other positions that the law advocates. If this is right, it will have two consequences for the issue I am considering here. First, it will explain Maimonides' changing attitudes toward Plato and scripture. Second, it will explain exactly what his evidence for creation ex nihilo is, and I will return to the second ramification below.

If Plato's view is acceptable from the point of view of the law, the question of why it needs to be rejected remains. I argue that what should be concluded from the tension in Maimonides' presentation is that Plato's position is the only one of the three that Maimonides can be sure is false. This is because he presents Plato's position as an incoherent mixture of ideas. In the end, Maimonides' varying attitude toward the Platonic view can therefore be explained, because he takes a different stance toward it depending on the point of view from which he is discussing it. Furthermore, if the Platonic position is equivalent to the literal sense of scripture, Maimonides' ambivalent attitude toward scripture can also be explained.

To clarify a little further, both Aristotle's position and that of the law are considered to be philosophically acceptable. The reason Maimonides prefers to side with creation is evidence taken from the law, dialectical rather than demonstrative evidence. If not for the law, Aristotle's position would be perfectly acceptable. The same is not true of the Platonic view. The reason for rejecting it is not that it is opposed to the law. The dialectical evidence of tradition does not hold any sway over it. Rather, Maimonides rejects it primarily because it does not satisfy a basic truth condition, coherence, and therefore cannot be true.

Like a number of other thinkers, Maimonides links belief in the eternity of the world to a belief in the world's necessity.[34] The latter appears to be a corollary of the former. If this is granted, then there is an immediate problem with the Platonic and scriptural positions, since they posit the eternity of time without accepting the necessity of the world. So both of the two positions toward which Maimonides appears to adopt an ambiguous attitude contain two elements. First, both assert, along with Aristotle, that the world is eternal a parte ante. Second, both assert that God acts through purpose. This is why they can be broken down into two parts, one of which, divine purpose, is acceptable and one of which, the eternity of time, is not. This position must therefore be false and is unacceptable.

Maimonides' view that the world must be either eternal and created through necessity or created ex nihilo and through divine purpose sheds light on his overall attitude toward the Platonic view. When Plato asserts that the world does not exist of necessity, Maimonides finds his position acceptable. In this case, if Plato's belief is to be consistent, he would also have to posit a first moment in time. However, when he asserts that time is eternal, his position must be rejected, as it implies its corollary, necessity. From this second point of view, if Plato is to be consistent, he must accept the view that God creates through necessity. Since in neither of these two cases can both elements of the Platonic position be accepted as part of a cogent teaching, taken as a whole, Plato's position is incoherent and therefore unacceptable. The same holds for Maimonides' view of the literal sense of the scriptural passage on creation. It, too, teaches Aristotle's notion that things cannot come to be from nothing, while simultaneously ascribing purpose to God and rejecting the notion that the world is necessary. This position is unacceptable to Maimonides, because it posits eternal time. However, it is acceptable because it teaches that God acts through purpose, and that is in accord with the law. Scripture literally teaches both the eternity of time and that God creates through purpose. Since Maimonides clearly connects the notion of necessity with that of eternity, it does not make sense for him to affirm both of these as true at the same time. If this is what scripture teaches, then, the truth of the literal sense of scripture can be accepted only with regard to one of these factors. On the one hand, it agrees with Aristotle, while on the other, it agrees with the law and the general message of scripture.

2.5   ACCEPTING THE LITERAL MEANING OF SCRIPTURE

There is a further difficulty that has to be explained before my interpretation can be accepted. Although the above account may hold for the Platonic position, it is not yet clear why it would hold for scripture, implying that the two might yet need to be distinguished. In the case of Plato's position, Maimonides agrees that one can accept it and still adhere to the law. However, he does not say that it makes a claim on the believer. The reader of the *Guide* is nowhere instructed to accept Plato's position and is free not to do so, should he or she wish. The same is not true of the scriptural view. Maimonides explicitly instructs the reader to take scripture literally in the case of creation, as mentioned above. I now turn to the chapter in which the advice appears; it will aid in understanding Maimonides' presentation of Plato, since it is in the discussion of Plato that the advice emerges.

The purpose of this chapter of the *Guide* is to discuss the conditions for reading scripture correctly. Maimonides explains that it is always possible to interpret scripture as teaching something that appears to counter the plain meaning of the text: "the gates of interpretation are not closed in our faces."[35] He explains that this is what happens in the case of the scriptural texts that seem to teach that God is corporeal. Although there are many biblical accounts of God that depict God as a body, the intention of scripture is that God is incorporeal. This must be the case, because the true meaning of scripture is in accord with demonstrated philosophical truth. Accordingly, were eternity demonstrated, it would be possible to interpret scripture in line with eternity as well. Maimonides states that it may even be easier to do so.

Maimonides then offers two reasons for why it is not necessary to interpret scripture as teaching that the world has existed eternally. The first reason is that eternity has not been demonstrated. There is no need to interpret scripture to accord with an opinion that has not been demonstrated and is not even more likely than another meaning to be true. Maimonides contrasts the texts teaching that God is corporeal with those about creation. The former must be interpreted, because it has been demonstrated that their surface meaning is false. By contrast, it is unnecessary to interpret those teaching creation, because they have not been shown to be literally false. The issue here is not that scripture literally teaches one position over the other. Maimonides is simply explaining why it is necessary to interpret scripture in one place but not in another. While the discussion does imply that there are texts in the Torah that teach creation ex nihilo, Maimonides also says that there are many texts that seem to teach eternity. Apart from the examples explained here, he also openly says that there are many texts in scripture that, on a literal reading, support Plato's opinion.[36] However, the intention of the texts as a whole should be considered. Maimonides always considers any truth that has been demonstrated to be the intention of scripture. Therefore, if the literal sense of scripture is demonstrably false, it must be interpreted, as is clear from his comments about interpretating scripture when it appears to teach that God is a material being. However, when the external sense is not demonstrably false, it is not necessary to interpret it. As yet, however, it would seem that it is permissible to interpret scripture even in that case. Maimonides has not yet forbidden such action. Therefore, he has not given any clear instructions for how to understand scripture when there is no demonstration. This is particularly true of the case under consideration here, in which to take scripture literally is no help at all, as it can lead to adopting a false belief. The literal sense of the scriptural passage must be false in one of its two elements, but there is no demonstration regarding which.

A second reason that Maimonides does not see the need to interpret scripture to be teaching eternity is that eternity uproots the law by introducing necessity into God's creation.[37] This objection applies only to Aristotle's understanding of eternity. It is in this context that Maimonides' positive attitude toward Plato emerges. Plato's belief does not imply necessity, so it is acceptable. The issue is necessity versus freedom. Hence, in this respect, the position of Plato, which accords with the scriptural account of creation, is preferable. So as far as the question of God's creating freely through purpose as well as will is concerned, the literal sense of scripture is correct. At the end of his exposition of the second reason,

Maimonides explains how to escape this difficulty. He says that in the absence of any demonstration, one should construe scripture literally and accept that the law teaches something that human intellect cannot understand. The question here concerns which aspect of the literal sense of scripture to accept, and for this, it cannot be judged only on what it teaches about creation but must be considered along with the matrix of intertwined beliefs that make up the law's teaching. The intention of scripture must be considered as a whole. Scripture teaches, along with the law, that God acts through purpose. If that is so, then when it is properly understood, it cannot also teach eternity. Therefore, taken as a whole, the literal sense of scripture must be considered to teach creation ex nihilo. This is the case even though the creation story on its own may easily be construed to teach eternity.

There is another conundrum to unravel in Maimonides' comments about the acceptability of interpreting scripture. On the one hand, he states that it is always acceptable to interpret scripture if necessary. On the other, he seems horrified by the suggestion that it may be acceptable to interpret the miracles in scripture. He explains that Aristotle's view of eternity uproots the law and gives the lie to the miracles

> unless—by God!—one interprets the miracles figuratively also, as was done by the Islamic Esotericists [ahl al-bāṭin min al-islām]. This, however, would result in some sort of ravings [haḍayān].[38]

This comment is puzzling. It is difficult to see how interpreting miracles figuratively as natural events constitutes a "raving." Natural events should not be considered to be ravings. On the contrary, Maimonides would be more likely to label belief in an act that goes against the usual natural order of things as a raving. He regularly interprets miracles in a figurative manner and tries to naturalize them as far as possible.

These difficulties are eased by paying attention to the particular interpretations Maimonides has in mind here. He writes that the interpretations of miracles that are to be rejected are those of the Islamic Esotericists. This is a term regularly used of the Ismāʿiliya, and Maimonides' comment must be seen in the context of the polemics that took place against that movement after the demise of the Fatimid dynasty in Cairo. For more than two and a half centuries, they had ruled until they were deposed in 1171, only shortly before Maimonides wrote the *Guide*. Sarah Stroumsa notes that "Ismāʿīlī taʾwīl incorporates miracles in the general theurgical system, which claims to control and manipulate the world by scientific methods. For Maimonides, the whole system is false and accordingly deserves the name 'ravings.'"[39] The idea that miracles can be a result of a prophet's knowledge of the way in which the created cosmos works may well be behind his negative comment. However, it could reflect Sunni polemical treatises against Islam rather than genuine Ismaʿili ideas. One such polemic is al-Ġazālī's" *Obscenities of the Esotericists (Faḍā'iḥ al-Bāṭiniyya)*, which he was commissioned to compose in order to refute Ismaʿili doctrine. Ġazālī includes a section on the way in which they interpret scripture symbolically. There he lists a number of particular interpretations of specific miracles, which he describes as some of "their ravings" (*haḍayānahum*).[40] This is yet another system in which the miracles are possible, although Maimonides and the law object to that system as well. The reference requires prior knowledge on the part of the reader in order to understand the import of Maimonides' statement. It is necessary to disentangle Maimonides' critique of Aristotle, whose teaching disagrees with the law, from his critique of the Internalists and those who share their views. Here again, there is a comment that the reader needs wider knowledge to understand. Without considering the context of each comment, and whom Maimonides is commenting about, the reason for his objection to interpreting miracles cannot be understood.[41] More about miracles and about how Maimonides argues backward from the law will follow in the next chapter.

2.6 SUMMARY

It is worth pausing here to consider what has been argued so far and what still remains to be shown. Although Maimonides appears to make contrasting assertions about both the Platonic view and the literal sense of scripture, he is actually saying different things in different places. There is no contradiction when the chapters on creation are considered as a whole. Scripture is to be taken literally inasmuch as it affirms that God acts with a certain purpose and that it rules out the notion that the world is necessary. This, in turn, means that it teaches a first moment in time, although it does not do so openly. In order to be taken literally in its general teaching that God acts through purpose and freedom, scripture is to be interpreted, because the literal sense seems to teach that "there was time before the existence of this sun," and when understood properly, that implies that God does not act through will and purpose.

On the one hand, the Platonic-scriptural position is grouped together with Aristotle inasmuch as it posits something eternal. As a consequence of eternity, God's creation must be considered necessary, a teaching that is contrary to the law. Therefore, the Platonic-scriptural position cannot be accepted. On the other hand, the Platonic-scriptural position posits a creation that occurs as a result of God's will and purpose. From this point of view, it is acceptable because scripture, Plato, and the law all allow for divine freedom and purpose and hence miracles, as well as reward and punishment. The entire law is based on certain beliefs that are tied up with creation through purpose. The law provides answers to certain theological questions that Maimonides raises. However, the Platonic-scriptural position cannot be correct on both counts.

The literal sense of scripture is accepted in that it teaches purpose and is rejected inasmuch as it teaches eternity. Plato's belief may therefore be adopted inasmuch as it allows for purpose. On this point, the law teaches a position that could not otherwise be known. It teaches that God acts through purpose. The question of creation is ultimately decided according to which position accords with the law's view that God acts through purpose.

CHAPTER 3

Necessity and the Law

A number of matters arise from the consideration of creation in chapter 2 above but remain unexplained. Maimonides repeatedly connects Aristotle's belief in the eternity of time with a belief that creation is necessary. Some other theologians argue that God's free creation could be consistent with the existence of an eternal world, so Maimonides' connection of eternity with necessity needs explaining. Another issue concerns his arguments for God's existence, which he seems to undercut by rejecting Aristotle's views on eternity. The reason it may undercut those arguments is that Aristotle's view provides one of the premises that Maimonides uses in them. Those arguments are presented as demonstrative, and in that case, they are undoubtedly true and ought to follow only from certain premises. I will explain how Maimonides can use an uncertain premise in this particular demonstration. There is an element of dialectic in his method of argumentation, and the argument does not show Maimonides to have presented contradictory positions. That leads to a discussion of what the problem with Aristotle's view might be. That is, how exactly does affirming eternity with its corollary of necessity undermine what Maimonides considered to be important? Maimonides objects to Aristotle because necessity rules out certain beliefs that are integral to the worldview that the law espouses. The final part of this chapter will therefore be dedicated to outlining what those matters are and why, if they are true, they are evidence in favor of creation de novo.

3.1 ETERNITY AND NECESSITY

Maimonides prefers creation ex nihilo to Aristotle's belief in eternity because the former implies that God creates with both will (*irāda*) and purpose (*mašī'a*). Aristotle's position, on the other hand, while it may accept the presence of will in God, rules out the possibility of God's creating through purpose and therefore introduces necessity (*luzūm*) into creation.[1] Maimonides presents necessity as a corollary of eternity. He states that nothing moved by accident can be moved eternally:

> Everything that is moved owing to accident must of necessity come to rest, inasmuch as its motion is not in virtue of its essence. Hence it cannot be moved forever in that accidental motion.[2]

On this basis, if an eternally moving world is posited, the motion must be necessary. It must be included in the world's essence. Accordingly, since time is an accident of motion, if the world exists for all time, it would exist of necessity, because the existence would have to be implied by the world's essence. If the existence of the world is eternal, then, existence cannot be accidental to the world; the world exists necessarily. As explained in chapter 2 above, Maimonides takes Aristotle to hold that the world has always existed in its present form and will continue to do so for eternity. For that reason, he presents Aristotle's view as an opinion that the world is necessary. Consequently, Maimonides says, were Aristotle's position on eternity accepted, the law's understanding of the nature of many crucial theological phenomena would be falsified.[3] As Maimonides interprets the issue, many of the opinions of the law as a whole are at stake. In fact, the very basis of the law would be removed were Aristotle's view to prevail. So Maimonides rejects Aristotle because of the consequences that follow from the Aristotelian premises when they are pushed to their logical conclusions. In short, since necessity is a corollary of eternity and necessity implies that certain beliefs are false, Maimonides argues that eternity must be rejected. So far, however, it is unclear why the question of necessity is important and what the implications are.

Because Maimonides does not explain why necessity is considered to be a corollary of eternity, one can only speculate about why he may have thought them to be mutually implicatory. He seems to adopt the assumption from previous sources without questioning it.[4] Certainly, the notion that everlasting beings are necessary beings has a long history.[5] Nevertheless, one way to challenge this reading of the Aristotelian position might be to distinguish between eternity and necessity. Consider the following proposition granted: [P] if the world is eternal, it is necessarily eternal. There are two different ways in which that statement could be understood.

1. If the world is eternal, it is necessarily true that it is eternal.
2. If the world is eternal, it is true that it is necessarily eternal.

On reading [P1], all that is being asserted is that if something is true, it is necessary that it is true. This is like stating that "if the world is eternal, the world is eternal," and the necessity stems from the tautology. From this reading, deriving a sense in which it is true that "it is necessary that the world exists" is easy. If it is true to say that the world always exists, it is false at any one time to say that it does not exist. So if the world always exists, it is impossible for the proposition "the world does not exist" to be true. In that case, it is necessary that "the world exists" is true. On this reading, the statement [P] means that if the world always exists, the contrary is impossible. Reading [P2] attributes a kind of necessity to the world's existence that is not dependent on a conditional antecedent. Instead, it claims that the world is necessarily existent. In this case, if the world is eternal, it must also possess the property of necessity, and that is what Maimonides wishes to avoid. Now, it may be asserted that a being can be possible in its own right but necessary through its cause. Maimonides even makes use of that notion when he argues for God's existence.[6] That is not the issue here, though. Maimonides wishes to avoid the notion that there is anything intrinsic to God's nature, or intrinsic to the world's nature, necessitating God's creative action. God's creation must be absolutely free. That, he claims, would not be the case if the world is eternal. It would be eternal of necessity.

The first of these two options may be the obvious reading of [P]. However, Maimonides seems to think that the second is implied also. For that reason, there seems to be a problem with his view. It seems to conflate two kinds of possibility: a logical kind [P1] with what might be considered a theological kind or a metaphysical kind [P2]. To make the metaphysical point, rather than merely a logical one, the argument needs to equivocate between possibility as possessed by a statement that can be true and false and possibility as contingency of existence possessed by concrete objects. It would have to assume, as Maimonides seems to, that there is no real difference between the two readings of [P]. But a distinction should be drawn between them. As an illustration, consider a sitting man. A man who is always seated of necessity cannot be standing, although one could imagine him standing up. There is nothing about his being a man that precludes his standing up, even if he happens to be seated throughout his life. It is only impossible that the man is at any point standing if it is presupposed that he is always sitting. A person who is sitting is necessarily sitting but does not sit of necessity.[7]

Similarly, a distinction could be drawn between a world in which there is no possibility of nonexistence and a world that does admit of such a possibility but in which that possibility is never realized, as the world is eternally held in being by God. In the case of the first world, God could not be said to will that the world exist, since the world must exist. In the case of the second, however, it is possible for the world not to exist, and therefore God could be said to choose the world's existence. God would be able freely to will the eternal existence of the world. The sense in which these two worlds are said to be necessary differs. The first might be necessary in itself, but the second would be eternally contingent on the only being that is self-sufficient and thereby necessary in its own right, God. Maimonides holds that the second of the two worlds would not really admit of nonexistence, and therefore God would have no choice but to create. So much is clear from his statement that those who posit a world created eternally but as a result of God's will change the word *necessity* but retain its meaning.[8]

Why Maimonides makes this assumption is unclear. Why could God not choose eternal existence? If God is deemed incapable of freely creating an eternal world, is that not a limitation of God's power? Perhaps an explanation can be found if more general principles are taken into account, namely that possibility can be connected to potency as opposed to act. One reason the connection might have seemed obvious to many could be as an extension of the view that what endures is what is actual. Form is that which causes a thing to be actual. Matter, on the other hand, is the source of potentiality. Beings composed of both matter and form are actualized by their form and endure because of it. Their tendency to decompose and take on a different form stems from their matter. Act is therefore connected to existence and permanence, potency to transitiveness. That which is more actual is that which endures for a longer period of time. If something were to last forever, it would then be closely connected to act rather than potency. Since potency is what allows the nonexistence of a being, if there is no potency in a thing, it would be necessary.

If this argument is what is behind the implicit and assumed connection between necessity and eternity, the basis for the link is in the metaphysical beliefs on which the Aristotelian worldview is built. That might explain why thinkers such as Maimonides seemed to accept it without comment. To assert that the world has always existed and will always exist would amount to an assertion that it contains no potency. It would only be possible to know that the world is eternal if one knows that it lacks the potency toward nonbeing. For the world to be eternal, then, it must be permanently actual and in that sense necessary. To say that an eternal being could possibly not be would amount to a contradiction. The only way to argue that Aristotle's position must be affirmed would be to argue that the world does not possess a potency for nonbeing. Therefore, the conclusion could be drawn that there is something about the world that necessitates its existence. If, on the other hand, the world contains the possibility of nonexistence, it would be impossible to know that the world is eternal.[9] That would be why Aristotle's belief must be an opinion rather than absolutely certain knowledge that the world is eternal: he cannot know that the world has no potency, and it is therefore always possible for it not to exist. If the world began to exist, it would have done so as a result of God's choice, rather than because there is anything necessitating the world's existence.

All of this is speculative, since Maimonides does not explain the connection between eternity and necessity. Perhaps it is an issue for which he had no solution, or maybe the question never arose for him. Alternatively, it could be a matter that he hoped his readers would puzzle over without his supplying an easy answer. What is clear, though, is that he presents necessity as a danger to the law. For that reason, it seems strange that in his own demonstrations for God's existence and unity, the very foundations of his metaphysical beliefs, he insists that the best way to proceed is to begin from the premise that the world is eternal. So in the next section, I consider why Maimonides does not undercut his own arguments regarding the world's creation when he offers demonstrations of God's existence.

3.2 CAN GOD'S EXISTENCE BE DEMONSTRATED IF CREATION IS TRUE?

Maimonides makes use of the premise that the world is everlasting in order to prove God's existence, even though that premise is opposed to his own belief. He even goes so far as to say that if an argument is to be demonstrative, it must be based on Aristotle's view, since only then can it be proven according to all possible positions.[10] His own arguments, he says, are demonstrative, and for that reason, he appears to endorse Aristotle's view. He argues that those who try to demonstrate God's existence through a proof containing the premise that the world is not preeternal fail. They do not provide any successful proof at all. Maimonides states that they are unaware of the difference between dialectic and demonstration.[11] He is aware of the difference, and he makes use of dialectic in his own demonstrations. As mentioned above, one of the ways in which dialectic is useful is in order to examine scientific discussions.[12] This fact, rather than the presence of a hidden position, makes sense of his arguments.

The second part of the *Guide* begins with a list of twenty-five scientific statements that Maimonides uses as premises for his arguments. All of these, he says, have been demonstrated elsewhere.[13] Since Maimonides does not intend the *Guide* to be a book of demonstrative philosophy, there is no need for him to repeat those demonstrations. The reader is expected to know them from previous philosophical studies.[14] These premises are used to demonstrate three things. Maimonides' first aim is to establish that God exists. Second, they also demonstrate that God is incorporeal. Third, they demonstrate that God is simple (*basīt*).

If the premise of eternity is accepted, the conclusion that God exists is harder to prove, since it is not simply given to the intellect. Maimonides wishes to demonstrate beyond any doubt that God's existence can be proved. Since the particular demonstration in question cannot proceed on the basis of premises that are certain, this will involve arguing the case even with the least favorable assumption. Consequently, in addition to these twenty-five, there is one more premise that Maimonides says is necessary in order to understand the demonstrations: the eternity *a parte ante* of the world. This premise, he says, has not been demonstrated but represents Aristotle's opinion (*ra'y*), which is based on proofs (*dalālāt*) rather than demonstrations (*barāhīn*).[15] He presents demonstrations based on Aristotle's undemonstrated premise of eternity.

In the chapter under discussion, Maimonides enumerates four proofs of God's existence. It is appropriate to outline one as an example, without going into great technical detail. In the first of the proofs, Maimonides attempts to explain the fact that the world is in motion. He sets up a series of disjuncts and concludes that there are four ways in which motion might be imparted to the world. First, motion could be caused by an external material entity. Second, it might be caused by a separated immaterial being. Third, it may be caused by a force pervading the entire sphere. Fourth, its cause may be a force in a part of the sphere. Once the premise that the world is everlasting is introduced, the second is the only acceptable alternative. The first is ruled out by the second of the twenty-five premises, which states that an actually existing infinite body is impossible.[16] Therefore, the total of bodies that exist, since it is finite, could not contain the infinite force required to move the world for eternity. The third and fourth alternatives also posit forces that cannot be infinite and so must be ruled out. God's existence is thus established on the basis of the premise that the world is everlasting.[17]

As is clear from this proof, without Aristotle's premise, the demonstration collapses, and the existence of an infinite, incorporeal being cannot be shown. Since Maimonides insists that there is no doubt of God's existence, he appears to need Aristotle's premise to be true. If that is so, Maimonides would need to reject the position on creation that he openly defends. The problem can be stated even more emphatically: since demonstrations move from true premises to true conclusions, the premise that the world is eternal has to be true if the arguments are indeed demonstrations, as Maimonides says they are. Further, demonstrations move from certain premises to certain conclusions, so the implication is that there is no doubt that the world is eternal.

No such conclusion should be drawn, however, since it relies on a fallacy. The argument breaks down as follows:

- If the world is eternal, God exists.
- God exists.
- Therefore, the world is eternal.

In order to conclude that God exists, Maimonides needs to say also that the world is eternal. Therefore, if the world is created, it becomes possible that God does not exist. When the consequent of the above argument is negated, the conclusion must also be negated. That is, given the first premise, if "God exists" is false, "the world is eternal" is also false: if God does not exist, the world is not eternal. From here, it is easy to see why one would be tempted to say that Maimonides undercuts his insistence that the world is created when he uses the premise that God is eternal in his arguments for God's existence. To deny that God exists is to deny that the world is eternal, which means that if the world is not eternal, God does not exist. So to assert that God exists is to assert that the world is eternal. If Maimonides continues to maintain that the world is created, it seems that he has no grounds for arguing that God exists. In its present form, however, the argument would only work with the additional qualification in the major premise that God exists only if the world is eternal. Maimonides claims that this is not true. Rather, he argues, it is a primary notion (*ma'qūl awwal*) that if the world began to exist, it must have been caused to exist by something else.[18] That cause must be God; otherwise, it would be part of the caused order that it explains.[19]

Maimonides' point is that God's existence is demonstrable even though neither position on creation is. Creation or eternity is not at issue when he presents the arguments for God's existence. The argument based on eternity can therefore be clarified by prefacing it with other premises, thereby making the demonstration into a dilemmatic argument as follows.[20] The world is either eternal or created. If it is created, God exists. If it is eternal, God exists. Therefore, God exists. That is why Maimonides can offer a demonstration even if the premise he uses may be false. It is true that this kind of demonstration does not provide a complete Aristotelian demonstration, because it does not explain why the conclusion must be true, only that it must be. Nevertheless, to assert that eternity is true on the basis that it must be used in this particular demonstration would betray no less of a misunderstanding of dialectical argument than that of the *kalām*.

If this reading is correct, there is no need to posit a hidden position on the basis that Maimonides grants Aristotle's position as a premise in his own arguments. He does not use the seventh contradiction in this discussion. Rather than offering individual interpretations of the contradiction and applying them to the question of creation, then refuting each in turn, I point the reader toward chapters 7 and 8 of this book for my interpretation of the seventh contradiction. In the meantime, I will limit myself to the observation that when Maimonides' argument is read carefully and thought through properly, he does not seem to see a contradiction between the assertions that God's existence is demonstrable on the one hand and that the world is not eternal on the other.

3.3 THAT NECESSITY UPROOTS THE LAW

Maimonides rejects eternity because it implies necessity. Necessity must be rejected because it is opposed to the law. It is opposed to the law because it rules out God's creating with purpose. That raises the question of what it is about the law that would be undermined were the world necessary and why. The notion of purpose is vital for understanding Maimonides' view of God's action in the world. All of God's actions are good, and therefore God must carry them out for a purpose. Maimonides explains that a good action is one that aims at a certain intelligent goal and achieves it; it is carried out for a purpose, and it fulfills that purpose.[21] If God creates through purpose, God creates a universe that is ordered and in which nothing is out of place or arbitrary from God's point of view. Rather, everything aims at the fulfillment of God's will.[22] Even if human intellects are incapable of understanding exactly what God's purpose in creation is, God has a purpose in view; God's action is good.

> A man endowed with intellect is incapable of saying that God is vain, futile or frivolous. According to our opinion—that is, that of all of us who follow the law of Moses our Master—all his actions are good and excellent. He says: "And God saw everything that he had made, and, behold, it was very good." Consequently everything that he, may he be exalted, has done for the sake of a thing is necessary for the existence of the thing aimed at or is very useful.[23]

There is a close connection between actions that are performed for an end and actions that are performed through the purpose indicated by creation.

> One of the strongest proofs for the production of the world in time is the fact, demonstrated with reference to natural beings, that every one of these has a certain final end, some of them existing for the sake of others; for this is a proof of purpose on the part of a being possessing purpose.[24]

Although a full consideration of Maimonides' explanation of miracles is beyond the scope of the present work, there is one consequence of asserting that miracles occur that is relevant.[25] It is connected to the extent of God's knowledge and also to the limits of human knowledge. Maimonides writes that necessity gives the lie to the prophets. Miracles are supposed to count as evidence for the truth of the law and the prophets.[26] Maimonides severely limits the application of this idea in his *halakic* works.[27] The point here must therefore be different: miracles are evidence of God's knowledge of particulars and hence of the message of the law. They do not authenticate the prophets' view in themselves, but they do authenticate the law as a whole, which teaches God's knowledge of particulars. In Maimonides' view, prophecy is a natural phenomenon, although the miraculous is not ruled out.[28] When a person has followed the correct procedure of actions and study and reached the kind of intellectual perfection required, prophecy automatically ensues. This is the opinion of Aristotle, and so far as it goes, Maimonides agrees with it. However, he adds an extra condition. The law agrees with Aristotle but teaches that should God wish, God could withhold prophecy from one who is correctly prepared. This is miraculous, since God's action temporarily alters the nature of the thing on which the miracle is carried out. By nature, humans prophesy when they have reached a certain level of perfection, but God can suspend that prophecy. God can stop a natural event from coming to be by suspending the usual course of nature and not creating what would ordinarily be created.[29] In that case, Aristotle's view, in which miracles are considered impossible, would not destroy prophecy entirely but would destroy the law's understanding of prophecy. Prophecy would not be uprooted; the law's stance on it would. The law's view includes the possibility of miracles, which illustrates God's involvement with particulars within the world.

This account explains why Maimonides supports the view that God creates through purpose on the basis of its consequences for miracles. Maimonides explains that miracles are events that are built into the created order of things. They are not deviations from the divine course of events, although they do change the nature of the individual thing that they happen to.[30] It is a sign of the purpose in nature, and of the perfection of God's work, that God has created a world that does not need to change. Miracles must therefore be seen as events that are caused by God to fulfill an individual purpose and that are just as ordered as any other events that take place, rather than permanent changes required to improve the created world. If miracles are to be an ordered result of God's creative agency, they must be a result of God's purposive choice rather than a necessary result of the divine nature. Miracles are events that occur to individual things rather than to generalities of creation. Therefore, if they are to be the result of God's purposive action, the kind of involvement that the law requires of God necessitates God's knowledge of particulars. Miracles are then possible as a result of God's knowledge. They do not occur only because of their nature; they come about as a result of God's will. Their purpose is defined and decided by God's will.

There is purpose and reason for all of the theological issues for which the law offers explanation. Since Maimonides asserts that there is nothing arbitrary at all in creation and since God creates all things as a result of God's wisdom and will, it follows that God knows all individual things. The doctrine of God's omniscience is, then, another crucial aspect of the view of the law that Maimonides is attempting to defend. To anticipate what I will discuss in a later chapter, the fact that God's knowledge extends to particulars is one of the major differences between human and divine knowledge.[31] Humans cannot be said to intellectually apprehend particulars, because the intellect deals with universals. Particular things are perceived by the senses, but the senses alone do not provide knowledge as such.[32] For knowledge to come to be, the intellect must abstract from sense perceptions. By contrast, God knows all things as their cause and for that reason knows particulars. In order to defend this position, Maimonides needs to insist that God creates the entirety of all things rather than fashioning something that exists independently in its own right. Because God's creative act is ex nihilo, it is unlike any other actions, all of which take place within a created context. God's creation must be free, unconstrained by any presupposed thing.

These questions are all included in Maimonides' discussions of the law in 2:25, the chapter in which Maimonides discusses interpreting scripture. Plato's view does not uproot the law because it allows for miracles and prophecy. They are matters taught by the Mosaic view, because the law teaches God's knowledge of particulars. An important issue not raised in 2:25 is the overall purpose of the world. Maimonides does discuss the issue in a later chapter, though, in which he says that the world does not exist for the sake of anything other than God's will. Consequently, no kind of being in the sublunar world, including humans, is the purpose of creation, a point Maimonides considers important in order to respond to a number of problems.[33] He argues that humans cannot know the true purpose of existence. The only explanation for why things exist and why they exist in the way that they do that is available to humans is that God willed things to be the way they are. No ultimate scientific explanation of the final end of the universe can be given.[34] The distinction between human and divine knowledge shows that humans cannot hope to have a unified scientific understanding of everything. Since humans know universals rather than particularities and since the cosmos includes miracles, which cannot be known as universals, human knowledge cannot extend to absolutely everything that exists. That they are not understood by science does not mean that they are impossible, since science aims at understanding generalities abstracted from matter, not at understanding all particulars. The law draws limits to what humans can know and protects against intellectual hubris.

Maimonides considers all of these notions to be included within the position he presents as that of the law. He then argues back from issues entailed by the law to a position on creation. From his assertion that God knows all things as their creator, he is able to say that miracles are possible. Miracles can only be brought about if God, the creator, is able to act on individual things. In order for miracles to be possible, then, God must be omniscient. It follows from this that God's creation is ex nihilo in the sense that it does not rely on any presupposed thing. There can be no hint that God is constrained by God's own nature or anything else. Rather, God's creation is totally free. Maimonides considers creation ex nihilo also to imply creation de novo. He therefore affirms the position of the law over those of the competitors.

Like the position on creation, the law's view of God's knowledge cannot be demonstrated. So when Maimonides writes that he prefers the law's view, which asserts that God knows particulars, he says the following:

No demonstration at all can be obtained with regard to these great and sublime notions, either for our opinion—that of the community of those who adhere to the law—or for the opinion of the philosophers, even if one considers all the differences among the latter with regard to this question. And with regard to all the problems with reference to which there is no demonstration, the method used by us with regard to this question—I mean the question of the deity's knowledge of what is other than he—ought to be followed.[35]

Worth noting is the fact that there is no mention of the Platonic view here. Although Plato allows for God's knowledge of particulars and therefore for the law's view of all the questions raised in 2:25, his position is not an option. The choice is between the Mosaic and the Aristotelian views.

3.4 SUMMARY

In order to uphold the position of the law, Maimonides rejects the belief in the eternity of the world and its ruling out of divine purpose. His arguments on the basis of eternity are dialectical. They do not hide a secret acceptance of the Aristotelian position. The issues connected with divine purpose involve God's knowledge of particulars. If God is to create individual miracles, God must have knowledge of more than the generalities. The question of God's knowledge will therefore be the overarching theme of the next three chapters. The discussion will take place within the context of Maimonides' discussion of divine attributes. In order to show that he does indeed predicate knowledge of individuals in God, it is necessary to contend with the claim that such predication would run contrary to his discussion of negative theology. Therefore, I now turn to that famous section of the *Guide*.

CHAPTER 4

⌒⌒

Religious Language (A): Negative Theology and Divine Perfections

One can only be silent when speaking of God. Nothing can be known about the infinite divine essence, and no words can communicate God's glory. Maimonides' adherence to such an uncompromising and extreme negative theology is perhaps the matter for which he is most famous or, in some circles, notorious. He is often thought to be too negative because of his refusal to countenance using any words at all to refer properly to God. Since Maimonides is so keen on negative theology, scholars have pointed out a conflict between his doctrine of religious language on the one hand and what he says about God's knowledge and intellect on the other. The conflict itself can only be discussed after Maimonides' view of God-talk is appreciated, but it is important to note it here since I argued in chapter 3 that Maimonides asserts a belief in creation ex nihilo because it is connected to his view of God's knowledge. The law's position as a whole depends on the belief that God has knowledge of particulars.

As with the chapters on creation, the parts of the *Guide* that I will deal with now contain dialectical elements. Positions that Maimonides ends up rebutting are adopted and taken to their ultimate conclusions. However, they are not always identified explicitly as rejected positions; the student must be sensitive to what exactly each chapter is discussing in order to avoid confusion. Imitating oral teaching by demanding independent thought on the part of the reader is a prominent method in the *Guide*, and students are also expected to read other texts and possess sufficient background knowledge. Maimonides does not explain his view on religious language in full detail, and he does not consider all of the potential difficulties in the positions he advances. Rather, he assumes familiarity with the wider philosophical discussion and mentions ideas that someone familiar with that discussion would recognize. His strategy leaves a text requiring clarification: there are inconsistencies that need to be reconciled. Among those are apparent contradictions, one of which is the alleged contradiction between Maimonides' doctrine of negative attributes and his assertion that God knows all things. I will argue that when these two doctrines are understood properly, there is no such contradiction: Maimonides attributes knowledge to God consistently with his general statements on divine predication. Far from opposing one another, they turn out to be complementary.

Ultimately, Maimonides' theory of religious language is based on his argument that it is possible to demonstrate the existence of a creator and, as a corollary to this, that the creator is a simple unity. The notion that God is one seems to make it impossible to predicate perfections of God: if God has multiple perfections, God's essence is a plurality of perfections. So divine unity and religious language need to be investigated together. But that is for later; the first task is to show that Maimonides, contrary to popular opinion, accepted that God contains all perfections and that in his negative theology, he maintains that words cannot directly refer to those perfections.

4.1 MAIMONIDES' REPUTATION AS A "NEGATIVE THEOLOGIAN"

Opposition to Maimonides' perceived excess has come from different sides. One reason for the objections is his attempt to purge the concept of God of any anthropomorphism and the allegorization of scripture to which that led. The rise of kabbalah contributed to the view that Maimonides was a staunch defender of a philosophy opposed to religious ideas.[1] Such criticisms have continued into more recent times; Franz Rosenzweig commented that at the end of the theologian's journey, "negative theology and atheism can shake hands."[2] Medieval philosophers also disagreed with Maimonides' evaluation, usually arguing that more than he allows can be said; notable examples are Gersonides and Thomas Aquinas, both of which critiques I will consider briefly later for the light that I think they can shed on Maimonides' view.[3] There were also more sympathetic accounts, although they do not all agree about what Maimonides' message is.[4]

4.2 ALTERNATIVE UNDERSTANDINGS OF THE DOCTRINE OF NEGATIVE ATTRIBUTES: SYMBOLS OR PERFECTIONS?

In Harry Wolfson's interpretation, Maimonides' negative theology indicates the presence of perfections in God, as far as it is possible to do so in human language. On this account, Maimonides' negative theology is aimed not at denying perfections of God but at denying that they can be reflected in human language:

God, by virtue of His absolute perfection in every sense, has an infinite number of aspects in His essence; and had we only the means of doing so, we should be able to express them all in human language. But on account of the unknowability of the divine essence we express none of its infinite aspects in positive terms; one can only hint at them by negating of Him our own knowable perfections.[5]

Wolfson's opinion was contested by Julius Guttmann, who disagreed with the view that Maimonides attached any positive meaning to attributing perfections to God. Guttmann's reading of Maimonides has proved the more enduring of the two, perhaps because of the inherent difficulty of trying to explain what a divine perfection might be and how negative attributes can point toward it.[6] In chapter 5, I will suggest a way in which that is possible and how Maimonides' negative theology is used to indicate that God is perfect through divine, uncreated perfections that are sufficiently different from created perfections as to be predicated only by way of equivocation. Guttmann's position has recently been developed by Ehud Benor, who argues that Maimonides develops a system in which he is able to predicate certain perfections of God "symbolically"; in his view, "intellect" is one of those symbols.[7] However, I contend that Benor's explanation can only provide a partial solution. In supporting the view that Maimonides does believe that absolute perfections exist in God, this chapter, along with the next two, contains an argument in favor of Wolfson's view against that of Guttmann.[8]

4.3 THE NEGATIVE MOTION: WHAT IS TO BE DENIED?

How far does Maimonides' negative theology go? The doctrine of divine unity (*tawḥīd*) is paramount, and Maimonides is concerned to protect it from any hint of compromise. This concern is what drives his theories of religious language. There are a number of sections of the *Guide* in which he opposes different ways that people may associate something nondivine with God and therefore, perhaps without intention, impute plurality into God's essence. Among these sections are the chapters between 46 and 59 of the first part. Indeed, this is the section that contains Maimonides' most detailed exposition of religious language and negative attributes, and it is a section of which opponents of Maimonides' views are sometimes critical.[9] In these chapters, he explains why attributes of action are the only positive attributes that ought to be predicated of God. Here, too, is the idea that perfections should not be affirmed of God, but, rather, the negation of their privations should be asserted.

Maimonides nowhere denies that God is perfect, possessing all perfections in a manner appropriate to the divine nature. What he denies is that such perfections can be subsumed under the same definition as created perfections. Maimonides' concern is language's ability to represent divine perfections. This is crucial and is an aspect of Maimonides' arguments that is often neglected. Once it is taken into account, Maimonides' arguments become intelligible: he posits the existence of divine perfections, as he claims to do in various parts of the *Guide*, without thereby undermining his understanding of divine unity and transcendence or his insistence that divine and created perfections can only be referred to with an equivocal use of language. His position is neither incoherent nor esoteric. Rather, it is not spelled out with great clarity, since it is an area in which Maimonides relies on the pupil's ability to think the matter through, for all the reasons given.

To account for such a common misinterpretation is not easy. The first step is an explanation of what Maimonides is getting at in a couple of chapters that may give the impression that he is as pessimistic as the most "negative" interpretations take him to be. Subsequently, I will offer evidence that Maimonides did posit perfections in the divine nature. Following that, the question of divine perfections and divine simplicity needs to be considered: can God contain multiple perfections while remaining simple? Finally, I will address the question of whether attributing perfections to God finishes up in anthropomorphism. These tasks constitute the rest of this chapter and the next. In chapter 6, I will offer further evidence that my explanation is germane to an understanding of the *Guide*. I will argue that the extended discussion that Maimonides presents of God's knowledge fits with the account of divine perfections and their predication.

4.3.1 Association of Created Perfections (1:56)

One way in which Maimonides' discussion follows a dialectical course is displayed in chapter 56. There he adopts the position of the "attributists," and after presenting what they do say, he shows what he thinks they ought to say if they are to follow their own premises consistently.[10] This method of presentation needs to be recognized for the chapter's thread to be followed. Commentators often ignore the fact that Maimonides is arguing against a position in a dialectical fashion. A reader may easily be tempted to place too much emphasis on certain parts of this chapter and take his explanations of the attributist position to represent his own opinion.

Maimonides explains that those who predicate essential attributes of God inadvertently reject the belief that God is simple by importing multiplicity into God's essence. Such theologians posit a "likeness" (*šabah*) between divine and created attributes. He explains that those theologians who predicate attributes of God tend to predicate perfections of God. They think that the divine perfections are to be defined in the same way as the perfections they find in people, "so that both notions would be included in the same definition."[11] According to this account, the difference between the way they exist in God and in humans is a matter of degree rather than of kind. The divine perfections would therefore be of the same species as created perfections. Thus, the theologians mistakenly posit a likeness between divine attributes and created attributes.

Likeness is a relation (*nisba*). Therefore, it only exists when there is a relationship between two things. Maimonides explains that "attributists" are able to posit a likeness, and hence a relation, because things falling under the same species are alike inasmuch as they are part of the species no matter how much they differ in other ways. They are then able to use comparative terms to distinguish between the perfections as they exist in God on the one hand and as they exist in humans on the other. On their account, God possesses the same attributes but in a perfect way: divine perfections are more intense than created perfections, but they are still instances of the same perfection. According to Maimonides, such comparisons can be made only when words are used univocally.

In truth, Maimonides says, there is no relation between God and humans. There can therefore be no likeness between them. Those who believe in essential attributes seem to be aware of this. According to their own statements, these attributes should not be like the attributes of other beings; what they ought to say on the basis of their own premises is that there is no likeness between divine and human attributes. "However, they do not act upon this opinion," since the way they predicate the terms of God implies a relation in God to creatures.[12] So in a dialectical fashion, which is appropriate for testing the coherence and therefore the possibility that these statements might be true, Maimonides has explained that the attributist position is incoherent. It is clear that "existent" should be truly predicated of both only in a purely equivocal sense (*bi-štirāk maḥḍ*), just like "knowledge," "power," "will," and "life."[13] This even rules out the possibility of predicating them "amphibolously" (*bi-taškīk*). Maimonides explains that a word is used amphibolously when it is said of two things that have different essences but are alike in their accidents.[14] Predicating attributes of God in such a way would liken God to other things by attributing accidents to both of them, but God possesses no accidents, according to all who reflect (*āhl al-naẓar*).[15] This is a decisive demonstration (*burhān qaṭʿī*) that attributes have only the name in common.

By likening God to creatures, those who posit positive attributes reduce God to an inhabitant of the created universe. They assert that certain attributes inhere in God, and they claim that these attributes are of the same kind as the attributes possessed by things in the world. On such an understanding, there is a difference only in degree between the attributes ascribed to God and those ascribed to creatures. Nevertheless, in ascribing such attributes to God, theologians compromise God's transcendence and unity. They do not recognize the absolute difference between God and everything that is created and so conceive of God as the equivalent of a perfect created thing. Maimonides writes that such people have unknowingly abolished their belief in God altogether.[16] Their belief is nothing less than idolatrous, since it is a belief in a false god.[17]

In chapter 56, Maimonides rejects the notion that God has essential attributes (*ṣifāt ḏātī*). He objects to the way in which members of a certain group use language about them. However, if one were to accept that the perfections in question cannot be captured at all by the meaning of the words we use, then he would have no objection to the doctrine. What Maimonides understands by "attributes" cannot include "absolute perfections," and this is why attributes, including created perfections, must be negated with respect to God.

4.3.2 The Five Types of Attributes

In chapter 52 of the first part of the *Guide*, Maimonides outlines the kinds of attributes, dividing them into five types: the first two are essential attributes; the third is accidental; the fourth is relational; the fifth is action carried out by the subject.[18] God can have no essential, accidental, or relational attributes at all. The only attributes predicable both of God and of other things are attributes of action. This is as clear a place as any in the *Guide* that appears to support the view that language used of God should be interpreted as attributes of action.

The first group that Maimonides discusses is definitions. They are attributed to a thing when the nature of that thing is explained.[19] These are essential attributes and may not be predicated of God. The second group is what is meant by a part of a definition.[20] They are also essential attributes. Both of these groups of attributes imply composition (*tarkīb*), and therefore multiplicity, since they rely on definitions, and definitions always contain both genus and differentia. They must therefore be denied of God. Properties external to the essence described, accidental properties, are the third group of attributes.[21] These neither constitute nor perfect a thing's essence but are qualities attached to it. If a quality existed in God, God would be a substratum for accidents. Positing a quality, then, would imply multiplicity, since the quality would qualify the essence and thus be added to it, thereby making the thing into a plurality of essence plus quality. Maimonides explains that these also must not be attributed to God, since they imply composition, as they require a substratum. Furthermore, since quality always qualifies, it likens the qualified thing to something else. One who believes that there are accidents in God always qualifies God, thereby likening God to something else. As explained above, Maimonides considers that unacceptable. He enumerates four genera of qualities, all of which require composition: (1) speculative or moral habits, (2) natural faculties and dispositions, (3) passive quality or affection, (4) quantity. Since none of these is applicable to God, God cannot possess a quality.

Next, Maimonides discusses relational attributes.[22] He admits that attributes of this fourth group do not seem to compromise God's unity. They do not necessarily imply plurality, as they are not the essence of a thing, nor do they subsist in its essence. Consequently, it may be thought that they are applicable to God. However, as shown above, Maimonides rules out attributing a relation to God when he rules out likeness. Here he elaborates further. Relational attributes must be denied of God, as the relation has to be a relationship to time, to place, or to another individual. In order for there to be such a relationship, it needs to be possible to invert the two things that are related while maintaining their relation. In the cases of all of the relations that Maimonides mentions, neither of the two related things can be thought of without the other. For example, a slave is only a slave if he has a master, and a master can only be a master if he has a slave. Similarly, a father is only a father if he has a son, and there can only be a son if there is a father. With God, however, such is not the case, as the necessary of existence could exist without the existence of anything contingent, but contingent existents cannot exist without a necessary existent.[23] This is what Maimonides means when he writes that "there accordingly can be no correlation between them."[24] The relationship that does hold between God and creation is unlike these or any other relation. Since this chapter of the *Guide* discusses relations that are common to a variety of different things, the unique relationship of creator to creature is not considered.

Relations across different species and genera are the fourth kind of attribute, an example of which is that between quantity and quality. Ultimately, this kind of relation is accidental to a thing even though it is not an essential accident.[25] However, it may seem more fitting to apply relation to God, "for it does not entail the positing of a multiplicity of eternal things or the positing of alteration taking place in his essence, may he be exalted, as a consequence of an alteration of the things related to him."[26] This implies that although in repudiating attributes Maimonides is chiefly concerned with denying any multiplicity or change of God, there is another problem that he is reacting to. He wants also to safeguard God's uniqueness, and that would be compromised by positing a relation. Any relationship requires commonality. As explained above, in all related things, there is something that is shared by them. Things that have no commonality of species or of genus cannot be related through the species or genus. In that case, they are not subject to this kind of relationship. Nevertheless, even if they have no common species or genus, there may still be a commonality between the two things, as they both have existence in common. However, there is no such commonality between God and creatures, because God exists necessarily, whereas creatures exist contingently, and these kinds of existence are totally different from each other. Once more, then, the relationship between God and creation is not subsumed under this kind of relationship.

The final type of attribute Maimonides mentions is attributes of action: "when a thing is described by its actions."[27] These refer to something that someone has made. For example, if a door was built by Zayd, it is attributed to Zayd.[28] Such attributes are remote from the essence of the thing, and therefore it is acceptable to predicate them of God. The attributes are about the thing made rather than the maker. Because the attributes in question only refer to the effects, they can be predicated of God and of other things. God has been demonstrated to exist as the creator, so the world can be referred to as God's action. Maimonides specifies that these can be used because a plurality of actions does not imply plurality in the essence of the agent.[29] As in the case of the third kind of attribute, there is a seeming similarity between the fifth and the kind of relationship that holds between God and the world. Again, though, the similarity is merely superficial. Maimonides would have to insist that the need to distinguish God's actions from a person's actions remains. The following two propositions differ because creation is not like any other act of bringing into being: this door was made by Zayd; the world was created by God.[30] Maimonides states that only God acts through essence rather than an added notion. Nothing else is creative by its very essence, so this distinguishes God's acts from those of other things. However, the attributes of action are not to be distinguished in such a way, since they are about the things made, not about the maker. Neither are they about the act by which the thing was made, because attributes of action do not refer to the ability the agent possesses through which actions are acted out.[31] Therefore, as with the previous attributes, these particular kinds do not define the unique relationship that holds between God and creation.

So in this chapter, Maimonides discusses all of the attributes that he thinks can be ascribed to a thing. He concludes that only one of them can be used of God. This is not something he "grudgingly accepts."[32] Rather, it is a logical point. No attribute claiming to refer to God can be used, but since attributes of action are about the world, they are acceptable. Attributes of action do not refer to God's essence at all. Therefore, inasmuch as they refer to the things made, no distinction can be made between the attributes of action of God, who acts through essence, and creatures, who act as a result of attributes they possess. When saying that attributes of action can be predicated of God, Maimonides means that they are the only kind of attributes that can be predicated in the same way of God and of humans, which, for Maimonides, is the same as saying that they are the only attributes that can be represented properly by human language and can be fully understood by humans. The reason for this is that they are about the patient rather than the agent. The attributes themselves do not refer to the essence or accident in question in either case. Returning briefly to chapter 56, there Maimonides states that if attributists are to follow through on their convictions that God's essential attributes are unlike created attributes, they ought to interpret them as attributes of action. That is because they could then attribute things with the same definition to God, while still maintaining that God's essential attributes are different from those of humans.

4.3.3   Negative Attributes

Maimonides denies that any attributes signifying the essence of a created being, or a similarity between two beings, can be attributed to God. Rather, they must all be negated of God. However, this is not the heart of the famous doctrine of negative attributes. So far, the only kinds of attributes I have mentioned are those that may be applied to created things. No explanation of the kind of negative attributes that Maimonides writes may be attributed to God can be found in the chapters so far examined. They show that all positive attributes should be denied of God. However, it turns out that Maimonides argues that they are not the only things that should be so denied; there are some negations, or privations, that should themselves be negated. These are privations of perfections.[33]

It is important that the idea that privations of the perfections are to be negated of God is not mentioned in chapter 52. The purpose of that chapter is to discuss positive attributes that are helpfully used of created things and to consider which of them can be used to refer to God. Negative attributes are attributes that might not be used helpfully about created things, as they can only limit knowledge. They cannot provide information about what exactly the nature of the object to which they are attributed is, unless some prior knowledge of the things defined through negations is possessed.[34] Ontologically, they are not attributes at all.

Maimonides offers an example of how negative attributes work. If someone is aware that there is an object in a room but unaware of what that object is, a helpful way to proceed would be to negate all of those things that the object is not. So, in the case of a boat, one might begin by negating "animal" or "plant" of the object and continue negating things until the only remaining object is a boat. The person now knows that the object in the room is a boat. There is an obvious problem with this example. It works in the case of a boat because boats are present in the list of things that we already know about. The object must be a boat, because it is nothing else on that list. Negative attributes can be helpful in referring to created things but only if there is sufficient similarity between the things negated and that of which they are negated. So, for instance, a boat is not a single piece of wood, but if it is made entirely of wood, denying that it has any other material will teach something about the boat.

However, as an analogy for coming to know God, the example is limited. God is not a boat, and God is not like a boat. But that is not the point of the analogy; it is simply an example of how to proceed. Negative attributes of this kind can teach about things that do fit into the list of known, created things. They are used helpfully of God, since there is no other way of referring to God's essence. This is simply the best available attribute. Their purpose is to "conduct the mind towards that which must be believed with regard to God."[35] The mind can understand only that God exists and cannot understand anything at all about God's essence.

Therefore, no language can refer to God. Words must be taken as negations of perfections if they are supposed to refer to God's essence, because they cannot properly refer to God's essence. Language ultimately cannot provide positive information about God, and language cannot refer properly to a divine perfection. Hence the silence that must result from a correct application of the doctrine of negative attributes need not extend to attributes of action: it is possible to refer properly to the world but not to God.

Maimonides advocates negating privations of perfections. He does not argue that the perfections themselves ought to be negated, as long as those perfections are not limited by being attached to a created thing. This might be because he does ascribe absolute perfections to God, but the purpose of negations is to deny that anything that is on the scale of created perfections can be ascribed to God. Regular negative attributes are helpfully used only when there is some similarity between the thing aimed at and the attributes denied. Maimonides explains that "an attribute does not particularize any object of which it is predicated in such a way that it is not associated by virtue of that particular attribute with other things."[36] Likewise, negative attributes particularize by excluding "what has been negated from the sum total of things that we had thought of as not being negated."[37] In the case of God, regular negative attributes are only appropriate up to a point. They do not particularize God, because every attribute must ultimately be denied. This is true even of perfections, because perfections are attributes and are always limited and qualified by the thing they perfect. "For all perfections are habits, and not every habit can exist in every being possessing habits."[38] Therefore, even negative attributes must be used in a special way when they are used of God. "Even those negations are not used with reference to or applied to God, may he be exalted, except in the respect, which you know, that sometimes that which cannot fittingly exist in a thing is denied of it."[39] God is not the kind of thing to which any of these deficiencies can apply. Therefore, even regular, created perfections cannot exist in God, because all created perfections are perfections of a created thing and therefore limited to perfecting the essence or an accident of a thing: all things other than God are deficient in some way. The only way that negations can bring one closer to God is if they are used properly to show that God shares nothing with creation. To explain his point, Maimonides uses an analogy. He says that denying deficiencies of God is like denying sight of a wall. Denying that the wall can see does not negate of it a perfection that ought to pertain to it as a wall, since a wall is not a seeing thing. The wall would not be a more perfect wall were it able to see. Similarly, when denying that attributes can be applied to God, the intention is to stress that God is not the kind of thing that attributes can ever possibly apply to. However, the limitations of the analogy must be recognized. Although negating sight does not make a wall a deficient wall, it does deny it a perfection of some sort. The wall does not have the deficiency of blindness, but it does not possess the perfection of sight.

Vision is negated of a wall because the wall is a restricted being. God, however, is the fullness of being rather than a restricted being, so the reason for negating attributes is not exactly the same. This means that all deficiencies must be denied of God, and perfections also imply deficiency because they are perfections of inherently deficient things. "In relation to God all things that we consider perfections are the very extreme of deficiency."[40]

It is more proper to negate the perfections' privations, since the perfections do exist in God, although not in a way in which they can be understood or truly referred to using language derived from experience of the created world. The way that Maimonides proposes to refer to "absolute perfections" without compromising their difference from created perfections is to negate the privations of perfections. Negating the privation of the perfection is particular to God-talk. God-talk is silence because of such negations. Unlike regular negations, they do not teach the mind anything at all about their subject, because the mind can understand only perfections that are limited by the thing they perfect. However, God "does not possess a thing other than his essence, which is his perfections, as we have made clear."[41] God's perfections are therefore not limited by being perfections of something other than themselves. I will say more about this later. Now I turn to what Maimonides writes about the existence of perfections in God.

4.4   THE QUESTION OF DIVINE PERFECTION

The next stage of my argument involves offering evidence that Maimonides does believe that perfections exist in God. This will establish the basis for the contents of the next chapters, where I offer an interpretation of how it may be possible to understand what Maimonides means by divine perfections. Characteristic of a divine perfection is that it is unknowable and therefore cannot be defined. For now, though, explaining some of Maimonides' statements on divine perfection will be sufficient.

When summing up chapter 52, Maimonides reiterates that of all of the attributes discussed in it, only attributes of action can be predicated of God. However, he also points out that in addition to these, some attributes are used in order to indicate perfections:

> some of them, as we have made clear, also with a view to indicating his perfection [*kamālihi*] according to what we consider as perfection.[42]

They indicate what humans consider to be perfection because the "Torah speaks in human language." [43] The only way in which words can indicate is by reference to things that humans know, and this is why they are insufficient. Because scripture always uses words indicating perfections when it uses words of God, it limits itself to those anthropomorphisms that are considered to be perfections in people. They are words with positive meanings. Although they are used in order to indicate divine perfections, their true meaning is reflective of created perfection. However, as mentioned above, when scripture uses them of God, they are supposed to indicate "absolute perfection." This is why they are mentioned in this chapter while negative attributes are not: negating the privations of perfections is a particular way in which Maimonides tries to refer to God without referring to created perfections.

Maimonides seems to have introduced this concept into the chapter quietly and without support or discussion, so it is easy to ignore. It is inconspicuous because the purpose of his chapter is to discuss those attributes that can be used of creatures and to consider which of them can also be used of God and why. The perfections that are attributed to God by scripture and by people indicate perfections in creatures, since that is the only kind of perfection that humans are capable of grasping. However, the meanings of perfections ascribed to God are different. Since chapter 52 concerns attributes that can be intelligibly predicated of creatures, those perfections that are in God but not creatures are not discussed in detail.

Furthermore, as Maimonides explains in the following chapter, although they cannot be used properly of God, attributes are sometimes used in scripture in order to signify absolute perfection:

> Every attribute that is found in the books of the deity, may he be exalted, is therefore an attribute of his action and not an attribute of his essence, or it is indicative of absolute perfection [*kamāl muṭlaq*].[44]

The perfections are not included among the five attributes. However, this does not mean that Maimonides denies their existence in God. Rather, the fact that they are not mentioned in chapter 52 indicates that they are not "attributes" in any normal sense at all.

Here Maimonides explicitly returns to explaining the correct meaning of scripture. That reminds the reader that the purpose of the *Guide* is exegesis. The exegetical strand is also evident at the beginning of the section on divine attributes, when Maimonides explains why such attributes appear in scripture. The reason given is that people need to be taught truth in a way that they can understand. So they are told that God contains all perfections, even if perfections as they exist in God cannot be understood. "Necessity required that all of them be given guidance to the belief in the existence of God, may he be exalted, and in his possessing all the perfections."[45] And again, "he is perfect in various manners of perfection."[46] Things are figuratively ascribed to God "in order that his acts should be indicated by this means. And those particular acts are figuratively ascribed to him in order to indicate a certain perfection [*kamāl*] that is not identical with the particular act mentioned."[47]

This shows that, at the very least, Maimonides thought that it was proper for the general populace to believe that God contains certain perfections. It may be possible to argue that Maimonides only wanted the masses to accept this notion so they would adhere to the law. That would place it in the category of necessary rather than true beliefs.[48] In such a context, a necessary belief may be one that is not literally true but has some pedagogical merit in leading people to act in a certain way for political welfare.[49] Such beliefs would hold out a reward for good actions that encourages people to act well, even if the reward, taken literally, might not come about. For example, a biblical passage promises that rain will fall at an appropriate time if the people obey the commandments, but Maimonides did not believe that rainfall is causally dependent on keeping them. However, the balance of evidence favors the notion that Maimonides really does believe that perfections exist in God.

There is no doubt that Maimonides considers it necessary to teach the masses certain doctrines without fully explaining all of the subtleties to them. Nevertheless, the necessary beliefs he mentions, namely God's unity, knowledge, power, will, and eternity, should be taught to the masses not for the sole reason of persuading them to act in a certain manner but also because they are true.[50] Maimonides states that these doctrines should be taught to the masses on the basis of *taqlīd*, which "means the unquestioning acceptance of the guidance of others or the uncritical acquiescence to the opinions and teaching of people whom one holds in esteem."[51] These same doctrines should ideally be studied and properly understood by all who are capable. Although acquiescence to truth is far inferior to sound assent based on knowledge (*taṣdīq*), it is still better than total neglect of true doctrines.[52]

In a later chapter, Maimonides expands on the claim that scripture uses attributes that are perfections in humans in order to teach people that God is perfect. He explains that those who posit essential attributes in God were led to do so because they took scripture literally. They believed that scripture teaches that God contains perfections in the same way that humans do. In truth, Maimonides says, "the purpose for which all these attributes are used is to predicate perfection of him, but not the particular notion which is a perfection with respect to creatures possessing a soul."[53] This is a clear statement that perfections occur in scripture not only to persuade people to act in a certain way, although that element is present, but also to indicate real perfections in God. There is also a comment about attributes of action that accounts for some of these perfections: "most of these attributes are attributes pertaining to his diverse actions."[54] That Maimonides says "most" is important, as it indicates that this is not true of all of them. Again, the indication is that there is more to understand.

The fact that Maimonides argues that the only attributes that are common to God and creatures are attributes of action does not imply that he rejects the notion that perfections exist in God. Although he must think that those perfections are totally different from created perfections, it seems that Maimonides does consider perfections to exist in God. These perfections are utterly unlike human perfections but are indicated in scripture by human perfections since that is the only way human language can refer to them.

4.5 SUMMARY

In this chapter, I have aimed to achieve a number of things by way of introducing the issue of Maimonides' negative theology. He focuses on the need to negate attributes of God, rather than explaining how it may be possible to assert that God is perfect in all ways. This fact may go some way toward accounting for the emphasis that later interpreters have placed on the negative motion at the expense of Maimonides' references to God's perfections. Maimonides does not say that there are no perfections in God in this section of the *Guide*. On the contrary, he insists in a number of places that perfections do exist in God but that those perfections have nothing in common with the perfections in creatures. He insists that the words that scripture uses to describe God are not to be taken univocally. The issue he addresses, then, is not whether humans can know that God should be considered to contain all perfections without compromising the divine simplicity or falling afoul of anthropomorphic statements. Rather, it concerns the question of whether or not words can express those perfections. He argues that any words used equivocally of both God and creation would be guilty of implicitly denying God's unity. Nevertheless, it does not follow that Maimonides wishes to deny that perfections exist in God in an uncreated way. In order to sustain his position, Maimonides insists that since perfection terms are derived from created things, they refer properly and primarily to created perfections. That means that if they are also used to refer to divine perfections, they will associate those perfections with members of the created world, and that is unacceptable. Given this problem, how can Maimonides continue to insist that perfections do really exist in God? Chapters 4 and 5 below will explore a possible solution to the problem by explaining how uncreated perfections might be pictured and how they could be sufficiently different from created perfections so as not to be encompassed by the definition of the created perfections, thus avoiding Maimonides' critique of positive attributes.

CHAPTER 5

✦

Religious Language (B): Perfections and Simplicity

T his chapter builds on the arguments of the previous one as part of a progression toward offering a solution to difficulties many have raised concerning Maimonides' view of what can be known and said about God. There is an extent to which this chapter in particular could be viewed as an exercise in using the *Guide* in the way in which Maimonides advises the reader to do so. As explained in the first chapter of this book, Maimonides writes his *Guide* in such a way as to make sure that it reveals only so much as is appropriate for each individual reader. One of the ways in which he tries to achieve this goal is by instructing the reader to read other works dealing with the issues he includes, thus ensuring that any understanding of those issues requires the ability to penetrate philosophical discussions; those discussions are often aimed at advanced students rather than beginners. Furthermore, he relies on the reader's own capability to think through the issues independently. Both of these pieces of advice must be taken into account in an interpretation of the part of the *Guide* concerned with divine attributes, because the issue of divine simplicity and religious language in the *Guide* is obscure; background issues are not explained extensively, and connections are not explicitly drawn. It may be argued, then, that no interpretation can appeal to a particular text in the *Guide* for confirmation of all details. Nevertheless, there are allusions and pointers that help the diligent student, and Maimonides' explicit statements may still tend toward a certain view. The first task of this chapter is to explain and expand on the little that Maimonides says about divine simplicity. The second task is to explain how the doctrine fits with the issues considered in the previous chapter: how can God be an indivisible unity and also contain all perfections?

5.1 GOD AND EXISTENCE

The obvious question facing anyone who predicates perfections of God is how to square such predication with the divine unity. The question is pertinent to Maimonides' own project, since, as related in chapter 4, he opposes those who predicate normal perfections of God. He presents the doctrine of divine simplicity as an explanation of what is meant by the statement "God is One." The statement needs to be understood in a particular way, because attributing any number, including unity, to something attaches an accident to it.[1] Maimonides explains that "one" and "many" are accidents in the genus of "discrete quantity."

> Oneness and multiplicity are accidents that attain to an existent thing with regard to its being many or one.[2]

However, the necessary existent can have no accidents. Therefore nothing falling under the genus of quantity, including the number one, may be predicated of it.

> To ascribe to him whose existence is necessary, who is truly simple [basīṭ], to whom composition [tarkīb] cannot attach in any way, the accident of oneness is just as absurd as to ascribe to him the accident of multiplicity.[3]

When God is described as "One," it must mean something other than what is normally meant by the word *one*. Accordingly, the chapter closes with the following explanation:

> when we say one, the meaning is that he has no equal and not that the notion of oneness attaches to his essence.[4]

These quotations show that Maimonides employs the doctrine of divine unity to safeguard the distinction of God from the created world in two respects: uniqueness and indivisibility.[5] The easier of the two to grasp is the assertion that God "has no equal." God's uniqueness does not involve God's being the only member of a species, though, since it does not mean that "the notion of oneness attaches to his essence." This, too, means something different. The first aspect of the doctrine follows from the second: God is unique because God is not composite. That God is simple, then, is the second respect in which God is one, and that is what is meant by the assertion that there is no composition in God. Any attributes God has must be identical with God's essence; otherwise, God would be composed of both essence and the attribute in question. Even the most fundamental distinction that exists in all created things, that of essence and existence, does not apply to God. God's existence is necessary, so God's essence is identical with God's existence. So in order to secure the two implications of God's unity, Maimonides uses the distinction between existence and essence to show that God is the necessary of existence. In the case of God, by contrast with other things, the distinction does not hold, so God is both unique and absolutely indivisible.

5.1.1 Existence

Maimonides' explanation of existence is very brief. The nature of existence is one of the matters of which the reader is expected to possess a certain amount of prior knowledge. Here Maimonides expects the student who would understand these matters fully to read widely and think independently. What Maimonides does say appears in the context of his explanation of the meaning of an uncaused, and therefore necessary, being. His clearest expression appears immediately before his explanation that number cannot attach to God. He states that in all things that are caused, "existence is an accident happening to the existing thing" (*'araḍ 'āriḍ lil-mawǧūd*).[6] Maimonides thus distinguishes existence from essential attributes. The consequence of asserting that existence is accidental is that it must be seen as "something additional to the quiddity of that which exists."

The notion that existence is distinct from essence is common among medieval thinkers. It is developed by Alfarabi as a means to distinguish the first, God, from all other things.[7] It is taken further by Avicenna, who uses "accident" (*'araḍ*) to describe the relationship of existence to essence. The way in which Maimonides words his statement is similar to Avicenna's numerous expressions of the idea and appears to be an allusion to the Avicennan view.[8] By adopting that position, Maimonides perhaps opens himself up to a misunderstanding and consequent critique, which became common as a result of Averroes' critique of Avicenna.[9] Ḥasdai Crescas is an example of a later Jewish author who took both Avicenna and Maimonides to task for describing existence as an accident:

> Avicenna and al-Ġazālī,[10] and the Rav who follows them, hold that existence differs from quiddity and that it is an accident happening to it. . . . A not inconsiderable doubt occurs according to the opinion of one who says that the existence in the rest of the existing things [besides God] is other than the quiddity, and that it is an accident occurring to it. This is because if the existence is an accident, it follows necessarily that it exist in a subject. The existence would therefore have existence. . . . Thus, it would follow necessarily that if this accident bestows the existence and the continuity on the essence it would be prior to the subject in terms of the essence. . . . But it has already been posited as an attribute! This inconsistency cannot hold.[11]

Crescas is here accusing Avicenna and Maimonides of a serious and elementary mistake: the belief that existence bears the same relation to things as other nonessential properties. In truth, Avicenna held no such position, and neither did Maimonides. By describing existence as an accident ('araḍ), Maimonides cannot intend to characterize it as an accident like other accidents, since all other accidents add something to the essence to which they are attached by inhering in the essence. By contrast, unlike other accidental or nonessential properties, which inhere in a prior subject and add something to the essence of that subject, existence does not inhere in a subject. That would be impossible, because inhering requires a preexisting subject; existence cannot inhere in a prior subject, since there would be no prior subject for it to inhere in unless that very property, existence, is already present. Existence therefore adds nothing to the essence of the thing to which it attaches because it is presupposed to the essence. For Maimonides, the fact that existence is not an essential attribute is enough to mark it out as accidental; that is simply his way of distinguishing it from essential attributes. Whatever the relationship between an existing thing and its existence, the two are not identical. It remains the case, however, that existence is related to the existing thing differently from the way in which other properties are related to that thing.

5.1.2 Instances of Properties: Accidents and Existence

Nowhere does Maimonides go into great detail explaining exactly why existence can be considered an accident and how, if at all, it differs from other properties warranting the name *accident*. In order to clarify what he might be driving at, the reader must consider more than only what is in the *Guide*. My account draws on the work of recent philosophers who argue that existence is a "rich" property, containing all perfections in an unlimited way.[12] As Maimonides does, they argue that God should be seen as the only necessarily existing being, a being that contains all perfections but remains simple. To prepare the ground for this claim, let me first examine how one might think of existence and its relationship to existing things. Considering the difference between existence and other accidents provides a useful way in.

Some properties are instantiated in individuals as accidents. The properties themselves do not exist independently but only as properties of a substance. Since in Maimonides' view, "no species exists outside the mind," instances of properties must be dependent on a substance.[13] The subject in question, which is defined by its essence, is therefore always logically prior to its accidents. There are two ways in which this is true: in respect of individuation and in respect of actuality. These two ways need to be clarified before any discussion of the relationship between essence and existence can proceed.

The first way in which substance is prior to accident is in respect of individuation. This means that accidents depend on their subjects to be distinct from other accidents of the same sort. For example, one instance of a color may be differentiated from another instance of the same color by inhering in a different subject. Even if the two subjects are of the same species, they remain distinct, because they are two instances of that species. Matter is the differentiating principle of substances, and substances differentiate their accidents from those of other substances. Only by virtue of a substance's existing are its accidents different from other instances of the same property, those instances being accidents that inhere in different substances. So an accident can be said to be parasitic on the existence of its substance for its own individuation. The second respect in which a substance is logically prior to its accidents is in respect of actuality: the substance is the subject in which the accidents inhere, and the accident depends on the subject's actuality for its own actuality. This means that an accident can only exist if there is a prior existing subject in which it can inhere. It is only actual inasmuch as the subject is actual, and therefore its existence is parasitic on that of the substance.

In the case of existence, the same is true in one of these two respects. The existence of a particular thing may be distinguished from other instances of existence of the same kind of thing because it exists in a subject: the subject is that which distinguishes one instance of existence from another. In respect of individuation, then, the existence of that thing is posterior to, and dependent on, the subject with which it is connected. The existence is individuated in a substance because of that substance, not because of the existence. Existence, therefore, shares the first aspect of the relationship to essence with accidents: it depends on its substance in order to be individuated. This may be why there is a similarity and why existence warrants the term *accident*. There is a way in which existence must be considered to be logically prior to essence, however, and this is the cause of Crescas's unrest and the reason existence must be distinguished from a regular accident. Unlike other things that Maimonides may term accidents, existence must be assumed in order for there to be a subject in which properties may inhere. A property cannot inhere in a subject unless the subject exists, but a subject cannot exist before receiving its existence. Therefore, unlike in the case of an accident that inheres in a prior existing subject, existence cannot be a property that inheres in a substance. and a subject cannot be prior to its existence. In other words, it cannot be because of the substance that the substance itself exists, since existence is not a part of what it means to be that substance. Therefore, a thing's existence is not parasitic on its subject. If anything, the opposite is true, and the substance must somehow depend on its existence.

So a regular accident is individuated by a substance and also inheres in that substance, thereby deriving its actualization from the substance. By contrast, existence, although it is individuated by a substance, cannot be said to inhere in a substance and depend on it for its actuality. Existence is the actuality of the thing, so existence cannot be actualized by the thing. In concrete terms, this may be explained in the following way. Take an accidental property attributed to a thing, the color green ascribed to a ball, for example. A ball cannot be green if it does not exist. It cannot possess any color at all without the prior act of existing. However, when the terms are inverted, the fact that it exists would not imply that it has certain other properties such as being green. It could just as easily be pink. Existence does not imply or assume any other property. Although any existing thing must possess properties, the identity of those properties is not determined by the fact of existence. By contrast, all other properties assume existence. Existence must be logically prior to the substance, and existence is the only nonessential property of which this is true. The alternative would be that existence inheres in the ball, like the color green, which already somehow exists. That would mean that the ball would have to be logically prior to its own existence. However, that is impossible, because in order for existence to inhere in a subject, there would have to be a subject that already existed. In that case, the existence inhering in the subject would not be that by which the subject exists, and there would have to be another existence already attached to the thing. That, once more, is Crescas's objection, but, as mentioned above, there is no evidence that either Avicenna or Maimonides adhered to such a position. There is no suggestion that either considered things to exist with one kind of existence and then, after actualization, to exist with another, more complete kind of existence.[14]

By describing existence as an accident, Maimonides distinguishes a thing's existence from its essence. He may also be comparing existence to other accidents in that both depend on an essence for their individuation. However, in doing so, Maimonides does not go into detail to explain the relationship between substances and their instances of existence. It is clear, nevertheless, that he considered existence to be prior to essence in terms of actuality.[15] Although they may have the same extension, their intention differs. That is to say, there might not be anything that is not an existent or an existence that is not a thing, but to consider something inasmuch as it is a thing is different from considering something inasmuch as it is an existent. Essences remain prior in terms of individuation to their existence, however, since an essence distinguishes the instance of existence from other instances of existence.

5.1.3 Existence as a Bound

If the above argument is correct, existence is related to things differently from the way in which other properties or, in Maimonides' terms, accidents are related to things. Nevertheless, individual things do possess existence, and they are distinct from one another. There must therefore be some way in which existence somehow belongs to the substance without inhering in it. There must be a relation of some kind between the individual and its existence. Existence must be able to be individuated by a thing without inhering in it. So it is necessary to work out how a thing can be logically posterior to its existence while its existence remains a real property of the thing.

The relationship could be explained if a thing's essence is that which restricts its existence. The essence binds the existence and prevents it from being identified with other instances. In that case, the essence of a substance is related to that thing's existence as its bound. Both conditions of the relationship between essence and existence would then be fulfilled. Essence would be prior to existence in respect of individuation, thereby fulfilling the first condition, but posterior to existence in respect of actuality, thereby fulfilling the second condition, too. To elaborate slightly, a thing's existence would be dependent on its bound, and therefore posterior to its bound, in order to be distinct from other instances of existence: a thing would be logically prior to its existence in respect of individuation. However, a bound must be logically posterior to the thing it bounds, since there must be something for it to bind. In the present case, that thing is the existence of the individual. Hence, the fact that essence is the bound of its existence means that a thing's essence is logically posterior to its existence in respect of actuality.

Because Maimonides does not explain the relationship between essence and existence in any great detail, there are no texts within the *Guide* that could obviously be cited either to corroborate or to oppose the interpretation offered here. Nevertheless, there is evidence that it is germane to his position. Apart from explaining the difference between existence and other accidents, it is also implied by Maimonides' view that there is a hierarchy of being. If there is some kind of hierarchy in which those beings possessing the best faculties are higher up the scale, it would follow that the ranking depends on how many properties, and of which kind, are possessed by each member of the scale. This is because a bound would be seen as more restrictive the more properties it excludes.

Without considering exactly how the scale is made up, it is safe to say that Maimonides does believe in a hierarchy of increasingly perfect beings within the cosmos. So much is evident from a number of his ideas. The most basic ranking of things within the sublunar world is seen in Maimonides' ranking humans above animals, which themselves are superior to plants, which, in turn, are superior to inanimate beings.[16] Even within these divisions, there are further hierarchies. One example is in Maimonides' discussion of human perfection, where it is clear that some people are more perfect than others.[17] The same is true of prophets: some are more perfect than others.[18] Furthermore, the heavenly bodies are superior to the greatest beings in the sublunar realm, humans.[19]

5.2 NECESSARY EXISTENCE

This account of existence and the way it might be related to essence is helpful in the current context because it serves to clarify exactly what might be meant by the doctrine of divine simplicity, which states that there is no composition in God. To apply the discussion of existence to a necessarily existent being is no simple task, though. Since there is no composition in God and since God's existence has been established, there is no distinction between God and God's existence. This means that there is a fundamental difference between God and created things. Accordingly, Maimonides explains that existence may be termed an accident only in everything that has a cause for its existence.[20] In the case of something that is uncaused, God, the distinction between essence and existence does not hold: there can be no distinction between God's essence and God's existence.[21]

5.2.1 The Difference between God's Existence and Created Existence

Because God is God's existence, there is no need to search for a cause for God's existence beyond God's essence.[22] Therefore, both conditions relying on the distinction between essence and existence cannot hold of God. The above argument shows that in beings that do not possess existence as part of their essence, an individual is the bound of its existence. An individual is prior to its existence in respect of individuation and posterior to its existence in respect of actuality. Both of these conditions rely on there being a difference between the individual and its existence. That is, there must be a difference between bound and bounded. Because there is no distinction between essence and existence in God, it is impossible for one to be prior to the other. In the case of a being to which existence does not attach as a nonessential property, because its existence is identical with its essence, essence cannot be posterior to existence in respect of actuality, since essence and existence are identical. Whereas what holds of the relationship between a created thing and its existence depends on there being a distinction between the two, what holds of God and God's existence cannot, since there is no distinction. Consequently, God cannot be prior or posterior to God's existence in respect of either actuality or individuation. However, if the account I have offered is correct, there cannot be an identifiable being that is not distinct from its existence. It seems, then, that the above account of the relationship between essence and existence cannot be applied to God.

So there seems to be some difficulty with the doctrine of divine simplicity. It asserts that there is no difference between God and God's existence. But I have argued that for a thing to exist, it must have an essence distinguishing its existence from the existence of other things. The statement that God's essence is identical to God's existence appears to be incoherent for two reasons. First, existence cannot serve as a bound to existence. Existence is that which is bounded. If it were also to be the bound itself, there would be a bound that bounds itself. In that case, there would be nothing logically prior to the bound and hence nothing to bind. The consequence of asserting that God is God's existence therefore seems to be that God cannot have an actual instance of existence, since that would require the bound to be actualized by what is bounded, its existence. Second, it is through its bound rather than its existence that a thing is individuated, so if a thing's bound is nothing other than its existence, there would be no individual. Since God lacks an individuator, a bound, God cannot be an individual existent distinguished from other individuals that exist. In sum, if existence is conceived along the lines that I have explained here, the idea of a necessarily existent being seems to be incoherent. It would amount to a claim that there can be a being in which the bound (essence) and the instance (existence) are identical. But Maimonides says that this is precisely how God should be thought of. Does this show that Maimonides could not have thought of existence as a bound? Not at all. Because he distinguishes between accidental existence in created beings and necessary existence in God, there is yet more work to be done before a conclusion can be drawn. This difference between uncreated existence, which is unique to God, and derived existence, which is possessed by everything else, turns out to be key. Taking it into account renders intelligible the assertion that in God, essence and existence are the same.

5.2.2   Uncreated Existence/Uncreated Perfections

So far in this chapter, I have concerned myself with matters preliminary to further consideration of those treated in chapter 4. The time to connect them has now arrived. The question raised in chapter 3 was how the existence of divine perfections can be squared with Maimonides' negative theology. The aim of his negative theology is to prevent improper use of language from compromising divine simplicity and thereby inappropriately comparing God to creation. I have explained that Maimonides does not differentiate between God and God's existence. In order to preserve the unity of God, God must also be identical with all of the divine perfections. Working out how it could make sense to say that God is God's essence, in spite of the seeming incoherence of such a position, will help to explain how Maimonides can insist that God contains all perfections without compromising divine simplicity and while maintaining that they differ from created perfections in a way that precludes univocal predication.

As in the case of perfections, Maimonides states that existence can only be attributed to God and other things by way of "absolute equivocation."[23]

How can he attribute perfections and existence to God while maintaining that any language used to refer to God's perfections and existence must be used of God and creation by way of equivocation? How can Maimonides assert that perfections really exist in God and that God is God's existence, both of which he clearly does, without falling afoul of his own critique of those who attribute perfections of the same species as created perfections? To offer an answer to these questions, the following must hold. If perfections are to exist in God but are to be totally different from perfections that exist in created beings, uncreated perfections must not be defined in the same way as created perfections. They cannot possess the specific characteristics of the created perfections.

If something is said to be good, the meaning of the word *good* is always defined by the subject to which it is attached. Nevertheless, there is a community of meaning among different goods. The more a created thing approximates the form of the thing it is, the more perfect it is said to be. Avicenna explains that things strive for their own actualization. They desire their own existence. In doing so, they desire to be the best possible instance of that which they are. "The good in general is that which everything within its bound desires and through which its existence is completed."[24] Things are good inasmuch as they are in act. They are good if they are actually that which they are supposed to be, rather than being deficient. They are bad inasmuch as nonexistence and deficiencies are attached to them. In such cases, they do not exist properly as that which they are essentially. Good and existence are therefore equal. Avicenna's conclusion is echoed in the *Guide*. Maimonides also states that "the good [ḫayr] is existence [wuǧūd]."[25] The idea pervades his work and is obviously present, for example, in his explanation of the presence of evil in the world.[26]

Consider two different kinds of things as examples. A person is more perfect the more virtuous he or she is. An apple is more perfect the tastier it is. In both of these cases, the good is defined and limited by the thing it is said of. It is defined along with the definition of the thing to which it belongs. All of these attributes may be found in created objects to a greater or lesser degree. The most perfect of any of these perfections would contain the perfection in question to the highest possible degree. It would constitute a limit beyond which there could be no greater degree of that perfection. For example, the most perfect apple would constitute a limit beyond which apples cannot pass, as no apple could be better than the most perfect possible one. These perfections would then be of the same species as all other similar kinds of perfections.

This kind of limit is the maximum or minimum of a particular scale. So, for example, the limit of speed is the speed of light.[27] This is the maximum possible speed; nothing can travel faster than light. It may be considered the most perfect speed. Similarly, the limit of human knowledge would contain everything that a human could possibly know, and it would contain it in the same way as humans know. A limit of any attribute, then, is the maximum, or perfect, instance of that attribute or, mutatis mutandis, the minimum of the attribute. It is important to note that such a limit remains a member of the scale or species of attributes of which it is a perfection. So a maximum speed is still a speed, or, to take another example, a perfect piece of music, should there be such a thing, remains a piece of music, albeit one that is vastly superior to other instances of music.

These are the kinds of perfections that Maimonides argues cannot be attributed to God. He rejects the claims of those who posit attributes in God, because they posit attributes that, although perfect, are still the same as crea-turely attributes, because they are both "included in the same definition."[28] If Maimonides wishes to attribute perfections to God, while maintaining that the perfections do not fall under the same definition as created perfections, he must be indicating that uncreated perfections do not share the characteristics of created perfections. Uncreated goodness would not be something limited to any category. It could not be the good of any particular genus or species and would therefore not be subject to the same definition of the species. In what way, then, could it be considered a perfection?

Besides the kind of limit that is a maximum or minimum of a scale, a limit might be thought of as different in kind from that which it limits. Such a limit occurs when the defining characteristic of the scale in question is varied to the extent that it no longer exists. That accounts for the fact that the limit is not a part of the scale it limits, since it does not possess the specific characteristic of that scale; it is not a member of the species it limits, since it does not possess the specific difference of that species. For that reason, it cannot be subsumed under the same definition as the scale. Such a perfection would therefore not be subject to Maimonides' critique of applying ordinary attributes to God. A series of polygons is an example of a limit in which the defining characteristic of the scale in question is multiplied out of existence. Ordinarily, there could not be a limit of polygons possessing the maximum number of sides a polygon could have. No matter how many sides a shape has, it could conceivably have yet more. It will always remain a polygon until it has an infinite number of sides, but then it would become a circle. So the limit of polygons could be considered a circle. Although a circle is not a polygon at all, it is that toward which polygons, in a series of ever increas-ingly sided shapes, tend. This is because in order for a series of polygons to morph into a circle, the defining characteristic of a polygon would have to disappear. The specific difference would be multiplied out of existence. Limits like these could be considered analogous to the kind of uncreated perfections that would be perfections without being subsumed under, and therefore limited by, the definitions of the kinds of things they are perfections of. While an uncreated perfection would not bear exactly the same relationship as a circle does to a set of polygons, or as motionlessness does to speed, the analogy is helpful. Circles can be represented in human thought and language.

Uncreated perfections cannot. The point is that thinking of uncreated perfections as limits that do not belong to the scale that they limit allows those perfections to be unlimited by definitions. They are perfections of a scale, but as limits of it, they are unlimited by it.[29]

Maimonides is often taken to mean that perfections do not exist in God. However, what he rejects is the idea that created perfections exist in God. His objection to those who believe in attributes is that they compromise God's simplicity. If "absolute perfections," or limitless perfections, do not compromise divine simplicity, he would accept that they can do so. The notion of uncreated perfection makes sense of the idea that God is identical with all perfections and remains simple. It also preserves total ignorance of God's essence.

5.2.3 Uncreated Existence

I mentioned above that Maimonides holds to a metaphysical system in which existence is the richest of properties and in which there is a hierarchy of being. I argued that this fact indicates that essence should be seen as that which limits existence to a particular, containing only those perfections within the essence's limit. It is clear from his own statements that he considers God to be a simple necessary being and that what he means by this is that God is God's existence and is uncaused. What is not clear is how such a statement might be understood. If uncreated, unlimited, absolute existence is similar to the unlimited perfections outlined above, Maimonides' assertions are intelligible. Before applying the above distinction between kinds of perfections to them, then, it is appropriate to consider whether an uncreated instance of existence might be explained in such a way.

Maimonides does not use the Arabic term for "absolute existence" (*wuǧūd al-muṭlaq*), but in a different context, he does refer to God's existence as "the most perfect of existence" (*wuǧūdihi akmāl al-wuǧūd*).[30] Apart from terminological considerations, though, there are other reasons for thinking that Maimonides accepts the possibility of an unlimited instance of existence. It is implied by the idea that essence is related to existence as its bound, which in turn, as I argued above, is implied by the notion that there is a hierarchy of being. Before arguing this point, let us consider what an unlimited instance of existence would be by comparison with unlimited perfections. Unlimited perfections were seen to be completely different from those things constituting the scale of which the perfections are a limit. That difference lies in the fact that such perfections do not possess the specific difference of the things in the species that the perfections limit. Therefore, they are not on the same scale as the species or, indeed, the perfection. To apply the same method to existence, if the essence of an existing thing is characterized as the bound of the thing's existence, if this is its specific difference, as I argued above, an unlimited instance of the scale of existing things would have no bound. If it did have a bound, it would not be an unlimited instance, since it would fall under the same definition as the members of the scale it limits, and that is what Maimonides wishes to avoid. By contrast, existence that is unrestricted by a bound would not be definable, since the bound is the essence, and the essence is what is subject to definition.

In order for there to be an unlimited instance of existence, there must be a series of things that can be ordered to form a scale of existent things. Now, because existence is bounded, it is restricted by the essence. That is what makes it an individual particular. Things exist in many different ways, but no one thing contains every mode of existence. A bound is more constricting the more properties it excludes. Given that a thing contains fewer or more perfections depending on its bound, which is its essence, a thing that contains no bound at all would be considered a limitless instance of existence. That is because the extent of the bound would have been multiplied out of existence, and all that remained would be unbounded, limitless existence.

The argument can be even more forceful. The existence of a scale of existing things not only allows limitless existence but even points toward it. Therefore, if one is to assert that there is an unlimited instance of existence, one must also assert that there is some kind of hierarchy of being. That hierarchy would be a scale by which things could be ranked according to the degree of existence they have, according to the amount of existence the bound allows within itself. The less limited the existence of a thing is, that is, the less limiting its bound, the more existence it could be considered to have. It would thereby be closer to the perfect instance of existence. However, any instance of existence must always be bounded as an instance is individuated, and only through its bound can it be individuated from other instances. An instance of existence, therefore, can never contain all things that could exist, unless that instance is considered to be the aggregate of everything in existence. Hence no individual could ever be the limit of existence. Such a hierarchy, however, could point toward an unlimited instance of existence in which the bound was widened so far as to be extended out of existence. This would be the unrestricted limit of existence. It would obviously not be an instance of existence, though, since it lacks a bound, and the bound, being the individuator, is what makes an instance of existence an "instance." It would therefore differ absolutely from any instance of existence, despite retaining the similarity in existence.

Since Maimonides is working with such a hierarchy of existence, he can accept the notion of an unlimited instance of existence in which the characteristic by which the individuals on the scale are ranked, their bound, has been expanded so far as to have been widened out of existence altogether. The unlimited existence would therefore be an instance of existence with no bound at all.

5.2.4 The Identity of Instance and Bound in God

An unlimited instance of existence is allowed, and even implied, by Maimonides' belief in a scale of existence and also by the notion that existence is a bound. Considering God to be an unlimited instance of existence solves the difficulties involved in suggesting that there is no distinction between God's essence and God's existence and that God is an uncreated and therefore necessary being.

The first difficulty is that since there is no difference between bound and bounded in God, God lacks any incompleteness in respect of individuation and so lacks an individuator. If God is understood to be a limited instance of existence, this makes an assertion of identity between essence and existence in God incoherent, because it asserts that what essentially has a bound, an instance of existence, has no bound. If Maimonides is understood to be making an assertion concerning an unlimited, because uncreated, instance, however, the problem is irrelevant, since an unlimited instance is by definition boundless. There is no inconsistency in saying that an unlimited instance of existence is not bounded, because an unlimited instance of existence cannot be bounded. The second difficulty is that in order to exist, a bound needs to bind prior existence. Once more, however, if the instance in question is an uncreated instance of existence, then the problem is irrelevant. An uncreated instance of existence does not need to bound prior existence, since, again, it is by definition boundless. Therefore, not only does it not need to bind prior existence, but it cannot bind prior existence.

This discussion dovetails with Maimonides' interpretation of God's uniqueness. There can only be one unlimited instance of existence. If there were many, they would be individuated and would require a limiting essence restricting their existence from one another. They would not then be unbound and unlimited. So if there is an unbound instance of existence, there can only be one unique one. God's absolute uniqueness has consequently been preserved. However, that there is only one God then becomes a statement with different meaning from that there is only one world, since in the case of God, there is no individuation as such. Therefore, just as "instance of existence" in "unlimited instance of existence" is different from "instance of existence" in "limited instance of existence," "one" has different meanings when applied to the unlimited existence and when applied to all other instances of existence.[31] There is an important sense in which God is not individuated and thereby distinguishable from other things. This is what is meant by God's transcendence, and it follows from the claim that there is absolutely no similarity at all between God's necessary existence and the existence belonging to any created being.

A further consequence is that if God is to be identified with God's existence, God contains all perfections but can still remain simple. A bound is a restriction. Consequently, the tighter the bound, the more restricting it is and the more perfections it excludes. The less restricting the individual bound, the more properties the individual contains. Unbounded existence—an unlimited, uncreated instance of existence—will therefore contain all perfections. An uncreated instance of existence can be seen to include all perfections within itself. So Maimonides states that God exists in the same way that God is living, powerful, and knowing: "he exists not through existence. In the same way he lives not through life, is powerful not through power and his knowing is not through knowledge."[32]

5.3 USING ANALOGICAL LANGUAGE TO REFER TO GOD

Maimonides concludes that although perfections exist in God, perfection terms can only be used of God and humans equivocally. He insists that negation is therefore the most proper method of referring to God.[33] Maimonides writes that even existence is predicated of God and creatures by way of absolute equivocation (*ištirāk maḥḍ*).[34] If existence is always an accident in created things and all human knowledge and language derive from experience of created things, it seems to follow that it is impossible for humans to know, or to speak about, something that possesses existence in any way except as accidental. If this is true, it would be impossible to know or speak about a necessarily existent being.

According to many theologians of the time, it would still be possible to use language to refer to God by arguing that certain terms are used in a prior way of God and in a posterior way of created things. Aquinas's strategy here is informative. He builds on a distinction between the thing signified and the way in which it is signified.[35] This distinction facilitates his claim that the attributes are only different in the human manner of signifying but are the same in themselves. He is then able to argue that perfection terms can be predicated "primarily of God and derivatively of creatures."[36] The words have a literal meaning that humans cannot understand. Therefore, the way in which they are used, their *de dicto* or analogical sense, means something quite different from their real, *de re*, sense.[37]

This distinction is what allows Aquinas to appeal to analogy. He argues that perfection words are, in fact, used properly of God and analogically of creatures, since God contains those perfections in a pure form. They are different in the way they are signified by creatures, but in God, since God contains all perfections in a simple manner, they are the same. Therefore, he is able to argue that God possesses both perfect wisdom and perfect power at the same time without that implying plurality in God's essence. He says that the attributes are different in our way of signifying but are the same in themselves. Maimonides, on the other hand, makes no such distinction. He is prepared to allow only the sense of a word that can be understood by creatures, which is the meaning deriving from creatures, to be its true sense. He must therefore conclude that those words must be used equivocally of God and creatures.

One way in which Maimonides could have expressed a use of equivocal terms that would allow something like Aquinas's position, is by describing the relationship between the terms predicated of God and of creatures as amphiboly (*taškīk*). Amphibolous terms can signify a relationship of priority and posteriority.[38] Such a relationship between divine attributes and created attributes is offered in response to Maimonides by Gersonides, among others.[39] As discussed above, however, Maimonides does not use the term in such a way in the *Guide*.[40] It is possible for him to agree that *prior* and *posterior* can be used of things in general but not of God, because he considers words to signify created things primarily. He cannot do otherwise, because he does not allow for the distinction between the way words are used and what they really mean. For Maimonides, language is derived from created things and signifies those things both in our understanding and in its true meaning. That is the root of the difference between Maimonides' doctrine of religious language and that of Aquinas.[41]

5.4 SUMMARY

I have explained a way in which Maimonides' position on divine simplicity and religious language can be understood to be consistent with his repeated assertions that perfections exist in God. I have argued that his refusal to allow positive attributes does not imply that he fails to recognize the presence of "unlimited perfections" in God. Both his explicit statements and his metaphysical positions point toward the conclusion that he accepts that perfections exist in God. If a thing bounds existence, the conclusion that existence contains all perfections, which are exemplified by the things that bound it in a greater or lesser way, would then follow. So the very fact that God is considered to be a boundless instance of existence implies that God contains all perfections. Nothing with a bound, which is inevitably restrictive, can contain all perfections; boundless existence would contain all perfections. However, Maimonides does not accept that those perfections can be represented by human language or in the human intellect. His doctrine of negative attributes does not allow any positive language to be used of God, because the limits of language are defined by the limits of the intellect. On his view, terms denoting created perfections cannot be used to signify more than humans can know by them. We do not know God's essence, and we cannot refer to it. But we do know that God is the fullness of being, the necessary of existence, and that God contains all perfections. To deny that God has attributes is not to deny God. Nor is denying that humans can grasp anything at all about God's essence or use language of God the same as denying God.

Divine perfections are "absolute perfections," and, like the deity, they are limitless. They are therefore not limited by being an instance of the perfection. When Maimonides negates the privation of a perfection, the presence of an instance of perfection in God is what is denied. Instances of limited perfections are dependent on the individuator. They are posterior to the individuator and incomplete with regard to it. The situation is different in the case of existence, but that may be explained by the observation that existence does not inhere in an individual but is bounded by an individual. Therefore, in the case of an instance of existence, it is limited by the individual binding it. In the case of God, essence does not bind existence, since God is not limiting. God is limitless, and limitless, infinite perfection does exist in God. The claims that God is God's existence and that God is identical to all divine perfections are therefore intelligible.

In the next chapter, I will argue that knowledge is a divine perfection. As such, it is limitless. My argument will offer an answer to a problem raised in Maimonidean scholarship. Through an examination of Maimonides' text, it will also provide further evidence that Maimonides does believe that perfections exist in God and that those perfections should be understood as uncreated, limitless perfections.

∽

CHAPTER 6

Religious Language (C): God's Knowledge as a Divine Perfection

One of the discussions that can throw light on Maimonides' approach to religious language revolves around what he has to say about God's knowledge. His basic theological commitments include divine omniscience, but it is not immediately apparent how his negative theology, which includes the claim that "knowledge" can only be used equivocally to refer to both divine knowledge and human knowledge, can be squared with this. In order to show that they are compatible, then, I must consider some objections that have been raised to his account. It is regularly asserted that there are inconsistencies between what Maimonides says about God's knowledge and his doctrine of negative attributes, which I examined in chapters 3 and 4.[1] Such perceived inconsistencies have led scholars to drive a wedge between the two doctrines and either to posit an "esoteric" doctrine or to explain away the problems by neglecting some of Maimonides' claims. Close attention to Maimonides' arguments shows that he describes God's knowledge in such a way as to make it consistent with the idea of uncreated perfections that I explained in chapter 6. This is because Maimonides' exposition of God's knowledge requires him to argue that "knowledge" is used equivocally of God and of humans, consonant with his general take on religious language. Therefore, positing knowledge in God does not force Maimonides into simultaneously holding contradictory beliefs both to be true. The examination will provide further evidence that the notion of uncreated perfections is relevant to Maimonides' treatment of divine attributes in general.

6.1 GOD'S PRODUCTIVE KNOWLEDGE

The law teaches that God knows all things. "Nothing is hidden in any way from him, may he be exalted, but everything is revealed to his knowledge."[2]

In Maimonides' view, God knows all particulars in their particularity. He argues that God knows all particulars because God's knowledge is prior to, and somehow causative of, the things that it knows. This position appears to have some serious philosophical difficulties. Maimonides deals with these in the *Guide* when he replies to those philosophers who deny the law's opinion, and I will come to his response below. Nevertheless, the variety of interpretations of Maimonides' view on the topic show that his own position is still unclear.

In order to explain how God can know particulars while the difference between God's knowledge and human knowledge is preserved, Maimonides offers an analogy that, although imperfect, helps to illustrate his point.[3] He likens God's knowledge to that of a human craftsman in that both are causative. However, according to Maimonides, the fact that God's knowledge is causative ultimately differentiates it from human knowledge. That difference, along with the pervasiveness of God's causal activity, implies that God is omniscient.[4]

> There is a great difference between the knowledge that a maker [*'ilm al-ṣāni'*] has of a thing he has produced and the knowledge anyone else has of the same thing. That is that if the thing made is made in accordance with the knowledge of the maker, the thing that is made is a result of the maker's knowledge. The knowledge of any other who thinks about the thing made and comes to know it, on the other hand, is a result of the made thing. . . . And such is the case in the generality of existence and its relation to our knowledge and to his knowledge.[5]

There are two important differences between the knowledge that the creator of an artifact has of that artifact and the knowledge of an onlooker. The first is that a producer of an artifact is aware of the thing produced and understands all of its workings intimately before and after producing it. A second difference is that the artifact's form in its maker's mind acts as a cause in bringing the artifact into existence. Neither of these conditions applies to someone who knows the artifact by abstracting from experience and examining observations.

For the analogy, Maimonides uses the example of a water clock. The clock-maker knows exactly what the clock will do through his or her own understanding of the form of the clock. By contrast, a person examining the clock is unaware of how it works before beginning to examine it. Instead, the observer needs to investigate the workings of the clock and from them deduce what the clock will do at all times in order to understand its functions and to know what will happen in it. In this sense, the observer's knowledge of the clock is derivative of the clock's existence. An onlooker is therefore at a disadvantage by learning about the clock only from examining a limited number of its movements. Maimonides explains that "if you suppose that the motions of this instrument are infinite, the onlooker could never contain them in his knowledge."[6] The observer must make a judgment concerning the object's nature and the way it will always behave from the limited number of actions experienced. But the observer can never take into account all of the movements of the clock, so a judgment must always be made to include all of the particulars that occur at all times inside the clock by extrapolating from a limited number of the clock's movements. Knowledge proceeding through induction and gained from observation cannot have the same degree of certainty as that proceeding from a priori principles. The difference between induction from physical effects and deduction from metaphysical causes determines the epistemological status of the knowledge acquired. Maimonides is prepared to accept that sense experience affords undoubted premises. However, in principle, he is aware that more certainty can be had through knowledge of the general, which is then applied to the particular. The induction can become more certain the more cases are observed, but it can never be considered to be absolutely certain without any reservation, although it may be accepted as true.[7]

Maimonides is not alone in this but is building on a tradition of epistemology. He is applying a principle that can be found in Aristotle, who discusses the superiority of the properly scientific knowledge possessed by a scientist, *techne,* to the knowledge someone has as a result of experience, *empeirias.*[8] Aristotle considers how humans come to make universal judgments and how "art" subsequently comes into being. He explains that scientists extrapolate from their individual experiences and apply the knowledge they gain from those events to form a judgment about what occurs more generally. So, to use Aristotle's example, a doctor can know from experience of Socrates or Callias that some particular medicine will cure a certain ailment in those individuals. By making a generalization based on this knowledge, a doctor arrives at the scientific conclusion that the medicine in question cures the ailment when it is present in any individual. So scientific knowledge is superior to particular knowledge inasmuch as it is more general and therefore encompasses more things.[9]

Nevertheless, there is a respect in which experiential knowledge is superior to universal knowledge: only through experience can a scientist understand how to apply knowledge. This is because people who act do so through familiarity with particulars, since it is particulars that they are acting on and particular actions that they are performing: "all actions and processes of generation are concerned with singulars." One who possesses the universal knowledge required to heal someone will not be able to apply it without knowledge of the particulars that need curing. Although it remains the case that a scientist is considered wiser than an artist, because science requires knowledge of causes, there is a certain practical superiority possessed by one who has particular knowledge. For example, someone may know all of the principles of guitar making but might not be any good at building guitars.

By contrast, a skilled luthier would be able to create an instrument through past experience and practice, without knowing exactly why the properties of one piece of wood cause it to make a different sound from another piece of a different species.

So the knowledge that a scientist has is superior to that had through experience: universal knowledge is greater than particular knowledge, as it encompasses more. God's knowledge is universal, since it is productive and is self-knowledge. Maimonides likens the artificer's knowledge to God's, which is the cause of all things. In the same way that an artificer's knowledge is the cause of the clock, God's knowledge is the cause of the world.[10] Furthermore, in the same way that an artificer knows all of the actions that the artifact will undertake even before they occur, presuming it is not interfered with, God knows all of the things that happen in the cosmos at all times. This helps to bring out the difference between universal knowledge as it exists in God and as it exists in humans. In humans, particulars are apprehended through experience of those particulars, and universal judgments are made through experience of particulars. By contrast, God knows universals as their cause and so knows them through universals. Because of this, God's knowledge of universals is more "scientific" than human knowledge gained through observation.

In summary, the clockmaker's knowledge has two features that are absent from the knowledge of the clock's observer. The first is that it is prior to the artifact and causes the artifact, whereas the knowledge of an observer is posterior to the artifact and is caused by it. The second, which is consequent on the first, is that the maker's knowledge is more encompassing and, as such, enjoys a superior status. It can know all of the actions that the clock will perform without having to observe it. In the case of God, the type of superiority that knowledge of a particular affords is not lacking. God knows particulars as their cause. Therefore, God's knowledge does not lack at all in the ability to apply it.

To return to the question with which this chapter began, given that Maimonides seems to go to great lengths to deny that words can be used univocally of God and anything created, the fact that on this occasion he draws such a close parallel between God and a member of creation requires explanation.

6.2 AN INCONSISTENCY IN MAIMONIDES' ACCOUNT OF DIVINE KNOWLEDGE?

Maimonides argues in favor of God's knowing particulars, and he illustrates the superiority of God's knowledge by likening it to that of an artisan. Many scholars believe that this is an illegitimate move on his part. They claim that because he has put so much effort into distancing God from anthropomorphism, he is not entitled to use the analogy of an artisan's knowledge. Doing so is a flagrant abuse of his own extreme version of negative theology.[11] On the one hand, he stresses the inability of the human intellect to gain any grasp of God. On the other hand, when he draws a close parallel between God's knowledge and that of a human artificer, he seems to be positing a genuine similarity between God and humans. Since the two streams in Maimonides' thought are thought to be in conflict with each other, it is thought that they represent two irreconcilable views. Therefore, Maimonides' real opinion must be sought in one or the other or perhaps in neither. So the conflict between Maimonides' negative theology in part one of the *Guide* and his theological assertions in part three are considered a sign of esotericism.[12]

If this is indeed an instance of esotericism, the conflict seems to be far more obvious than has been made out, because there is no need even to connect parts one and three in order to discover it. Maimonides points out that "knowledge" must be used equivocally of God and of humans in the middle of his discussion of God's knowledge in part three. That is, in the same place as he predicates knowledge of God, he reiterates the very doctrine that is said to be inconsistent with that predication: "this knowledge is not of the same species [*naw'*] as ours so that we can draw an analogy with regard to it, but [it is] a totally different thing."[13] So great is the difference that there is no similarity at all between the two types of knowledge, and the word is used equivocally (*ištarāk*). "There is a community only in the terms whereas in the true reality of the thing there is a difference."[14] There is no need to connect diverse chapters of the *Guide* in order to discover the inconsistency, as Maimonides instructs those who would understand him properly to do; it does not seem to be a well-hidden secret.

In light of the distinction between uncreated and created perfections and Maimonides' claims that "absolute perfections" can be predicated of God, a possible solution opens up. If Maimonides' statements about God's thinking describe an uncreated instance of knowledge, he can preserve sufficient similarity between God's thought and human thought to warrant using the term while still insisting that it must be used equivocally. A more detailed examination of the chapters that Maimonides dedicates to the issue of the divine knowledge will show that Maimonides does, in fact, take God's knowledge to be a limitless, uncreated perfection. In the end, the apparent anthropomorphism is exactly what saves Maimonides from the charge of acting against his negative theology. His account does preserve the absolute difference between God's knowledge and human knowledge. He is able to posit knowledge in God as something that cannot be understood by humans or likened to human knowledge in much the same way that he was able to deny perfections of God, while simultaneously affirming that they exist in God in a completely different way.

6.3 THE STRUCTURE OF MAIMONIDES' ARGUMENTS FOR KNOWLEDGE IN GOD

To argue that the conflict between the two positions is apparent rather than real, I now turn in greater detail to the chapters in which Maimonides treats the differences between divine and human knowledge. The idea that God's knowledge is causative occurs, in different forms, in chapters 19 and 21 of part three.[15] Chapter 20 appears to be an interlude, but it is actually part of a progression. I will follow Maimonides' progression and begin with chapter 19.

6.3.1 Chapter 19: God's Knowledge and Providence

Chapter nineteen connects the previous section on providence, comprising chapters eight to seventeen, with the discussion of God's knowledge of particulars. One of the issues Maimonides considers when he addresses providence is evil.[16] Chapter 19 is not only about God's knowledge; it is also a continuation of the discussion of providence and evil. Maimonides' purpose now is to point out that the presence of evil in the world does not prove that God is ignorant of human affairs. He uses rhetorical means in order to persuade the reader that God does, in fact, have knowledge. Toward the end of the chapter, he writes:

> My entire aim in this chapter was to make it clear that this speculation is very ancient; I refer to the notion that God lacks apprehension [*idrāk*], which has occurred to the ignorant in view of the fact that the circumstances of individual humans, which by their nature are contingent, are not well ordered.[17]

Maimonides explains that some deny God's knowledge of individual events because what happens to humans seems to be disordered; joy and suffering do not seem to be a result of righteousness or evildoing. He writes that the objection was formulated in ancient times, and a response can be found in the Bible. The author of the Psalms, traditionally David, asks of those who deny that God knows their sinful actions, "he that formed the eye, shall he not see?" Maimonides explains that the verse means that someone is able to make an instrument only if he or she has some idea of how that instrument is to be used. The argument is based on the premise that in order to make an object, the agent must know that object. Since God is the maker of the world, God must know the world.

Rather than a complete argument for divine omniscience, this argument is a response to those who argue against God's knowledge on the basis of the presence of evil. It is not as sophisticated an argument as that which Maimonides presents in chapter 21, and it is not a response to the philosophers.

What the philosophers say about God's knowledge of particulars is outlined later on. He does not intend by the argument in chapter 19 alone to respond to the arguments of the philosophers who deny that God knows particulars but only to convince the less sophisticated that God has knowledge. The argument has a rhetorical aim, since it is intended to persuade people. It does not prove that God knows particulars in their particularity, although Maimonides does not openly say so. Only those who do not understand the difference between knowledge of individuals and knowledge of universals would be convinced. That is, the argument would only persuade people who do not understand that the intellect deals with universals.[18]

A brief consideration of the analogy suffices to show that Maimonides cannot use it to show that God knows all particulars. He writes that "unless a smith had a conception and an understanding of the meaning of sewing he would not make a needle in that form which alone permits the act of sewing."[19] Maimonides says that in the same way, God must know what it is to see in order to create an eye. God must also understand the workings of all of the other created things in order to create them in such a way that they function correctly, as, in Maimonides' opinion, they manifestly do.[20] Therefore, God must have a knowledge of the things in the world. So in Maimonides' view, the order in the universe indicates the existence of an intelligence ordering it. That intelligence cannot be nature itself, since "nature is not endowed with intellect."[21] There must therefore be some intellect ordering nature.

This argument purports to show that God must possess some knowledge. However, it leaves the nature of that knowledge open to question. To use Maimonides' own example, a smith needs to know how a needle is to be used and what is involved in sewing but need not know all of the individual occasions on which that needle is used. It is enough to understand what sewing is. Furthermore, the smith does not need to be any good at sewing. God's knowledge could likewise be a general knowledge in which God knows and understands exactly what must be created in order for the world to run in a smooth, orderly manner. The analogy does not show, nor does it attempt to show, that God knows individuals.[22]

Maimonides has refuted the claim that there is no knowledge in God. However, he has not yet explained all that he himself affirms about the matter. Since the belief that God knows individuals as individuals is what is described as the law's position, Maimonides has not yet argued in favor of the law. The proper subject of chapter 19 is not the details of God's knowledge but the problem of evil and a defense of providence. Maimonides distinguishes God's providence from God's knowledge, since he argues that God has knowledge of all particulars, but he claims that God does not have providence over the particulars of any species other than humans.[23] Accordingly, Maimonides finishes this chapter with the following comment:

As for what should be said concerning his knowledge, may he be exalted, of all things, I shall inform you of my opinion concerning this after I have made known to you the matters about which there is general consensus and that no one endowed with intellect can contradict in any point.[24]

First, then, Maimonides writes about something on which he agrees with the philosophers. He then proceeds to inform the reader of the part of his opinion that goes beyond what he argues in chapter 19 and beyond the opinions of the philosophers.

6.3.2 Chapter 20: The Five Differences between Divine Knowledge and Human Knowledge

In chapter 20 of the *Guide,* Maimonides explains why the philosophers think that the law's opinion is false. In doing so, he outlines the philosophical difficulties to which he must respond in order to defend the law's position. He then argues that the philosophers are wrong to dismiss the law's view. As with the treatment of creation, there is a distinction between what has been demonstrated and what is asserted as the opinion of the law without demonstration.[25] As with creation, God's omniscience is defended from the attacks of the philosophers who have not succeeded in demonstrating their own position. Then it is asserted as the position of the law and the true meaning of scripture. Maimonides defends its possibility rather than its certainty.

Chapter 20 begins with the statement that it is generally agreed that God does not acquire knowledge at one time that was previously absent. This is a consequence of God's being simple and unchanging and therefore totally actual. These principles are asserted by both the philosophers and the law, since they are demonstrably true. This, then, is that "about which there is general consensus."

> A matter concerning which there is a general consensus is that it is not true that new knowledge should come to him, may he be exalted, so that he would know now what he did not know before. And it is not true, even according to the opinion of those who believe in the attributes, that he should have many and numerous insights.[26]

Maimonides mentions that it has already been demonstrated that God's knowledge cannot change, because God's knowledge is God, and God does not change. He then proceeds to introduce a further opinion, which he describes as that of "the community of those who adhere to the law."[27] The community of the law asserts that God's knowledge has multiple objects but that it remains simple. Although the point is not made in such a way in this statement, the law's opinion amounts to the belief that God knows particulars. Combining the demonstrated position and the position of the law results in an assertion of God's omniscience. Maimonides expresses this in the form of differences that, according to the law, obtain between human knowledge and divine knowledge. As a result of God's knowing all things, five differences obtain. According to Maimonides' theory of divine predication, they show that "knowledge" must be used in an equivocal manner of God and of humans. So Maimonides avoids anthropomorphism by asserting that God's knowledge does not possess certain properties that human knowledge does. The five differences are as follows:

1. God knows multiple things of differing species, while God's knowledge remains simple.
2. God's knowledge encompasses nonexistent things.
3. God knows infinites.
4. God's knowledge does not change when things God knows change.
5. God's knowledge of a thing does not make that thing necessary.

The first difference was mentioned above as the law's position. The second difference is that God's knowledge encompasses that which does not exist. Humans cannot know that which does not exist, since the nature of human knowledge is that it is abstracted from things that do exist. If a thing does not exist, knowledge cannot be abstracted from it. However, Maimonides says that something that never exists is not an object for God's knowledge.[28] The second difference, then, must mean that the things that do not exist must be things that have not yet come to exist: future contingents. The third difference is that God's knowledge includes that which is infinite. This difference is entailed by God's knowing particulars. Humans can only know particulars through experience, and experience of an infinite number of particulars is impossible. Furthermore, such knowledge differs qualitatively from universal knowledge. Infinite particulars can only be known indirectly, that is, inasmuch as they fall under a universal. When Maimonides states that God's knowledge encompasses all individual things, he expresses a difference in the way in which God knows. God knows particulars with a more direct knowledge than humans do. He also expresses a difference in the number of things known, which in the case of God is unending. This is required by the possibility that the world is eternal *a parte post*. As explained above, Maimonides believes that such a kind of eternity is compatible with the law. He even thinks that believing in this notion is more in keeping with the law's view than disbelieving in it.[29] The fourth difference is that God's knowledge does not change when things come into being and pass away, even though God knows things as they exist. The fifth difference is that God's knowing that something is the case does not make it necessary. In the case of humans, this would not hold, since then they would possess not "knowledge" but "opinion." Human knowledge is not causative, so it cannot necessitate consequences; God's knowledge is causative but still does not make the consequences necessary.

Given these differences, there may be reason to think that God's knowledge should not be referred to as knowledge at all. It seems to be nonsense to say that God has knowledge because what is being affirmed is not relevant to any instance of knowledge. However, chapter 21 indicates that God's knowledge is an uncreated knowledge like the absolute, unlimited perfections I discussed above. So Maimonides is still able to refer to it as "knowledge" even though the word is used equivocally, since God's knowledge is not a bounded instance of knowledge.[30] Predicating knowledge of God does not compromise divine simplicity but, rather, preserves Maimonides' claim that the word is used totally equivocally of God and humans.

The five differences must be recognized if one is to assert the law's position on God's knowledge, and they entail that any use of "knowledge" has to be equivocal if it is to encompass both divine and human knowledge. The reason people confuse the issue of God's knowledge, Maimonides says, is that they fail to acknowledge the equivocation when they discuss the divine knowledge. Presuming that knowledge is used in the same way in both cases, the philosophers ignore the five differences and apply what they know about human knowledge to God's knowledge and thus conclude that God cannot know particulars. Maimonides blames the "philosophers" more than he blames others. They should be perfectly aware of the equivocation, since they have demonstrated that God is simple. Since the philosophers are aware that humans cannot understand God's essence and since God's essence is the same as all of God's attributes, including God's knowledge, they should understand that humans cannot grasp God's knowledge. Furthermore, they should then understand that the conditions that apply to human knowledge do not apply to God's.[31] So if God has "knowledge" and knows particulars in their particularity by virtue of that knowledge, "knowledge" must be used equivocally. That is because humans do not know particulars by virtue of their intellect but by virtue of their senses.

Although the equivocality of "knowledge" is shown by these five differences, there must be enough similarity between the two to warrant Maimonides' discussion in chapter 21. If there is a contradiction between the two positions, Maimonides would probably not put them so close together and be so open about them. So something about the kind of equivocation Maimonides intends when he claims that attributes are totally equivocal when used of God on the one hand and humans on the other can be learned from this discussion.[32] He cannot mean that there is no relationship whatsoever, so that God's knowledge cannot be compared to that of an artisan in the relevant sense. Rather, it is precisely because that comparison is possible that the five differences obtain. Since it is those five differences that justify considering the term equivocal, it is because God's knowledge can be likened to that of an artisan that the term is equivocal. This is not to say that God's knowledge is really like that of an artisan. It is an analogy and so will break down. But the analogy is useful, because it illustrates the five differences between God's knowledge and human knowledge that make the two totally unlike each other. The analogy shows that God's knowledge is nothing like human knowledge; ontologically, it is not even like that of an artisan.

So Maimonides is able to predicate knowledge of God because he makes the qualification that the word is predicated equivocally (*bi-ištirāk*).[33] This is his strategy with other perfections as well, which he considers "absolute," uncreated, limitless perfections. If the specific feature of knowledge is in the abstraction, knowledge is not necessary for God, since the divine intellect is prior to what is abstracted. Another way of expressing this is that knowledge always needs to be brought out of potential by a cause. If it is accepted that the characteristic of knowledge is that it is derivative and that it abstracts universals from particulars, it follows that God's productive intellect is the unlimited, absolute perfection of created intellects; it is the divine limit of the created perfection, an unlimited instance of knowledge. The way in which Maimonides explains God's knowledge in chapter 21 indicates that this is exactly how he saw the issue. If the *Guide* is understood in such a way, the five differences, and thereby the equivocality of "knowledge," are explained.

6.3.3 Chapter 21: Explaining the Differences—God's Creative Knowledge

Maimonides has now explained in chapter 19 why he feels able to assert that God has knowledge and in chapter 20 that the divine knowledge is different from human knowledge in certain respects. However, he has not explained how he can hold that God knows all things without violating the rule that "knowledge" must be used equivocally. In chapter 21, Maimonides solves this problem by attributing a limitless instance of knowledge to God. He is thereby saved from inconsistency. Maimonides can predicate knowledge of God without compromising his doctrine of negative attributes because knowledge is an "absolute perfection" in God. It is therefore justified to understand his presentation of the law's position to be a presentation of a coherent set of doctrines.

In this context, it is significant that the image of the water clock explained above appears in the chapter immediately following that which contains Maimonides' explanation of the five differences. The chapter's purpose is to explain how Maimonides thinks it is possible to assert those differences; because God's knowledge is causative, like that of an artisan, Maimonides is able to assert that God's knowledge is different from human knowledge in four of the above five ways. The analogy shows several things about God's knowledge: it encompasses multiple things while remaining simple; it can encompass future things; it has no limit; it is changeless. Maimonides reiterates these after the analogy and explains that they obtain because God's knowledge is causative. The fifth difference is missing from this list; there is good reason for excluding it here.[34] In chapter 20, Maimonides stated that God's knowledge of a thing does not necessitate that thing. He does not repeat this difference after the water clock analogy, because, unlike the other four differences, it does not follow from the position that God's knowledge is causative. Rather, Maimonides specifies that he came to the belief that God's knowledge does not compromise human freedom from the texts of scripture, not through philosophical reasoning.[35] As with the view that God knows particulars in their particularity, the compatibility of human freedom and divine omniscience is something taught by the law but not demonstrated by reason. Unlike the other four differences, though, explaining that God's knowledge is causative does not explain how this fifth difference is possible.

To explain how viewing God's knowledge as causative solves the apparent contradiction, I return to the conclusions of chapter 5. There I argued that Maimonides accepts that perfections exist in God and also that those perfections may be thought of as unlimited perfections. Such an assessment allows Maimonides to assert that perfections exist in God but that the words describing those perfections must be used equivocally. To recap, an unlimited perfection is a perfection of a particular scale of things but is not circumscribed by the features of the scale. Members of the scale are all of the same species, but some of them possess a greater intensity of the specific difference of that species. The unlimited perfection occurs when the specific difference is made so great, or so perfect, as to be totally unlike anything that is on the scale. The unlimited perfection occurs when the perfection cannot be limited to any created being or the definition thereof.[36]

If the specific difference that characterizes human knowledge is that it abstracts from particulars given to the senses and is able to form an intellectual idea of those particulars, that is, to turn them into universals, an absolute perfection of knowledge would be a knowledge with no need to abstract anything from particulars, because it already knows all of them.[37] A knowledge that is not abstracted from preexistent things and is not bound by them, as it knows all of them, would be a causative knowledge. Hence an unlimited and uncreated perfection of knowledge would be a knowledge that contains knowledge of all things but is causative rather than derivative. And that is exactly how Maimonides explains the way in which the law's position should be understood when he uses the analogy of an artisan to characterize God's knowledge. Furthermore, if God's knowledge is causative, it is not bound by time. So Maimonides might be appealing to something like the notion that God's knowledge is eternal.[38] The five differences would then be explained in much the same way as they are when the problem is solved by considering God's knowledge to be causative and therefore not influenced by anything in the created order of things.

Maimonides uses another analogy to describe God's creating the world, which may support the view that God's causative knowledge entails the notion that it is eternal. In this analogy, Maimonides states that all things are created at once, but they are individuated at different times. That is to say that from God's eternal vantage point, there is no difference in the time the act was carried out, but from the vantage point of time, there is:

> Everything was created simultaneously; then gradually all things became differentiated. [The sages] have compared this to what happens when an agricultural laborer sows various kinds of grain in the soil at the same moment. Some of them sprout within a day, others within two days, others again within three days, though everything was sowed at the same hour.[39]

Time is measured according to the created order rather than in God's eternal mode of being, because time is created. Extrapolating from this to the idea of God's causative knowledge of particulars entails the belief that God can know all things in the eternal moment.[40]

Ehud Benor argues that the notion of eternity is implied by Maimonides' discussion of God's knowledge of future contingents. He argues that Maimonides asserts that God can know particulars and that such a view is intelligible when it is considered as deriving from an understanding of the eternal nature of God's knowledge. His approach is justified, so Benor writes, because it "offers the most coherent interpretation of Maimonides' pronouncements on the subject of divine knowledge."[41] I wish to make a bolder claim and argue that *eternity* should be used not only because of the coherence it brings to Maimonides' discussion but also because it is in accord with his explicit statement that God's creation of particulars occurs in a single moment from God's point of view. They are differentiated by time only from the point of view of created things, since time is dependent on creation. In light of the notion that God's knowledge is creative, the two may be linked, and God's knowledge of particulars can be explained in the same manner.

6.4 THAT KNOWLEDGE IS A DIVINE PERFECTION: PREDICATING DIVINE PERFECTION BY NEGATING THE PRIVATION

So the conflict between Maimonides' two positions is only apparent. This can be taken as evidence that Maimonides predicates knowledge of God as an uncreated, and therefore divine, perfection. Further evidence can be seen in the fact that he explicitly refers to God's knowledge as a divine perfection. Maimonides' arguments for knowledge in God include one in which he predicates an "absolute perfection" of God by negating the privation of the perfection of knowledge. This is because such kinds of negative attributes indicate the presence of absolute perfections in God. No instances of the perfections or their lack can be predicated of God, but a perfection that is not limited through instantiation can be.

At the beginning of part three, chapter 19, Maimonides presents an argument that God knows all things; he appears to acknowledge enough similarity between human knowledge and divine knowledge to use "knowledge" with the same meaning in respect to both:

> No doubt it is a primary notion that all perfections [*kamālāt*] must exist in God and that with regard to him all deficiencies must be denied. It is almost a primary notion that ignorance with regard to anything whatever is a deficiency and that he, may he be exalted, is ignorant of nothing.[42]

The argument can be broken down as follows:

1. All perfections exist in God, so all deficiencies must be denied of God.
2. Ignorance with regard to anything is a deficiency.
3. God is ignorant of nothing.

As do the comments about God's knowledge and intellect examined above, this argument appears to conflict with Maimonides' negative theology. Gersonides uses it as evidence that Maimonides is inconsistent in his application of the doctrines.[43] The reason it appears to be inconsistent is that if Maimonides were to maintain that "knowledge" is predicated of God and humans by way of pure equivocation, he could not advance this argument without falling afoul of the fallacy of the equivocated middle. Maimonides has to be using "ignorance" in the same way in both the second and third statements. Clearly, in the second he uses "ignorance" in a way in which it refers to ignorance possessed by humans. If there is no similarity at all between the perfection as it exists in humans and as it exists in God, then the argument does not work. It can only be a valid argument if the "ignorance" of the minor is used in the conclusion.

Although a full examination of Gersonides' use of religious language is not the purpose of the present work, a response to his assertion that Maimonides is guilty of inconsistency will help clarify Maimonides' intention when he negates the privations of perfections. Gersonides' criticisms are based on the notion that in order for Maimonides to conclude that God has knowledge, the ignorance that is denied of God must fall under the same category as the knowledge that would be predicated of God. Consequently, by denying ignorance of God, Maimonides would be able to assert that God is omniscient. On this interpretation, the argument could also take the following form, used by Harry Wolfson when he explains Gersonides' critique of Maimonides:

> If knowledge is a perfection in man, God has knowledge.
> But knowledge is a perfection in man.
> Therefore, God has knowledge.[44]

But Maimonides does not express the argument in such a way. At no point does he attribute the human perfection of knowledge to God. Rather, he follows his own interpretation of negative attributes in this passage. His affirmation of a particular perfection does not involve him clearly attributing a perfection to God. Instead, he negates the privation of the perfection. The privation can be of the same type, so the argument remains valid. Nevertheless, the perfection in question is, despite the required similarity, not the same as that denoted by the human word. A divine perfection, then, must be differentiated from human perfections, since the divine perfections are limitless and "absolute."

In reply to Gersonides, then, Maimonides does not understand the perfection that he attributes to God to be of the same species as the privation. So the perfection is not attributed. Rather, what is said to exist in God is the limitless, causative perfection. Gersonides argues that perfection terms are used properly of God and derivatively of humans. Maimonides' position differs from that of Gersonides concerning the question of prior and posterior, because in Maimonides' view, the first applications of words indicating perfections are always created perfections. That is why negations of perfections are denied but perfections themselves are not denied. For Maimonides, it is genuinely less correct to use perfections: a deficiency can be used univocally of what is described in the created world and denied of God; a divine perfection can only be described by words used equivocally of creatures and God. There can therefore be a middle term if the privation is used in the argument. Instances of perfections, or perfections in a form susceptible to being instantiated, must be denied of God, but "absolute perfections" cannot be so denied.

In summary, Maimonides does not make any positive attribution. His statements only appear to be positive if the difference between an uncreated perfection and a created perfection is not taken into account. If it is, Maimonides is able to attribute the "absolute perfection" of knowledge to God without compromising his doctrine of negative attributes. So the conclusion follows that, at least in the case of "knowledge," Maimonides attempts to signify an absolute, or limitless, perfection when he negates the privation of a perfection.

6.5 SUMMARY

This chapter has suggested an interpretation of the position on God's knowledge that Maimonides presents as that of the law. It is possible to understand his pronouncements on the subject if his explanations of God's knowledge and intellect are understood to be unlimited perfections of those characteristics in creatures. Statements about God's knowledge illustrate how he thinks negations of privations should be predicated of God. Since chapter 5 established that Maimonides only allows words to be used of uncreated perfections and created perfections equivocally, this chapter has offered a solution to difficulties raised in the secondary literature concerning the overall coherence of Maimonides' position. I have argued that there is a single coherent position that is openly presented in the *Guide*, although not necessarily clearly presented.

The law's position on God's knowledge also complements Maimonides' presentation of the law's position on creation. In chapter 3, I argued that in order to explain the importance Maimonides gives to God's purpose, it is necessary to assert that God knows particulars. Maimonides offers a coherent, unified metaphysical position as that of the law. Creation and God's knowledge are two connected issues. If God knows particulars in their particularity, as the law teaches, the miracles are possible, because God is able to build them into creation. Similarly, if the world is created ex nihilo, in the manner that the law teaches, the miracles are possible. The reason creation allows for miracles while Aristotle's view does not is that creation allows for God's knowledge of particulars. If God knows particulars, the miracles become possible, and the law's view of creation is implicitly true. Maimonides writes that he accepts this position himself. Perceived contradictions within his own account do not necessitate the conclusion that there is a hidden doctrine that represents Maimonides' true belief. I have argued that they are not contradictions at all, once Maimonides' philosophical assumptions are taken into account. In any case, the supposed contradiction between God as knower and negative theology would not result from the seventh cause of contradictions, because it simply does not fit the description.

6.6 APPENDIX: THE QUESTION OF THE DIVINE INTELLECT

Until this point, I have focused on a problem raised in relation to the third part of the *Guide*. There is another, possibly related problem, however, which has been discussed in connection with a chapter in the first part of the *Guide*: the depiction of God as intellect. As with the case explained in the body of this chapter, it is claimed that Maimonides appears to be compromising his negative theology by positing attributes in God and by describing God in an anthropomorphic manner.

In the first part, Maimonides makes the following statement:

> You already know that the following dictum of the philosophers with reference to God is generally admitted: the dictum being that he is the intellect ['aql] as well as the intellectual apprehender ['āqil] and the intelligible [ma'qūl], and that those three notions form in him, may he be exalted one single notion in which there is no multiplicity.[45]

If no anthropomorphic attributes are applicable to God, it would seem wrong to assert that God shares the substance of intellect with humans. However, Maimonides asserts that he is describing something common to God and to those humans who actualize their intellect. He states clearly that his comments about the divine intellect would be understood only by one who has studied works on the intellect. These works apply not only to God's intellect but to intellect in general.[46] That means that the intellect in question must be common to both God and humans.

> It is accordingly also clear that the numerical unity of the intellect, the intellectual apprehender, and the intelligible does not hold good with reference to the creator only but also with reference to every intellect. Thus, in us, too, the intellectual apprehender, the intellect, and the intelligible are one and the same thing whenever we have an intellect. We, however, pass intellectually from potentiality to actuality only from time to time.[47]

To evade the problem, Maimonides claims that the difference between God's intellect, which is permanently in act, and human intellect, which passes from potency to act, is such a vast one that it sufficiently expresses the absolute difference between God and people. I will return to this below, as it may support the idea that the divine intellect is a divine, unlimited perfection. First, however, I will discuss some previous responses to the problem.

6.6.1 Responses to the Problem

The apparent inconsistency has been pointed out by a number of Maimonides' interpreters. Pines argues that there are two incompatible concepts of God in the *Guide*: the completely transcendent, ineffable God and the concept of God as intellect:

> It is evident that the statement that God cognises and the consequent assertions that He cognises Himself, or Himself and the forms or essences assimilated to Himself, are positive statements and as such in contradiction with the spirit and tendency of negative theology.[48]

According to Pines, it is possible but highly unlikely that Maimonides was not aware of the inconsistency: "in this particular case this point of view would amount to a grave and, in my opinion, very implausible accusation of muddleheadedness directed against Maimonides." In this essay, Pines refrains from asserting which of the two he believed Maimonides to hold, since "prima facie either of them is admissible."[49]

This assessment of the incompatibility of the two doctrines has been accepted by many. Indeed, that there is a real contradiction resulting from the seventh cause seems to have assumed an almost dogmatic status in some circles of Maimonidean studies. Shoey Raz goes so far as to identify it as the major secret of the *Guide* and to connect it with Maimonides' interpretation of Ezekiel's chariot, a subject to which I will return later in this book.[50]

But if there is really an opposition and Maimonides is trying to hide one of the two positions, which is the one that he accepts? On this, scholars disagree. For example, Alexander Even-Chen, who describes the opposition between the two positions as "essential and indubitable," argues that Maimonides' true position is that God is an intellect. The reason for concealing his belief is that, according to Even-Chen, it implies that God knows only universals, and this is a position opposed by the law.[51] Alvin Reines argues that the idea that God has knowledge is Maimonides' expression of a God who is not absolutely transcendent. In Reines's opinion, transcendence is the concept that would be more difficult for the masses to accept and indeed most damaging to them. He therefore concludes that the position that God is an intellect must be the smokescreen.[52] Hannah Kasher argues that Maimonides accepted both of them, even though they cannot be reconciled logically. On this reading, Maimonides possessed a nuanced understanding of religious belief, one that allowed contradictory statements to be held simultaneously, thus expressing the nature both of religious belief and of human beings.[53]

It is plausible that this conflict is an instance of the fifth cause of contradiction, and some recent interpretations could fit this scheme. For example, Diana Lobel mentions that when Maimonides refers to God as intellect, he may be talking about one of the intelligences rather than the unknowable God.[54] Ehud Benor argues that intellect is "symbolic" of God's immaterial mode of being and of divine unity. It is part of Maimonides' advanced theory of how language can be used symbolically to point toward a reality that cannot be understood. On this account, Maimonides accepts the inadequacy of such symbols but holds that they provide a content for religious thought. Intellectual and ethical perfection are the two symbols he deems important, since humans imitate God through them.[55] "Both are employed as self-transcending conceptions; invoking a notion of perfection yet made transparent by their ever-apparent inadequacy, they point beyond themselves towards the inconceivable divine being."[56] Ultimately, according to Benor, "Maimonides uses the notion of the human intellect as a symbol for God's mode of being. Thinking of God as an intellect makes it easier for our mind to accept the reality of God's immaterial modes of being."[57] According to Benor, Maimonides could not have held that God is really an intellect. The reason one needs, on his account, to consider the depiction of God as intellect as symbolic is that it is opposed to Maimonides' "extreme version of negative theology."[58] So the purpose of stating that God is an intellect must be didactic: God is not really an intellect, but the student is taught that God is an intellect as part of an educational program. Once the student is ready to progress, a new opinion that seems to be opposed to the first can be introduced.

If this is indeed Maimonides' position, there would be precedents. First of all, Benor's position might be supported by the fact that Avicenna writes that immaterial substances are considered to be intellects inasmuch as they are immaterial.[59] So it could make sense for Maimonides to use intellect as a symbol of God's incorporeality as well. Furthermore, Ġazālī also argues that the philosophers' God is the first created being, arguing that Avicenna's God is an intermediary between the true God and creation.[60] Although Avicenna distinguished God from the first intelligence, which moves the outermost sphere, Maimonides could certainly have followed Ġazālī's take on the philosophers' God.[61] He could then have considered the depiction of God as intellect as the position "generally accepted" by the philosophers but one that just misses the mark. I would like to raise another possible solution, which is that the divine intellect described in 1:68 is an uncreated, limitless instance of intellect and that it is therefore compatible with Maimonides' negative theology.

6.6.2 How Would an Uncreated Instance of Intellect Be Indicated?

I argued above that Maimonides' account of God's knowledge should be seen as an account of the unlimited perfection of knowledge. The argument may be extended to include the chapter in the first part of the *Guide* as well, thereby defending Maimonides from the charge that he compromised his negative theology by describing God as an intellect or compromised his radical "intellectualization" of God with a more orthodox position of divine unknowability. As in the case of chapter 21 of part three of the *Guide*, chapter 68 in part one points toward the notion of an uncreated perfection. The implication is that Maimonides is able to consider God to be an intellect without compromising his explanations of religious language; both can be held in tandem and in harmony.

An uncreated perfection of knowledge would be causative rather than derivative, an interpretation that explains the five differences between the divine knowledge and human knowledge in part three. Throughout the chapter in the first part of the *Guide*, Maimonides insists on a similarity between the divine intellect and human intellect. That similarity is that both intellects are the same as that which they possess in abstract: both intellects have knowledge. Nevertheless, human intellect differs from the divine intellect, since human intellect passes from potency to act on a regular basis, whereas the divine intellect is permanently in act.

Maimonides mentions another difference between divine and human intellects, which is a corollary:

That which pertains solely to him, may he be exalted, and which is specific to him is his being constantly in act and that there is no impediment either proceeding from his essence or from another that might hinder his apprehending.[62]

Since God's intellect is permanently in act, there is never any impediment to its act. That is entailed by the fact that God's intellect is not at all derivative but is causative, and therefore nothing external to God can act on it. This seems to fit with a limitless intellect, which would be causative and would not have anything acting on it but would be permanently in act. It would not be ignorant and would thus constitute an intellect. The fact that it is permanently in act would mean that no matter, which is the source of passivity, attaches to it. That would be another reason to consider it an intellect, since the intellect is that which is immaterial and actual.

A totally actual knowledge will be permanently acting. It could not be derivative at all but would be causative. The doctrine of God as intellect would thus provide further evidence that a permanently active, causative knowledge can be considered an uncreated perfection and can therefore be ascribed to God. On Maimonides' account of divine predication, such ascription will have to be equivocal, as argued above. Maimonides is thus able to discuss God's knowledge and intellect without contradicting the statement that knowledge is predicated of God and of humans equivocally. Since God's knowledge is causative and since it causes everything, it is unfettered by any presupposed or preexistent thing. God's knowledge is therefore, like God, totally free.

There are, then, a number of possible solutions to this particular problem. Maimonides' description of God as intellect is intelligible if the description is a description of an uncreated perfection of intellect. A wholly causative intellect is not acted on but only acts on other things. The problems raised by this chapter of the *Guide* might therefore be solved in the same way as other limitless perfections. Solving the difficulty in this way would mean that there is no real contradiction when the two ideas are understood properly, although if they are not, it may seem that there is a contradiction. This response needs the reader to heed Maimonides' advice by undertaking much of the necessary work and thought without his direct guidance. It is, however, germane to what Maimonides writes, and it does not require the belief that he, apparently alone among his peers, considered negative theology to be built of contradictory premises to those that result in calling God an intellect. If there is opposition between the two doctrines, Maimonides might not have realized it. However, if such opposition is posited, and he is assumed to be aware of it, another solution is called for. One of those might be that of Benor, who argues that intellect is ultimately a symbolic way to refer to God's incorporeality. The contradiction would then be a result of the fifth cause, which Maimonides outlines in his introduction.[63]

Negative theology would constitute a stage beyond characterizing God as intellect. Alternatively, one might follow what seems to be Pines's lead and put it down to something like the seventh cause. Then the two ought not to be reconciled at all. However, an advocation of such a position would require detailed support and a theory that interprets the nature of the seventh contradiction in an appropriate manner. Although I shall not consider this issue in light of the seventh contradiction, as it does not seem to me to fit, I shall show how Maimonides uses the seventh contradiction in the next two chapters.

෴

CHAPTER 7

"Secrets of the Torah": Ezekiel's Vision of the Chariot

The opening of the book of Ezekiel is known in rabbinic literature as "the account of the chariot" (*ma'aseh merkabah*). Maimonides interprets it as a parable that uses a number of different symbols. The explanation of these symbols is scattered throughout the *Guide,* so understanding his interpretation requires the reader to piece together its different parts. Only in that way can one hope to understand Maimonides' true message. Such detective work will be the main task of this chapter, in which I will show that Maimonides believes the vision of the chariot to be a parable that has the constitution of the cosmos as its deeper meaning.[1] This deeper meaning is known by those who are educated in philosophy, although they might not identify the ideas behind the parable on first reading.[2] Maimonides writes his exegesis of Ezekiel as a hidden commentary addressed to the few who understand philosophy, pay sufficient attention to the hints scattered around the *Guide,* and are capable of connecting diverse chapters with one another; it is a puzzle that can only be solved by a reader who is both careful and well educated.

Ezekiel's vision should be taken as one of the "very obscure matters" to which Maimonides refers when he explains the seventh cause of contradictions.[3] There he states that when discussing such matters, it is necessary to reveal some things and conceal others. The way he goes about this in his biblical commentaries is through the allusions and pointers that reveal a surface meaning without revealing the inner meaning to any but those who are sufficiently trained. Maimonides feels the need to write this section of the *Guide* in such a way because the account of the chariot is a "secret of the Torah." The mystical "orchard" (*pardes*) is traditionally identified as the location of these secrets, and the Talmud warns people not to enter it.[4] I will address this a little further in chapter 8 below.

7.1 SECRETS OF THE TORAH

Discussions related in previous chapters of this work bear witness to how difficult it is to interpret Maimonides in general. However, with regard to the particular section of the *Guide* with which this section of the book deals, the problems are compounded. It is notoriously even more difficult to understand what Maimonides believes the true, inner meaning of "the account of the chariot" to be.

One of the main aims of the *Guide* is to explain the "secrets of the Torah."[5] These include the account of the chariot, the meaning of which Maimonides identifies with divine science, metaphysics, and the account of the beginning, the meaning of which he identifies with natural science, or physics.[6] However, the Mishnah forbids anyone to explain such secrets:

> One does not expound matters concerning sexual immodesty in the presence of three people, nor the account of the beginning in the presence of two, and the account of the chariot not even in the presence of one unless he is a sage and understands with his own mind. Even then one only gives him the heads of chapters.[7]

When explaining the accounts, then, Maimonides needs to tread carefully. He has to write in such a way as to prevent his explanation from being too transparent, and in his opinion, this is for the same reasons that the accounts are considered to be "secrets" in the first place: their difficulty and the danger they pose to those who have not been trained correctly.[8]

As I have pointed out, Maimonides does not have the advantage of educating pupils orally and assessing them individually, since the *Guide* is a written work addressed to a number of people and not to all of them directly. He is taking a risk, because it will inevitably enter the public domain. When it does so, Maimonides will be violating the warnings not to transmit the meanings of these two accounts to more than one or two people, respectively. In the case of the account of the chariot, there is another condition that must be met before it is taught. The account may not be taught to any pupil who is not wise and capable. There is no guarantee that Maimonides' readers will be wise and capable of such understanding.[9]

However, the final part of the Mishnah provides a safety net for this second violation. One who is able to understand alone is equivalent to one who can understand when only given heads of chapters; the worthy reader is expected to be able to understand "flashes" (*talwīḥ*).[10] Maimonides can therefore suggest heads of chapters without explaining them fully. That is how he tries to imitate the way that scripture and rabbinic literature communicated these matters but in a way appropriate to his own time. The reader's challenge is to identify those "heads" and order them so as to create a commentary on the entire text.

Despite only offering chapter headings, Maimonides feels the need to defend his decision to write a book explaining both the account of the beginning and the account of the chariot. He writes that the radical step he now takes is justified for two reasons. The first is that his actions are for the sake of heaven.[11] The second is that such steps have become necessary, since the knowledge he imparts is in danger of being lost to the nation.[12] Fortunately, he is set an important precedent, that of Jonathan ben Uzziel, to whom Maimonides refers in his commentary on the chariot. Jonathan used similar justifications to defend himself against a divine accusation after he had translated the prophets into Aramaic:

> The Targum of the Prophets was composed by Jonathan ben Uzziel under the guidance of Haggai, Zechariah and Malachi, and the land of Israel shook over an area of four hundred parasangs by four hundred parasangs, and a heavenly voice came forth and exclaimed, who is this that has revealed my secrets to humankind? Jonathan ben Uzziel arose and said, It is I who have revealed your secrets to humankind. It is fully known to you that I have not done this for my own honor or for the honor of my father's house, but for your honor I have done it, that dissent will not increase in Israel.[13]

Maimonides openly dedicates seven chapters to his explanation of *ma'aseh merkabah* at the beginning of part three of the *Guide*. His strategy in these chapters is to highlight sections of the account that require interpretation. In some cases, he also begins to explain what the correct interpretation is. However, the topic pervades the *Guide*, so one must study other chapters for most of the explanations hinted at in these seven chapters. Maimonides says as much when he concludes the seven chapters by saying that everything needed in order to understand his exposition of the chariot sufficiently is contained throughout all of the preceding sections of the *Guide*.[14] His comments are difficult to understand and are scattered throughout the whole of the first and second parts, as well as these chapters. This is how Maimonides goes about fulfilling his aim of explaining everything while appearing to explain nothing. He expresses his goal as follows:

> I shall interpret to you everything that was said by Ezekiel the prophet, peace be on him, in such a way that anyone who heard that interpretation would think that I do not say anything over and beyond what is indicated by the text, but that it is as if I translated words from one language to another or summarized the meaning of the external sense of the speech. On the other hand, if that interpretation is examined with a perfect care by him for whom this treatise is composed and who has understood all its chapters—every chapter in its turn— the whole matter, which has become clear and manifest to me, will become clear to him so that nothing in it will remain hidden from him.[15]

These warnings and comments about style are reminiscent of the introduction to the first part of the *Guide*. In both places, Maimonides instructs the reader to pay particular attention to every detail in the book in order to understand it correctly. In the first part, he also discusses the two different types of parables that occur in scripture.[16] Parables of the first kind contain only one meaning, which is elaborated throughout the story. In such parables, the esoteric meaning of the story might be worked out over the entire piece, or the extra words may simply be included for rhetorical purposes or in order to hide the inner meaning further. Parables of the second kind contain a number of different notions, and in this kind, different elements of the parable stand for different things.[17] The vision discussed here is clearly one of the second type of parables. It is not the case, however, that every single word in the passage needs to have a separate meaning. Some statements may be superfluous or repetitious, although Maimonides does not rule out the possibility that there is meaning in the repetitions as well.[18]

The fact that Maimonides' intention is to give to those who are unworthy of a full explanation the impression that he merely translates from one language to another is also reminiscent of the introduction to part one of the *Guide*. There he states that he could not write a book explaining the true meaning of scriptural parables without either making that meaning clear to everyone, including those to whom it should not be explained, or clarifying nothing at all by simply replacing one riddle with another.[19] His exposition of the chariot is a place in which Maimonides attempts to communicate different messages to different readers, replacing scriptural parables for some, without clarifying them, and presenting a riddle to solve for others.

In part 2 of the Guide, Maimonides offers a signpost pointing to the fact that he is about to discuss matters connected to the chariot. This section, which contains information about the nature of the spheres and the intelligences, appears in the middle of Maimonides' comments on creation. It follows an explanation that God's existence is demonstrated based on Aristotle's principles and also upon those of the law. He then interrupts the discussion with a "preface," which is of great importance for understanding Maimonides' commentary on the chariot. The interruption continues until chapter 13, where the discussion returns to the question of creation or eternity. Maimonides instructs the reader to pay attention to this preface,

> which is like a lamp illuminating the hidden features of the whole of this treatise, both of those of its chapters that come before and of those that come after.[20]

Both the content of the preface and the reason it is in this particular position are important. The content draws attention to the traditional "secrets of the Torah" and to the way in which Maimonides expresses his understanding of those secrets. The position indicates that what is to follow explains the account of the chariot.

What this preface says is crucial for understanding Maimonides' project in the *Guide*. He insists that his treatise is not to be used as a scientific textbook.[21] Then he writes that there are two realms concerning which he says nothing new: divine science and the nature and number of the spheres. In order to learn about these subjects, the reader is directed toward books written by others.[22] Maimonides' sole purpose is to explain difficult points of the law, and his explanations are often abridged. The implication is that when he discusses matters such as the existence of intelligences or the number and motion of the spheres, he does so only in order to explain those secrets of the Torah, so he writes as follows:

> I only intend to mention matters, the understanding of which may elucidate some difficulty of the law; in fact, many knots will be unraveled through the knowledge of a notion of which I give an epitome.[23]

Everything mentioned in this section is relevant to parables found in scripture and is useful for a proper understanding of those parables. Maimonides then connects the discussions with the opinions of the law and also with three specific points: *ma'aseh berešit, ma'aseh merkabah,* and prophecy:

> The reason why I mentioned, explained and elucidated that matter would be found in the knowledge it procures us of the account of the chariot or of the account of the beginning or would be found in an explanation that it furnishes of some root regarding the notion of prophecy or would be found in the explanation of some root regarding the belief in a true opinion belonging to the beliefs of the law.[24]

As mentioned above, the preface and all that follows until chapter 12 are an interruption of Maimonides' treatment of creation. Discussion of creation began in the first chapter with the argument that God is creator and the world is created, and it will continue in chapter 13 when Maimonides begins to address the question of whether the world had a beginning. In the meantime, the discussion turns to issues concerning the celestial chariot. The "preface" to this discussion is a clear indication that the section appearing during the interruption of the question of creation is supposed to aid in an understanding of the secrets of the Torah. It is also a clear indication that the subject of the chariot is to be found in that section.[25]

7.2 THE VISION OF THE CHARIOT AT THE BEGINNING OF THE BOOK OF EZEKIEL

Since Maimonides' examination of the account of the chariot is a commentary that is purposefully set out in an order that does not facilitate understanding, it will be useful to quote much of the first chapter of Ezekiel. I will split the chapter into sections, making it easier to explain Maimonides' commentary. In doing so, I do not follow Maimonides' purposeful disorder but try to turn his commentary into an orderly one by dividing the vision into the different parts he addresses. The commentary is a puzzle that must be solved by the careful reader. It is an example of an issue in which one needs to follow Maimonides' advice to connect different chapters with one another in order to understand the entire message. Once such a task has been achieved, it becomes clear that there are certain notions hiding behind the commentary that would be shocking to the average religious reader: Ezekiel's mistakes. I will deal with these in detail in chapter 8 below. The present chapter is simply an attempt to understand Maimonides' commentary and describe his interpretation of the vision and the way in which he presents it.

The fact that Ezekiel claims to have seen more than one vision is important.[26] Maimonides divides the account of the chariot into three parts. He says that this is because Ezekiel is relating three different visions with different meanings, each of which is introduced in the biblical text with the words "and I saw." The first "and I saw" does not occur until the fourth verse. Before that is a prologue.

The narrative of the vision as a whole, then, is divided into the following parts:

1. Prologue.
2. Description of the beasts.
3. Description of the wheels.
4. Description of the man above the beasts.

Maimonides states that the three visions represent differing degrees of apprehension and that the final vision, that of the man, "is the ultimate perception and the highest of all."[27] This is the order in which Ezekiel relates the vision. I mentioned above that the interpretation offered here follows the general lines of the medieval commentators, in taking it to be a pictorial representation of the cosmos.[28] The beasts are images of the spheres; the wheels represent the matter of the sublunar world; the man corresponds to the intelligences.

7.3 PROLOGUE: PROPHECY AND EZEKIEL'S VISION

[1] Now it came to pass in the thirtieth year, in the fourth month, in the fifth day of the month, as I was among the captives by the river Chebar that the heavens were opened, and I saw visions of God.
[2] In the fifth day of the month, which was the fifth year of king Jehoiachin's captivity.
[3] The word of the Lord came expressly unto Ezekiel the priest, the son of Buzi, in the land of the Chaldeans by the river Chebar; and the hand of the Lord was there upon him.[29]

So the book of Ezekiel begins. Maimonides points out a number of aspects of the passage. The first relevant point is that the place and date of the vision are both mentioned.[30] Maimonides draws attention to this fact immediately before emphasizing that the vision is just that, a vision. The specific dating and location teach that the vision could not have been one that happened in the public domain, that is, in the world of the senses outside of Ezekiel's mind, for others would have seen it. Because he attaches both place and time to the vision, it would be easy to falsify, as others who were there would be able to bear witness against the claim that this description is literal.[31] Since nobody else saw the vision, Maimonides says that Ezekiel is indicating that it is indeed meant to be a prophecy occurring in a vision or dream.

Another indication that Ezekiel is relating a prophetic vision is that he reports that the prophecy occurred next to the river Chebar. Maimonides takes the river to be fictitious. Its presence may teach that Ezekiel is reporting a vision that occurred in his imagination. The river indicates that all that is perceived is in a vision of prophecy received through the imaginative faculty. Maimonides also draws attention to the fact that Ezekiel states that the heavens opened.[32] He explains that this expression is often used in prophetic speech and that it is a key to an understanding of the whole parable. Elsewhere, he explains that the idea behind such a statement is like that behind the prophetic image of gates or doors opening.[33] It is obviously indicative of allegorical speech, since there are no gates or doors in heaven. Therefore, whenever such expressions are used in the prophetic texts, they are metaphorical (isti'ārāt). Again, Maimonides is drawing attention to the fact that he considers the vision of Ezekiel to be a vision couched in imagery rather than a literal description of reality. He is also claiming that Ezekiel uses metaphors to tell the reader this.

7.3.1 Representation of Prophecy in Ezekiel's Vision

Maimonides holds that the vision is a prophetic vision. For Maimonides, prophecy is essentially a natural phenomenon that occurs when a person is correctly trained, when all of a person's faculties—physical, moral, psychological, and intellectual—are perfect. Once these have been sufficiently trained, the person immediately becomes a prophet. Maimonides distinguishes the Mosaic view from that of Aristotle by finding a place for God's direct intervention. If God so wishes, God may prevent the properly prepared prophet from receiving prophecy. This, however, would be a suspension of the natural order.

On Šem Tob's interpretation of Maimonides, Ezekiel alludes to the idea that prophecy requires correct preparation when he mentions a rainbow:[34]

[28] As the appearance of the bow that is in the cloud in the day of rain, so was the appearance of the brightness round about.

Maimonides states as follows:

> The matter, the true reality, and the essence of the rainbow that is described are known. This is the most extraordinary comparison possible, as far as parables and similitudes are concerned; and it is indubitably due to a prophetic force. Understand this.[35]

Maimonides does not describe the nature of a rainbow or its relevance any further. It is one of the places in which understanding the *Guide* requires wider knowledge in order to recognize an allusion and the ability to understand independently why it is important. The relevant point about the rainbow is that it is considered a purely passive phenomenon. Avicenna explains that in order for a rainbow to occur, the air has to possess a certain level of humidity.[36] This is a necessary preparation, since the air acts as the material cause of the rainbow. In addition to its being correctly predisposed, the material cause also needs to be in a particular relation with the sun. When that relation is present, the sun becomes the agent that causes the rainbow to occur. The sun acts on a particular part of the atmosphere in such a way as to create a rainbow, because that section of the atmosphere contains the conditions necessary for the existence of a rainbow. It does not appear in another place, because the atmosphere does not contain the suitable qualities. So the rainbow does not occur in a particular place as a result of any choice or alteration on the part of the sun but because of alteration in the atmosphere. The change is in the material cause of the rainbow, and that change enables a relation between the agent and the patient to come into being. The agent acts permanently but only causes the effect when the patient is properly prepared.

Since Maimonides makes these comments when considering the prophetic nature of the vision, he probably draws attention to the rainbow because the process described in the previous paragraph is similar to that of prophecy. On his understanding of prophecy, the agent, the efficient and formal cause, is the active intellect, and the patient, the material cause, is the prophet. The active intellect is always in act. The impediment to its acting on human intellect in such a way as to cause prophecy is on the side of the human: because they are attached to matter, humans are incapable of uniting themselves with the active intellect, which is separate from matter. Maimonides explains that the prophet must remove this impediment as much as humanly possible by preparing all bodily faculties in order to receive prophecy from the active intellect, which permanently acts. Once this has been achieved, the prophet immediately, or automatically, prophesies. The person is the patient and needs to be correctly prepared in order to become a prophet, as the air needs to be correctly prepared to become a rainbow. The active intellect is the constantly acting agent that influences anything that is prepared to be influenced by it; it is the agent, like the sun.

In the passage quoted here, Maimonides states that the image of a rainbow is extraordinary. It fits the notion that prophecy is a result of natural processes perfectly. Furthermore, in order to understand the parable, one needs to be aware of the nature of a rainbow. That is something that would be familiar only to one who has already studied science, as Maimonides advises a student to do, so the reference would be picked up only by one who is learned and is also able to identify that it hints at an explanation of prophecy, one who is "wise and capable of understanding." For that reason, it is a suitable parable for representing prophecy. It is detectable only by one who is a sage and is capable of understanding alone, as reflected in the Mishnah's statement, a perfect example of the way in which a parable about the secrets of the Torah should be written.[37]

According to Moses of Narbonne, a thirteenth-century commentator on the *Guide*, the colors symbolize the imagination.[38] The imagination plays an important role in prophecy. In Maimonides' understanding, all prophecy except for that of Moses occurs either in visions or in dreams. Both of these take place in the imagination. One of the differences between a prophet and a philosopher, on Maimonides' account, is that the prophet possesses a more perfect imaginative faculty. This enables him to fulfill the task of leading the people.[39] Another quality that is possessed in a more perfect way by a prophet than by a philosopher is intuition (*hads*).[40] The prophet possesses a speed of understanding, and this distinguishes the status of prophetic knowledge from that of a philosopher. This probably builds on Avicenna, for whom *hads* is an ability to obtain knowledge of the middle term of a syllogism with uncommon speed.[41]

7.3.2   Prophecy in Alternative Accounts of the Chariot

Other biblical passages are connected to the matter of the chariot. Two important chapters add extra details about the general phenomenon of prophecy, and Maimonides has something to say about both of them in the seven chapters of the *Guide* that are devoted explicitly to the chariot. They appear in chapter 10 of Ezekiel and chapter 6 of Isaiah.

7.3.3   Ezekiel's Second Account of the Chariot:
The Role of the Intellect

Ezekiel repeats his vision of the chariot in chapter 10. He makes it clear that the cherubs he describes in that vision are the same as the beasts of the opening passage. Nevertheless, there are some differences between the two accounts.

The vision contains four beasts, each of which has four faces. In the first vision, one of the faces is described as that of an ox, but in the second, it is described as that of a cherub. Maimonides draws attention to the role of the active intellect when he notes one of those differences. He writes that Ezekiel exchanges ox with cherub in order "to draw attention to a certain derivation of words."[42] He states that a key to understanding some of the allusions appearing in scripture is to recognize that they are anagrams or plays on words. The relevance of this particular play on words, he says, "we have explained in a flash" (*laūḥnā*).[43] The "flash" connects the issue to the first part, in which Maimonides claims to be using flashes (*talwīḥāt*) in order to teach those who are worthy.[44] In order to understand the hint in this chapter, then, one must search other chapters for the relevant explanation, following Maimonides' instructions in the introduction. Pines notes that the "flash" appears in part two, chapter 43.[45] There Maimonides explains that one way in which prophetic texts play on words is by using a word containing radicals that can be rearranged to form a different meaning. It seems, then, that the ox of chapter 1 is replaced with the cherub of chapter 10 to draw attention to an anagram. If the word for "cherub," which contains the radicals *k*, *r*, and *b*, is an anagram, it can be rearranged in such a way as to make the word Chebar (*keḇar*), which, as mentioned above, is the name of the river by which Ezekiel claims to have received the prophecy. Thus, there is a hint toward the idea that Maimonides connects with the river: that it indicates the imagination.

7.3.4 Isaiah's Account of the Chariot: Levels of Prophecy

There is another vision of the chariot in chapter 6 of Isaiah. The vision is less famous, perhaps because it is somewhat less elaborate and fearsome. Maimonides quotes the sages who say that the two visions are essentially the same but that Isaiah is like a city dweller who sees the king, while Ezekiel is like a village dweller who sees the king.[46] Since Isaiah is more used to the sight, he describes less of the detail. The implication is that Isaiah is the greater prophet, since he apprehends what is seen in the vision of the chariot more regularly, an assessment supported by what Maimonides says about prophecy in part two of the *Guide*, in which he discusses different levels of prophecy. Excluding that of Moses, he counts eleven. Scripture introduces prophetic visions or dreams with particular language, and each of these eleven levels is introduced with different phrases. It is important for Maimonides' interpretation of the chariot that Ezekiel is only mentioned in the fifth level, and I will address this further below. Ezekiel is thus depicted as inferior to a number of other prophets. For example, Isaiah is mentioned when Maimonides describes the seventh level. As with the comment above, this indicates that his prophecy is superior.[47]

Maimonides excludes Moses from the eleven ranks of prophets. He writes that "prophet" is used of Moses and other prophets amphibolously (*bi-taškīk*).[48] He states that nothing that is said about prophecy in the *Guide* applies to the prophecy of Moses.[49] Throughout his career, Maimonides asserts that there are a number of differences between Mosaic prophecy and that of all other prophets.[50] Ultimately, these can all be reduced to the claim that Moses' prophecy is not constrained by material considerations. As explained above, imagination is used in prophecy. The prophet is superior to the philosopher in that the prophet possesses a superior imagination and also a stronger intuition. Moses' prophecy is superior, however, since, unlike all other prophets, Moses does not have to use his imagination to prophesy. His prophecy is purely intellectual, and this explains why all of the differences between Mosaic prophecy and the prophecy of other prophets hold.[51] When a prophet other than Moses receives a vision, the use of a bodily faculty, the imagination, causes a physical reaction. Hence Ezekiel states, "[28] . . . And when I saw it, I fell upon my face, and I heard a voice of one that spoke." In this context, it is worth noting that Maimonides claims to have attained his current level of understanding through speculation alone, not through prophecy.[52] One consequence might be that Maimonides wishes to distinguish knowledge achieved through natural reason from knowledge gained by prophecy. However, given that Maimonides claims to understand as much as, or perhaps even more than, Ezekiel, it might also be an indication that what can be learned through prophecy is no different from what is learned through rational speculation. Such an account would fit with the account of prophecy that Maimonides adheres to, in which perfecting one's physical and moral characteristics, and subsequently one's intellect, is what enables one to attain prophecy.[53] Prophetic knowledge may still be superior to philosophic understanding in the way it enables communication of truths to a greater number of people.

7.4 FIRST SECTION OF THE VISION OF THE CHARIOT: A PICTURE OF THE SPHERES

7.4.1 Number of the Beasts: A System of Four Superlunar Spheres

[4] And I saw and behold, a stormy wind came out of the North, a great cloud, with a fire flashing up, so that a brightness was round about it; And out of the midst thereof as the colour of electrum, out of the midst of the fire.
[5] And out of the midst thereof came the likeness of four beasts. And this was their appearance: they had the likeness of a man.
[6] And every one had four faces, and every one of them had four wings.

Most of this part of the first chapter of Ezekiel is concerned with a description of the beasts, which, on Maimonides' reading, represent the superlunar spheres. Maimonides does not explicitly state that he understands the beasts to represent the spheres. Rather, he hints at his interpretation by pointing out aspects of the scriptural account and explaining what is important about them. The reader is then expected to associate those explanations with explanations of other things elsewhere in the *Guide*. Once again, it is evident that in order to understand Maimonides' commentary on the chariot, one needs to follow his advice to "connect its chapters with one another."[54]

Maimonides presents his most detailed account of the beasts in part three, chapter 2 of the *Guide*. There he calls attention to the fact that there are four beasts, each with four heads, four wings, and two hands.[55] The biblical account does not mention the number two, giving Maimonides more cause to focus on the number four. There is no explanation of the numbers in this section of the *Guide*. Instead, the reason appears earlier on.

That there are four beasts representing the spheres would probably strike a reader unfamiliar with the second part of the *Guide* as strange. If a beast represents a sphere, then one would have to conclude that there are four spheres, but that was not a commonly held view in Maimonides' time. Furthermore, Maimonides assumes the existence of nine spheres throughout most of the *Guide*, as well as in MT.[56] In a slightly different context, he even writes that God necessitates (*awǧab*) that there be nine spheres.[57] However, in a section in part two, Maimonides argues that it is acceptable to posit the existence of only four spheres and then explains what the four-sphere theory amounts to. He claims that "the doctrine of all the ancients was that the spheres of Venus and Mercury are above the sun."[58] He then says to "keep this in mind," which is clearly an instruction to think about it while reading other sections of the *Guide* and try to apply the knowledge to what is said elsewhere. The other part of the *Guide* that is relevant is the commentary on Ezekiel.

Positing the existence of four spheres surrounding the earth is a system in which Maimonides has to manipulate the position of the stars in order to make them fit. He claims to be relying on a doctrine that was widespread in ancient times and refers to ibn Aflaḥ, who refutes the teaching.[59] The idea that there are four spheres facilitates Maimonides' reading of Ezekiel, as it enables him to state that Ezekiel depicts a cosmos containing only four animated spheres: the moon, the sun, the five planets, and the fixed stars. An outermost sphere containing no stars is also posited. Maimonides is then able to say that each beast represents a sphere containing stars. The fifth sphere is also mentioned in a later section of the vision, but it is not represented as a beast, since it is not animated.[60]

The spheres do not give off light in their own right, as they are colorless. It is the stars contained within them that emit light; the spheres are radiant by virtue of the stars.

[13] As for the likeness of the beasts, their appearance was like coals of fire, burning like the appearance of torches; it flashed up and down among the living creatures; and there was brightness to the fire, and out of the fire went forth lightning.

Maimonides probably offers the opinion that there are four spheres because this is what he considered Ezekiel to believe, rather than because it represents his own belief. The fact that this account contrasts with the description of the cosmos that Maimonides presents elsewhere in the *Guide*, as well as at the beginning of MT, and which he presents as undoubtedly true in those places, is evidence for this claim. I shall return to Maimonides' disagreements with Ezekiel below.

7.4.2   Faces of the Beasts

[10] As for the likeness of their faces, they had the face of a man; and they four had the face of a lion on the right side; and they four had the face of an ox on the left side; they four had also the face of an eagle.
[11] Thus were their faces; and their wings were stretched upward; two wings of every one were joined one to another, and two covered their bodies.

Maimonides seems to minimize the differences among the faces of the beasts. He states that they are all the same, as each is really the face of a man. Although they are named by different species, Ezekiel intends merely to "indicate the face of a man that tends to have a likeness to forms belonging to these species."[61]

With regard to each being human, Maimonides states that there is an important difference between the first account of the chariot and the second: the second describes the beasts as cherubs, as mentioned above. He explains that "cherub designates a human being of tender age."[62] This comment is connected to Maimonides' interpretation of "cherub" as a term used to denote an intellect.[63] Humans are the only creatures in the sublunar sphere that possess intellect. Since each sphere has an intellect corresponding to it, the most appropriate image from the sublunar world with which to represent this aspect of the sphere would be a human. The second vision, then, points out that the beasts are connected to intellects. So Maimonides hints that the faces of the beasts are human because the beasts represent intellectual beings.

Despite this interpretation, Maimonides places some importance on the different species given to the different beasts' faces. Although they are all human faces, they are named by different species to point out the fact that they are to be distinguished. Humans are all part of one species, so they differ as individuals falling under that species. The case of the spheres is different, however, although they belong to the same genus, because each sphere is a species in itself.[64] In Maimonides' account, Ezekiel makes the point that each sphere is a separate species, rather than merely a separate individual, when he likens each of them to different species existing within the world. The fact that the four faces are named by different species, then, shows that the spheres belong to different species. They are the sole members of their species.

So far, Maimonides' interpretation is that what Ezekiel describes in his vision of the living creatures represents the bodies, souls, and intellects of the spheres. Ezekiel's vision also relates further information about the nature of the spheres.

7.4.3 Hands of the Beasts: The Governance of the Spheres

[8] And they had the hands of a man under their wings on their four sides; and as for the faces and wings of them four.

Maimonides points out that the beasts have two hands and that they are the hands of a man. He explains that a man's hand is of a specific shape in order to facilitate working with practical arts and crafts (*ṣinā'a*).[65] In this way, Maimonides draws attention to the interpretation that Ezekiel ascribes two causative functions to the beasts. He also mentions the role of a craftsman when he discusses the two functions of the spheres in part two of the *Guide*. There he explains that the four forces that flow from the spheres can be divided into two species. The first type of cause creates, and the second type preserves.

> This is the meaning of "nature" [*ṭabī'a*], which is said to be wise, having governance, caring for the bringing into existence of animals by means of an art similar to that of a craftsman [*ṣāni'*], and also caring for their preservation and permanence through the bringing into existence of formative forces, which are the cause of the existence of living beings, and nutritive forces, which are the cause of their lasting for whatever duration is possible. What is intended hereby is the divine decree [*amr*] from which these two activities derive through the intermediary of the sphere.[66]

The reason for the beasts' possessing two hands, then, is that they are engaged in two activities characteristic of crafts. One is the creative act, and the other is a preservative act.

7.4.4 Motion of the Beasts: Circular Motion

Maimonides' discussion of the beasts' motion provides further evidence that he believes them to represent the spheres. The motion he says that Ezekiel figuratively ascribes to the beasts is exactly the same as the motion Maimonides has already ascribed to the spheres; they possess only one motion in which there is no deviation or curve.[67]

[9] their wings were joined one to another; they turned not when they went; they went every one straight forward.

It is accordingly possible to extrapolate that their motion is circular motion, which continues in one direction, rather than rectilinear motion, which can occur in a number of directions.[68]

[12] And they went every one straight forward; whither the spirit was to go, they went; they turned not when they went.

The circular motion of the spheres is extremely quick and returns to its source.

[14] And the beasts ran and returned as the appearance of a flash of lightning.

The lightning indicates both the speed and the fact that the motion begins and ends at the same place.[69] It is identical to the motion of a sphere, which, aside from having only one direction, always returns to its source and moves extremely quickly.[70]

7.4.5   Spheres' Motion and the Beasts' Legs

The legs of the beasts also teach about their motion.

[7] And their feet were straight feet; and the sole of their feet was like the sole of a calf's foot; and they sparkled like the colour of burnished brass.

Maimonides draws attention to two things about the legs of the beasts. One is that the legs are straight rather than divided into parts. This may perhaps be a reference to the notion that the spheres do not undergo change, neither in their speed nor in direction. Their matter is constant, as it is more perfect than the matter of the sublunar world. The second is taught by the sages when they state that "there is no sitting above."[71] In Maimonides' interpretation, this teaches that the motion of the spheres is eternal and unchanging. He makes a particular point of instructing the reader to understand this point.

Above I described a method of interpretation that Maimonides describes as "derivation of words."[72] With this in mind, consider that the soles of the feet are like the soles of a calf's foot. According to Maimonides, this indicates the spherical nature of the spheres. "Calf" translates as *'egel* and "round" as *'egol*. In order to derive "sphericity" from "calf," one merely needs to change the vowels in the word. Maimonides plays with them in order to argue that Ezekiel's mentioning that the foot of the living creature was like that of a calf might be an allusion to something round, so Ezekiel's description of the beasts' feet indicates that the sphere is round.[73]

Although he does not explicitly say so, Maimonides' explanation of the motion of the beasts clearly indicates that they are supposed to represent the spheres.

7.4.6 Beasts' Wings: Causes of the Motion of the Spheres

[6] Each one had four faces and each had four wings.

Each beast has four wings. Maimonides points this out but says nothing more about the wings apart from that they are separated from above. The meaning of "wing" in prophetic literature is explained during the lexicographical section of the first part of the *Guide*. There are a number of possible meanings when scripture uses "wings." The first is the literal one in which they teach about motion. They can also be used figuratively to signify the extremity of the earth. When applied to either God or angels, "wing" occurs in connection with something that is concealed:

> According to our opinion, the angels have no bodies . . . [so] in all cases in which "wing" occurs with reference to the angels it signifies that which conceals. Will you not consider the dictum of Scripture: "with twain he covered his face and with twain he covered his feet"? This means that the cause of his existence is most hidden and concealed, that cause being indicated by the expression "his face."[74]

The scriptural verse quoted in this passage is part of Isaiah's vision of the chariot. However, Maimonides directs the reader to yet another chapter in order to discover the meaning of wings that are used for flight, as they are in Ezekiel's vision. This tests the reader even further, since that other chapter is not devoted solely to a discussion of the intention behind scripture's use of flight. Its main purpose is to teach that the angels are incorporeal and to explain the different possible meanings that scripture might be indicating when it describes them in bodily terms. In that chapter, Maimonides explains the various meanings that can attach to scripture's use of flight. He then distances his comments from an interpretation of Ezekiel by instructing the reader not to

> be led into error by what you find especially in Ezekiel with regard to "the face of an ox" and "the face of a lion" and "the face of an eagle" and "the sole of the foot of a calf". For this has another interpretation which you will hear. It is also merely a description of the animals.[75]

Maimonides' next comment appears to divert attention away from the subject of Ezekiel's vision by stating that these quotations will be explained in their proper place rather than now.

> These intentions will be explained by means of hints [*išārāt*] sufficient to awaken [*tanbīh*] the attention.[76]

The careful reader can see, however, that Maimonides returns to the topic at the end of this very chapter. There he explains that

> the two wings are the causes of flying. For this reason the number of wings seen in the prophetic vision corresponded to that of the causes of motion of a moving thing. However, this is not the subject of this chapter.[77]

The final sentence is a signpost pointing to the fact that the comment is important even though it is a digression. It is also an example of Maimonides' scattering information concerning the "secrets of the Torah" in diverse chapters that do not seem to have those secrets as their topic. What is learned from the comment is that the wings seen in "the prophetic vision" stand for the causes of the motion of the beasts. Since the beasts have four wings, Ezekiel ascribes four causes for their motion. Similarly, there are four causes for the motions of the spheres:

> The causes of every motion belonging to the sphere are four: namely, the shape of the sphere, I mean to say its sphericity, its soul, and its intellect through which it has conceptions, as we have explained, and the separate intellect, which is its beloved. Understand this well.[78]

The wings, then, signify the causes of the spheres' motion.

Ezekiel states that the motion of the beasts does not occur because of the nature of the beasts themselves but because of the spirit that is present in them. Presumably, the spirit represents the soul. It cannot be the intelligence, because the spirit moves along with the beasts. The intelligences, being free from matter, do not move, although they are the cause of motion in the spheres. A soul, on the other hand, although being the cause of the motion of a body, moves only accidentally when the body to which it belongs moves.[79] So far, Maimonides has hinted that the living creatures consist of spheres and souls. His descriptions of the spheres elsewhere in the *Guide* accord with the brief comments he makes about the beasts in Ezekiel's vision. After following Maimonides' advice and piecing together chapters from different parts of the *Guide,* the reader is left in little doubt that the subject of the first vision of the *merkabah* is the superlunar spheres.

7.4.7 Further Details of the Beasts: The Music of the Spheres

Further information about the beasts is given later in the chapter. It occurs after the second description, which is about the wheels. As mentioned above, Maimonides divides the vision into three parts, each beginning with the phrase "and I saw." However, this section occurs at the end of the second part but shares its topic with the subject of the first vision. The order could be a problem for Maimonides, as it may be that his interpretation does not suit the text. Abrabanel argues that Maimonides must have interpreted the account of the chariot incorrectly, since his explanation does not accord with the text.[80] Perhaps there is no way to solve this problem, but Maimonides may have seen the anomaly as evidence for a lack of order in the vision.[81] He may also have been unconcerned by it. Even if Maimonides' account, on this reading, does not fit the text, that does not falsify the interpretation of the *Guide* that I present here.

The passage runs as follows:

[22] And over the heads of the beasts there was the likeness of a firmament, like the colour of the terrible ice, stretched forth over their heads above.

[23] And under the firmament were their wings conformable the one to the other; this one of them had two which covered, and that one of them had two which covered, their bodies.

[24] And when they went, I heard the noise of their wings like the noise of great waters, like the voice of the Almighty, a noise of tumult like the noise of a host; when they stood, they let down their wings.

[25] For, when there was a voice above the firmament that was over their heads, as they stood, they let down their wings.

The first piece of new information in these verses is that there is a firmament. Since Maimonides interprets the four beasts as the four animated spheres, it is reasonable to think that he takes the firmament to represent the all-encompassing sphere, which contains no stars. Maimonides conspicuously omits verses 24 and 25 from the *Guide* altogether. Both describe a sound made by the beasts, which represent the spheres, when they move. Similar verses appear in Ezekiel's second account, but Maimonides does not mention those, either. In a chapter in part two of the *Guide,* he says that the spheres do not make a sound. There he attributes the belief that they do to Plato and Pythagoras and also mentions that it was common among the ancient Israelites.[82] Those medievals who comment extensively on this part of the *Guide* believe that Maimonides attributes the belief to Ezekiel.[83] They take different attitudes toward the problem. Šem Tob is an example of one who seems to sympathize with Maimonides' claim. He explains that this chapter teaches that the prophet is not superior to the philosopher in matters of reason.[84] On the other hand, Abrabanel disagrees with Maimonides' reading of the *merkabah* and is happy to use the fact that Maimonides believes Ezekiel to have erred as evidence for the failure of Maimonides' interpretation.[85] He also argues that the plain meaning of the text indicates that the wings make a sound. The wings are the causes rather than the spheres themselves, so Maimonides' interpretation of the passage does not seem to fit its literal meaning.[86] According to Abrabanel, this shows that Maimonides simply did not understand Ezekiel's vision.

Maimonides would not have wished to make an explicit reference to these verses, because he does not wish to point out so openly that he believes Ezekiel to be mistaken. If he had wished, on the other hand, to make sure that no reader associates this chapter with Ezekiel, he could have specified that the relevant verses have a different meaning, as he does on other occasions.[87] Since he never openly states that Ezekiel is to be associated with those who believe in the sounds of the spheres and since he never refers to these verses, the only way in which he indicates his interpretation is through hints bringing to mind, once again, the introductions to parts one and three.

7.4.8 The Number Four

The number four is clearly of great importance to Maimonides. Ezekiel's vision is based around it. Furthermore, it connects the beasts with the cosmological theory that Maimonides outlines in the second part of the *Guide*, where he refuses to commit to any single cosmological theory. He affirms the possible existence of only four spheres, with the addition of the outermost sphere, which encompasses all of them and which Ezekiel calls the "firmament."[88] This may be justified by his claim that there is no certainty about anything that is above the realm of the sublunar sphere but that everything that Aristotle says about that which is below it is undoubtedly correct.[89] Accordingly, says Maimonides, Ezekiel relates not that he saw "four living creatures" but that he saw "the likeness of four living creatures," by which Maimonides indicates that the vision does not intend to relate demonstrable truth.[90]

The number recurs throughout the *Guide*, particularly in the sections concerning the chariot. It fits both with scripture and, to a certain extent, with the Aristotelian account of the universe. Although Maimonides has to force his cosmology into a system that is based around the number four, there are some Aristotelian ideas for which the number is particularly appropriate, such as the existence of four humors, four parts of the soul, or four elements. On Maimonides' reading, it is to the last of these, the four elements, that Ezekiel's account now turns when he describes the wheels underneath the living creatures.

7.5 SECOND VISION: THE CONTENT OF THE SUBLUNAR WORLD

7.5.1 Identity of the *Ofanim:* The Elements

[15] And I saw the beasts, behold one wheel at the bottom hard by the living creatures, at the four faces thereof.

Maimonides draws attention to the fact that Ezekiel describes the wheels (*ofanim*) as reaching from the earth to the beasts. It follows that their realm is below the beasts, which are the spheres.

> Accordingly he has made it clear that it was a single body whose one extremity was by the beasts while the other was on the earth, and that this wheel had four faces. . . . Thus after speaking of one wheel, he goes on to speak of four.[91]

As such, they can only be members of the sublunar sphere. The wheels, which are the second part of the vision of the chariot, represent the four elements of earth, water, air, and fire, which together constitute everything existing in the sublunar sphere. Again, Ezekiel mentions that there are four wheels, which is convenient for Maimonides, as it provides further evidence that the account is a description of the cosmos.

The wheels are described as a single body divided into four. They are described as four things, but they are not described as having the form of any living thing at all. They are merely bodies, albeit "great, terrible, and fearful." However, they are all described as making up one body. They all have the same "likeness"; as a whole, they are likened to beryl.

[16] The appearance of the wheels and their work was like unto the colour of a beryl; and they four had one likeness; and their appearance and their work was as it were a wheel within a wheel.

Maimonides considers the image of a beryl stone:

> With regard to his saying about them, like unto beryl, he interprets this also in the second description, saying with regard to the wheels: "and the appearance of the wheels was "as the colour of a beryl stone." Jonathan ben Uzziel, peace be on him, translated this: "like unto a precious stone." Now you already know that Onkelos used this very expression to translate: "As it were, a work of the whiteness of sapphire stone;" he says "as the work of a precious stone." There is consequently no difference between its saying, 'as the colour of a beryl stone,' and its saying, "as it were, a work of the whiteness of sapphire stone." Understand this.[92]

The translation Maimonides refers to here is of a passage in Exodus that is explained in the first part of the *Guide*. Maimonides presents his explanation of Onkelos as if it is a digression by stating afterward that "we have gone beyond the subject of this chapter in order to deal with a matter that will be made clear in other chapters."[93] The explanation of the chariot, so it would seem, is where the digression is relevant.[94] Onkelos's translation is of another passage of scripture, one that deals with the vision of the nobles of Israel who apprehended the sapphire stone. This vision has been dealt with in detail by Michelle Levine.[95] She writes that "the nobles of Israel cognise first matter under the heavenly spheres."[96] Perhaps, then, the sapphire stone of Ezekiel's vision is to be interpreted as prime matter.[97]

Evidently, in the chapters dedicated to exegesis of the chariot, Maimonides alludes to his interpretation that this one body represents prime matter, which is a single thing divided into four elements. Each of these wheels would then represent an element. Maimonides elaborates: "then [Ezekiel] explains with regard to these wheels that they were encased one within the other."[98] Maimonides contrasts this with what is said about the beasts. Ezekiel states that the beasts are "joined to one another," which, Maimonides says, shows that they are connected to one another with no spaces in between. Elsewhere, Maimonides explains that the same is true of the spheres.[99] In the case of the beasts, "within" is not used. "Within" refers to a property that they do not have, because they touch one another instead of possessing this property. By contrast, the wheels do not touch one another while remaining distinct; they are "encased one within the other." So the fact that there is a wheel within a wheel seems to be a reference to the idea that instead of remaining distinct from one another, the elements combine in such a way as to make up all existing things in the sublunar sphere. That is what Ezekiel expresses when he says that the wheels are full of eyes:

[18] As for their rings, they were high and they were dreadful; and they four had their rings full of eyes round about.

Maimonides explains, "as for the wheels of which he says that they were full of eyes, it is possible that he meant that they were really full of eyes."[100] If the wheels are "really full of eyes," they could be references to sublunar beings that have eyes: animals. Maimonides says that there are three other possible meanings for the word *'ein*. The first is that it represents color; the wheels have many colors. Maimonides explains that this is the meaning of the word in its plain sense when it occurs in another place in the Bible. The second meaning is that it could be translated as "likeness." The third is that the word could refer to "various states and attributes." This third meaning allows Maimonides to argue that Ezekiel teaches that the elements can take on different states and attributes, thereby becoming different things. One of the reasons the eyes are there is to show that matter becomes all things in the sublunar world by assuming different forms.

7.5.2 Motion of the Wheels: Rectilinear Motion

Maimonides' description of the wheels' motion leaves no doubt that he takes them to represent that which is beneath the sphere of the moon, rather than that which is above it.

[17] When they went, they went toward their four sides; they turned not when they went.

Of this verse, Maimonides states that "there was in their motion no curve, no turning, and no deviation; there were only straight motions that did not vary."[101] It can only be a reference to rectilinear motion. The elements move in straight lines. Maimonides proceeds to explain that the wheels have no essential motion of their own but are moved by the beasts, as Ezekiel indicates in the following verses:

[19] And when the beasts went, the wheels went hard by them; and when the beasts were lifted up from the bottom, the wheels were lifted up.
[20] Whithersoever the spirit was to go, as the spirit was to go thither, so they went; and the wheels were lifted up beside them; for the spirit of the living creature was in the wheels.
[21] When those went, these went, and when those stood, these stood; and when those were lifted up from the earth, the wheels were lifted up beside them; for the spirit of the beasts was in the wheels.

"The beasts moved in whatever direction it was the divine purpose that the beasts should move, and by the motion of the beasts the wheels were moved."[102] The reason for the motion of the wheels is that the spirit of the beasts is in them. This is reminiscent of the chapter in part one of the *Guide* in which Maimonides explains that the elements are moved by the motion of the spheres and that all motion is derived from that of the outermost sphere.[103]

The elements do have a natural motion of their own, and if left to their own devices, they would rest in their natural positions. Earth and water move toward the center. Earth is heavier, so its natural position is below that of water. Air and fire move away from the center. Since fire is lighter, its natural position is on top of air. Their motion away from these positions is a result of the influence the spheres exert, so the wheels are moved by the spirit of the beasts.

7.5.3 Connection between the Wheels and the Beasts

> In this second apprehension he also explains that every wheel is related to a cherub, saying: "one wheel beside one cherub, and another wheel beside another cherub."[104]

Maimonides points out that Ezekiel connects the wheels with the beasts by stating that each wheel is set against one of the four beasts. During his exposition of the cosmology, which is built around the idea that there are only four spheres, Maimonides explains that each sphere has a special relationship with one of the elements:

> Each sphere is also specially assigned to one of the four elements, the sphere being the principle from which the forces of that particular element exclusively derive and that in virtue of its motion causes the element to move in the motion of generation.[105]

The relationship that Maimonides posits here between the spheres and the elements is a confusing aspect of the *Guide*, and I will address it further below in chapter 8. Maimonides attributes a number of effects to the spheres' influence on the sublunar world. An example of the four forces is the influence on the different types of things in the sublunar world. One force causes the mixture and the composition of the elements, another causes the vegetative soul, a third causes the animal soul, and the final force causes the rational faculty. Maimonides specifies that these are a result of the motion of the sphere, but it could certainly be another example of the connection between the beasts and the wheels.[106]

7.5.4 Sublunar Knowledge Is Known through Demonstration

Maimonides seems to take Ezekiel's use of "likeness" in the vision to indicate a lack of certainty about what is seen.[107] But in contrast to the beasts, Ezekiel does not say that he saw a "likeness" of the wheels. In the case of the wheels, Ezekiel is certain of that which he relates. That is to say, Ezekiel has certain scientific knowledge of all that is below the sphere of the moon. This account echoes Maimonides' own belief that everything Aristotle teaches about that which is in the sublunar realm is true. Maimonides believes that demonstrative knowledge is possible in this realm and that it was taught by both Aristotle and Ezekiel.[108]

7.6 THIRD VISION: THE INTELLIGENCES

Maimonides' commentary on the third part of the vision of the chariot is unclear even by the standards of the *Guide* and has caused much confusion. Consequently, it is difficult to offer an interpretation of how to understand his comments with certainty. The interpretation offered below is, I believe, correct in its general thrust, but it remains speculative concerning a number of details. The variety of possible interpretations of these details attests to the difficulty of uncovering Maimonides' meaning.

[26] And above the firmament that was over their heads was the likeness of a throne, as the appearance of a sapphire stone; and upon the likeness of the throne was a likeness as the appearance of a man upon it above.
[27] And I saw as the colour of electrum, as the appearance of fire round about enclosing it, from the appearance of his loins and upward; and from the appearance of his loins and downward I saw as it were the appearance of fire, and there was brightness round about him.
[28] As the appearance of the bow that is in the cloud in the day of rain, so was the appearance of the brightness round about. This was the appearance of the likeness of the glory of the Lord. And when I saw it, I fell upon my face, and I heard a voice of one that spoke.

7.6.1   Identity of That Which Is Above the Beasts

The end of chapter 2 of this section of the *Guide* contains a very short overview of the third vision. Here Maimonides does nothing more than point out the parts of the third vision that have inner meanings. He singles out three things that are above the spheres.

> He starts to set forth a third apprehension that he had and goes back to another description concerning that which is above the beasts. He says that above the four beasts, there is a firmament; upon the firmament, the likeness of a throne; and upon the throne, a likeness as the appearance of a man.[109]

It is unclear exactly where the third apprehension is supposed to begin. Although Maimonides stated earlier that each vision begins with "and I saw," he includes images that are mentioned before that statement within this third vision. He points out three things that are in this passage. The first is the firmament, which is above the beasts. The second is the likeness of a throne above the firmament. The third is the likeness of the man above the throne.

7.6.2   Figure of the Man: A Symbol of the Intelligences

Although the man is the last of the three elements mentioned by Maimonides and the climax of Ezekiel's vision, it is also the least controversial element to interpret. It probably represents the intelligences, because, although it is above the spheres, it is not about God. Maimonides states that God is not mentioned in the vision at all.[110]

There are further points in this part of the vision to which Maimonides draws attention. His interpretation of *ḥašmal* is important. He draws on the Talmudic teaching that the word is composed of two ideas, "the intention being to combine through a simile two separate notions regarding two sides, above and below."[111] Through this comment, Maimonides again indicates that the man represents an intelligence. Each intelligence is caused by that which is prior to it and also causes something outside itself. That seems to be why he connects the man with what is above and also with what is below.

7.6.3 The Problem of the Firmament

In verse 22, Ezekiel had described a "likeness" of the firmament. In this passage, though, "he mentions the firmament in an absolute manner."[112] Maimonides does not offer any reason for the change, but he clearly considers it important. He writes that the change corroborates and explains the reason "likeness" is used at all. The identity of the firmament is disputed. Above I explained that Maimonides considers its first appearance to represent the outermost sphere. However, in order to explain the difference in Ezekiel's presentation, Schwarz notes that "firmament" may have multiple meanings, as explained earlier in the *Guide*.[113] He points the reader toward Sara Klein-Braslavy's book for an explanation of the two meanings. Klein-Braslavy explains that in the creation story, the word "firmament" (*raqiʿa*) is used in two ways. The first signifies the heavens, and the second signifies one of the strata of air in the sublunar sphere. Klein-Braslavy mentions that the first is that which Ezekiel refers to.[114] However, her focus is not Ezekiel's vision, so she does not go into further detail. If the alternative meaning that she suggests is applicable in the current discussion and the reference is to something in the sublunar sphere, the reference would probably be to the beginnings of the process whereby the elements are mixed up together. This would explain why the firmament is not referred to as a "likeness," since it would refer to something in the sublunar realm. As mentioned above, Ezekiel does not refer to anything that Maimonides takes to be below the sphere of the moon as a "likeness." However, this solution does not answer the question of why Maimonides includes it in the third vision. An alternative explanation might be that it is treated as certain in the third apprehension because it then becomes the basis of other notions. When used in later arguments, it would be granted as axiomatic and therefore treated as if it were certain. Another possible explanation lies in the nature of the system. Belief in the sounds of the spheres, which on Maimonides' reading is affirmed by Ezekiel, relies on believing that they are perfectly ordered and harmonious. Like musical instruments, they must have the appropriate distances between one another. In that case, there can be no doubt about what is above the lunar sphere in this system.[115]

7.6.4 The Throne of Glory

The identity of the throne of glory is perhaps even more confusing than that of the firmament. Maimonides writes that scripture generally uses the term to indicate greatness. Everything that is singled out to indicate God's splendor is called a throne. When the heavens are described as a throne, this sense is meant.[116] So perhaps the throne of glory stands for the heavens.

There are other alternatives. In verse 26, the throne of glory is likened to the whiteness of the sapphire stone. The similarity is also indicated in the second of Ezekiel's visions. Maimonides does not mention it, but Jonathan uses the same term, *eben ṭabah*, to translate the "whiteness of sapphire stone" at the beginning of the second vision. So the sapphire stone seems to be the same as the throne of glory, and this leads to three more possible solutions.

The first is that the throne of glory represents prime matter. This suggestion is made by Levine on the basis of her explanation of that term in relation to the passage in Exodus, as mentioned above. However, if the sapphire stone is the prime matter of the sublunar elements, Ezekiel should not situate it above the firmament. Furthermore, there would be no need to refer to it as a "likeness," since it would be a member of the sublunar sphere, like the wheels.

The second possibility, offered by Ḥoter ben Shelomo, avoids these difficulties. Although it occurs in his own exegesis of the chariot, he believes himself to be following Maimonides' explanation.[117] He explains that the sapphire stone in Ezekiel's vision is prime matter, but it is the prime matter of the superlunar world, the fifth element that constitutes the spheres. Ben Shelomo's explanation accords with two of Maimonides' comments. The first is that beryl is a color generally attributed to the heavens. If so, the prime matter of the heavens may be represented by an equivalent term. I explained above that Maimonides takes "sapphire stone" to be such a term. It also accords with Maimonides' exegesis of God's throne as meaning the heavens.

For the third possible interpretation, the "throne of glory" in this passage could represent the active intellect. In the chapter in which Maimonides explains the meaning of "throne," he does not present the active intellect as one of the possible meanings. However, there are times in the *Guide* when the active intellect is called the glory of God.[118] Maimonides' explanation of the sapphire in connection with Exodus might support this option.[119] Levine explains that what is important about the sapphire is that it is devoid of color. It is therefore totally receptive and able to take on all colors. Describing prime matter as "a work of the whiteness of sapphire stone . . . conveys the effect of the formless character of first matter on the transformation of the elements."[120] Prime matter is not the only thing that behaves in such a way, however. The hylic intellect must also be totally passive and devoid of form if it is to be able to receive all of the forms that it potentially possesses.[121] So the sapphire stone could refer to the human intellect. It could even symbolize the active intellect, since that is connected with human intellect but is part of the realm of the intelligences. Finally, in possible support of this last interpretation, it is worth noting that Narboni identifies the throne as "another sphere, which some of the early sages named *šmey ha-haṣlaḥah*." Although I am not certain what to make of this phrase, I would like to offer a suggestion. In medieval philosophical Hebrew and in some midrashic sources, the word *haṣlaḥah* is used to refer to the achievement of human perfection, or felicity. Therefore, a possible meaning is "felicitous heavens" or "eternal heavens," since those who reach happiness achieve everlasting life. One potentially helpful midrash reads as follows: "spirit and life-force is that which shall be wandering aimlessly; it shall be under the heavens, and will not leave to rise up to the bonds of life."[122] If this or a similar midrash is the source of the idea behind *šmey hahaṣlaḥah*, Narboni could be taking the throne to refer to the souls that break through the heavens to achieve eternal life. Similarly, Maimonides mentions the phrase "bonds of life" in MT when he explains that it is the highest possible reward and that it is another name for the world to come, or eternal life.[123] It is plausible, then, that Narboni may have had such a midrash in mind.[124]

The details of Maimonides' interpretation may be understood in a number of ways. That is true especially of the third vision, about which he says little. It is reasonably certain, though, that the main focus of the third vision is seen to be the intelligences.

7.7 SUMMARY

Maimonides interprets the vision of the *merkabah* as a cosmological description. The difficulty of the subject and the strictures of Talmudic stipulations prevent him from doing so in a clear and systematic way; "secrets of the Torah" are not supposed to be explained to everyone. So Maimonides presents his interpretation of the account of the chariot in a secretive manner. The chapters explicitly dedicated to explaining it are designed to reveal some parts and conceal others. What they reveal is enough to point the educated, discerning reader to a correct understanding, as long as the *Guide* is studied continually. However, they also conceal, since what is revealed is not enough to explain the full meaning. For that, the skill and dedication of a committed and wise reader are also required. In order to understand the commentary, the reader is required to consider comments that appear in various sections of the *Guide*. These comments include some that are not closely connected to the content of the chapters in which they appear. Maimonides often draws the reader's attention to such comments by playing down their importance for that which is focused on in the places that they occur. Seemingly innocuous comments turn out to be meaningful for an interpretation of other parts of the *Guide*. The commentary is written in such a way as to test the reader and make sure that only one who is able to understand hints and allusions may uncover its entire meaning. This "esoteric" writing does not have to involve contradictions, although the passages involved proceed on the lines of ideas that are opposed to ideas assumed in other parts of the *Guide*. Furthermore, it is unnecessary to understand Maimonides to be hiding his true metaphysical beliefs by presenting a qualified belief that is less "radical." What he indicates through hints is not a hidden belief in a doctrine that he professes to deny but, rather, his interpretation of recondite scriptural passages.

CHAPTER 8

∽

The Scope and Accuracy
of Ezekiel's Prophecy

In the account of the chariot, as Maimonides interprets it, Ezekiel presents
a picture of the cosmos through the use of symbols. Maimonides explains
the account using hints, but it is a picture taught explicitly in other sections of the *Guide*, even though he does not obviously link the picture with the
explanation. The first of Abrabanel's criticisms of Maimonides' interpretation
builds on this point. He argues that were the secret of the chariot nothing
more than a description of the cosmos, the sages would not have been so careful to hide its meaning, since such ideas are taught publicly in other nations.[1]
However, Maimonides' exegesis implies matters that are not taught openly in
the *Guide* or the discussions of other nations, namely Ezekiel's mistakes. Not
only does Maimonides allude to a different part of the *Guide* in order to teach
those who are worthy, but, by contrast with many of the ideas that he hints
are taught by Ezekiel, he never states these beliefs clearly at all. So they may
represent some of Maimonides' most secret beliefs.

8.1 SUBJECT OF THE *MERKABAH*

The account of the chariot is considered to be the deepest secret of the Torah.
For this reason, we are warned off studying it or using it in certain ritual contexts.[2] A Talmudic passage tells a story of four sages who enter the *pardes*, the
orchard of mystical secrets. One of the messages the story conveys is that
delving into these secrets can be harmful. Of the four sages, only one emerges
unscathed: Akiba alone "left in peace." Secrets of the Torah require pupils to
undergo the correct training.[3] They do not reveal themselves easily. Only of
Akiba is it said that he "entered in peace." The implication, perhaps, is that he

was the only one of the four who was properly prepared. Gershom Scholem argues that the *merkaḇah* of the Talmud is part of the same tradition as that represented in the *"merkaḇah* mysticism" of the *heḵalot* literature.[4] *Heḵalot* tracts describe the mystic's ascent through the heavenly palaces. Practices designed to produce ecstasy or to influence the divine realms are major parts of those treatises.[5] The account of the chariot is central for the rabbis, and the theurgical beliefs and practices that go along with it are of great importance. Maimonides' interpretation replaces those beliefs with ideas drawn from the Arabic tradition. The secrets themselves he takes to be philosophical ideas.

8.1.1 Summary of the Secrets of the Torah in MT

The opening of MT contains a clear summary of the contents of the two major secrets of the Torah: the account of the beginning and the account of the chariot. The first two chapters contain the doctrines concerning God, some of which I have examined above. The first chapter is connected to the nature of God rather than to the nature of created things. Some of the things that are discussed in chapter 2 are present in Ezekiel's account. Maimonides identifies *ma'aseh merkaḇah* with divine science, which is Aristotelian metaphysics.[6] Accordingly, at the end of chapter 2, he makes the following comment:

> What we have mentioned in these chapters concerning this matter is like a drop in the ocean of what needs to be explained concerning it. An explanation of all the roots ['*iqarim*] that are in these two chapters is called the account of the chariot [*ma'aseh merkaḇah*].[7]

Chapters 3 and 4 concern the constitution of the cosmos. Here Maimonides includes the existence of the spheres, their order, motion, and nature, and also the sublunar elements and souls. Toward the end of the fourth chapter, Maimonides states that the matters treated in the third and fourth chapters are very deep, "but they are not as deep as the matter of the first two chapters. The explanation of all the things in the third and fourth chapters is called the account of the beginning [*ma'aseh berešit*]."[8] The reason this does not seem to accord with the *Guide* is that it indicates that the above examination of the chariot is misdirected. Ezekiel's vision of the chariot is a parable of a description of the cosmos. Since what is primarily indicated by the term *ma'aseh merkaḇah* is Ezekiel's vision—it is indeed the inspiration for the term—there is a problem. Maimonides explains in MT that a description of the cosmos actually falls under the heading of *ma'aseh berešit*. But this is what Maimonides understands the inner meaning of Ezekiel's vision to be. So it seems that the matters in Ezekiel's vision, although they are secrets of the Torah, are not the deepest of those secrets. Of course, only someone who has managed to understand what Maimonides believes the chariot to represent would realize this. It is yet another matter that is well hidden from the masses.

Following the classification of subjects that Maimonides presents in MT leads to the conclusions that in Ezekiel's vision, only the image of the man, about which little is said, is a part of *ma'aseh merkabah* but not of *ma'aseh berešit*, and much of what is most important in *ma'aseh merkabah* is missing altogether. To Maimonides' mind, then, Ezekiel may not have reached the highest peaks of human perfection and the deepest secrets of the Torah are not contained in the vision of the chariot. Not only does Maimonides interpret the chariot as teaching science that is not essentially part of the Jewish tradition, but he even implies that there are theological matters that are deeper and more important than those in Ezekiel's vision. However surprising such a statement may be in the light of the status of both Ezekiel and the *merkabah* within the tradition, it is supported by some of Maimonides' own statements. This leads to consideration of how Ezekiel is supposed to have erred and why.

8.2   EZEKIEL'S MISTAKES

Maimonides implies that two major scientific errors should be attributed to Ezekiel. The first concerns the question of whether the spheres make a sound, and the second concerns the order of the spheres.[9]

8.2.1   Sound of the Spheres

The section in part two of the *Guide* in which Maimonides explains the doctrines in Ezekiel's vision contains a chapter explaining the belief that the spheres make sounds. Maimonides states that this belief depends on thinking that the sphere itself is stationary but the stars move. He attributes the belief to some of the sages of the Talmud and other philosophers, including, significantly, Pythagoras.[10] Maimonides argues that this position is wrong and that the spheres make no sound. Aristotle's demonstrations on the matter are true and are to be adopted. His beliefs in this case are preferable to the alternative, because any truth that has been demonstrated is to be accepted on the strength of the demonstration, no matter who the arguments are made by or with whom they disagree.

In pointing out the mistakes of the sages, Maimonides' explicit point is that demonstrated truth should be accepted on the strength of the demonstration. In the face of demonstrative arguments in favor of a position, no evidence indicating that its contrary is true can be accepted. Even the opinion of any prophet would not constitute sufficient evidence against what is demonstrated.[11] In Maimonides' chapter, there is no mention of Ezekiel or of the chariot. Nevertheless, it is generally thought that the chapter is relevant to Maimonides' exegesis. One reason for this may be its presence within the section describing the cosmos. As I mentioned above, the reader is alerted to the relevance of this section for *ma'aseh merkabah*.[12] While it may be possible that Maimonides intends nothing more than to comment about the spheres and the nature of rational authority, the chapter's position indicates otherwise. If it is not connected, it seems out of place. So the chapter seems to have an implicit point as well, which is relevant for Maimonides' interpretation of Ezekiel's vision.[13]

8.2.2 Number and Order of the Spheres

The second mistake that Ezekiel is supposed to have made concerns the number and order of the spheres. Because Maimonides understood the four beasts in the vision of the chariot to represent the superlunar spheres, he concludes that Ezekiel thought that there are four spheres corresponding to the four beasts. In order to explain how the four-sphere theory would work, he adopts a theory that has been refuted elsewhere and attributes it to Ezekiel. This theory forces five planets into one single sphere and places them above the sphere of the sun. Consequently, it posits four spheres, as follows: the moon, the sun, the five planets, and the fixed stars. Maimonides states that such a position is acceptable, although it is probably false. In general, the commentators believe that it is undoubtedly false and that this is another case of Maimonides attributing a serious cosmological error to Ezekiel.[14]

In summary, Maimonides believes that Ezekiel was mistaken concerning some important issues. In neither of the cases in which mistakes have been pointed out does Maimonides openly state that Ezekiel was wrong. Therefore, they are matters that are only hinted at and that can be uncovered only by the learned, careful reader. Furthermore, he does not draw the reader's attention to these mistakes at all during the section dedicated to explaining Ezekiel's meaning. That Ezekiel attributes sounds to the spheres is not mentioned at any other point in the *Guide,* either. Although Maimonides is more open about attributing the four-sphere theory to Ezekiel, since he draws attention to it even if he does not clearly explain it, he does not explicitly state that the four-sphere theory is undoubtedly wrong.

As a result of this "esoteric" method of writing, Maimonides cannot openly explain why he believes that Ezekiel made mistakes. So there are further hidden matters in Maimonides' exegesis of Ezekiel to uncover. The reasons for these mistakes turn out to be key to understanding Maimonides' explanation of the passage in Ezekiel. I will suggest that Maimonides attributes another mistake to Ezekiel that has been hitherto overlooked. This mistake is more deep-seated and serious than those discussed above, since it betrays the fact that Maimonides considers Ezekiel to hold a worldview that is connected with idolatry.

8.3 THE REASONS FOR EZEKIEL'S MISTAKES

Two explanations of why Maimonides attributes mistakes to Ezekiel have been offered. Shalom Rosenberg argues that Ezekiel's mistakes result from his historical situation. He argues that Maimonides does not believe science to have reached completion in biblical times, and Ezekiel's errors attest to this. Scientific knowledge is progressing.[15] In response to Rosenberg's explanation, Warren Zev Harvey argues that Ezekiel is presented in the *Guide* as the paradigm of a prophet who has not been trained in the correct way. Maimonides emphasizes the importance of progressing through studies in the correct order on a number of occasions. When an improper path is followed, it becomes impossible to perceive the truth.[16] The evidence that Harvey offers for this is found in the section of the *Guide* devoted to prophecy. He points out that Maimonides mentions Ezekiel when describing the fifth of the twelve levels of prophecy outlined in the *Guide*. This is a relatively low level, so it is perhaps unsurprising that he is thought to have made some mistakes. Harvey supports his view with reference to Abrabanel's second objection, which notes the order of the visions. Abrabanel expands on one of the matters to which Maimonides draws attention.[17] Maimonides states that there is some relevance to the order in which Ezekiel describes the three visions:

> You ought also to have your attention directed to the order of these three apprehensions. Thus he has put first the apprehension of the living creatures, for they come first because of their nobility and of their causality—according to what he says: "for the air of the beasts was in the wheels"—and because of other things too. After the wheels comes the third apprehension, which is higher in degree than that of the living creatures, as is clear. The reason for this lies in the fact that the first two apprehensions necessarily precede the third apprehension in the order of knowledge, the latter being inferred with the help of the other two.[18]

The final vision is preceded by the other two because they are preparatory to it. It is proper to proceed from the subject of the first two visions to that of the last one. This is clear and is consistent with Maimonides' demands to train the mind by learning preparatory sciences before progressing to deeper subjects.

However, Maimonides does not mention this reason when explaining the order of the first two visions. Instead, their order is reversed. Although the first apprehension precedes the second in Ezekiel's account, the second apprehension precedes the first in the order of knowledge. That is, it is proper to proceed from the second to the first. If the reason is that they follow the order of preparation, then these two are the wrong way around. In response, Maimonides argues that the reason for the order of the first two visions is that the first vision represents something that is more noble than, and causative of, that which is represented by the second vision. If this is the reason for the order, then the inconsistency is again apparent, since the third vision represents something that is more noble than, and causative of, both of the other two. But in that case, the prophet ought to have begun with the third vision, proceeded to the first, and ended with the second. So Maimonides offers two reasons for the order of the visions, neither of which fits the entire account. If the reason for the order of the visions is that it begins with the simplest, most preparatory science and progresses to more advanced and subtle sciences, until "the ultimate perception and the highest of all,"[19] the *ofanim* should precede the living creatures, but they do not. However, if the reason is that one begins with the most noble science, which is the science of the things most causative, then the entire account should be opened with the description of the man, but, once more, that is not what Ezekiel does.[20]

There is a hint that these are not the only reasons. After Maimonides explains why scripture prefaces the wheels with the beasts, he mentions that this happens "because of other things too" but does not say what those other things are. If Maimonides considers Ezekiel to be mistaken, then the other things might well be connected with the mistakes. Since Maimonides does not openly express the belief that Ezekiel made mistakes, he would not be able to express the reasons for those mistakes openly, either, at least not without betraying the notion that he is deliberately hiding. Therefore, these other things may be a hint toward the mistakes.[21] If this is so, perhaps the explanation given to the order of the second and third visions not only could be applied to the first two but should be. Hence, Ezekiel could be said to have attempted to understand the superlunar world before understanding the sublunar world. He would have reversed the proper order of study and consequently become confused. This could account for his false worldview.[22]

I think that both Rosenberg and Harvey have uncovered correct reasons. However, neither of these reasons tells the whole story. They are symptomatic of a much more fundamental and shocking reason: Ezekiel's worldview was, in Maimonides' opinion, similar to that of people he considered idolaters. Maimonides attributes another mistake to Ezekiel that makes this apparent: the connection between the individual elements of the sublunar world and the spheres.

8.4 A THIRD MISTAKE: THE INFLUENCE OF THE SPHERES

An important component of the four-sphere theory is the connection bet-ween the spheres and the sublunar world. The links are articulated in a number of ways. One of these concerns the connections between the four individual spheres and the four sublunar elements. This connection is a key to Maimonides' exegesis. If my argument is correct, it explains Ezekiel's mis-takes. The reason for them is far more deep-seated than has been suggested recently; Maimonides' assessment of Ezekiel's knowledge is more negative than has so far been thought.

8.4.1 The Views of "the Philosophers"

The two mistakes outlined above are explained in chapters 8 and 9 of part two of the *Guide*. Chapter 10 shares the subject of Ezekiel's vision with those two. It begins with an explanation of the influence that the spheres exert on the sublunar world. Maimonides mentions an influence twice in close proximity but in slightly different ways. Both explanations are attributed to "the philos-ophers," but the philosophers referred to in the first statement may be differ-ent from those intended in the second statement. Maimonides uses "philosopher" in two different ways.[23] Using words to mean different things depending on context is normal for Maimonides, and it is quite possible that he is doing that here.[24] The first statement is in accord with Maimonides' own expressed views, but the second is not. The second statement may then be taken to reveal Maimonides' interpretation of the chariot.

The careful reader, "with a view to whom the treatise has been written," would notice the distinction that may be drawn between the two statements. That difference is indicated by the language with which Maimonides describes the views: the first is attributed to "all" of them, while the second is not. Furthermore, Maimonides writes that he explains the first statement else-where in the *Guide* but makes no such claim for the second. He may be using the word in a general sense on the first occasion and in a particular sense on the second occasion. Not all of the philosophers included in the first statement, then, are also to be included in the second. A reader who does not recognize the two different senses may confuse the two groups he refers to. Maimonides would thereby convey the idea to some readers that the four-sphere system is authoritative by connecting it with the philosophers' beliefs. By connecting the second statement with the first and concluding that the opinion under discussion is generally accepted in all of the philosophical books, an insensitive reader might be led to believe that Maimonides lends greater authority to it than is the case. In this way, Maimonides further hides the secret. Those who notice the difference, on the other hand, would not be taken in.[25]

8.4.2 The First Statement of the Spheres' Influences

Maimonides comments that it is well known from "all the books of the philosophers" (*kull kutub al-falāsifa*) that the sublunar world is governed by forces deriving from the spheres.[26] It is stated that this has also been mentioned in the *Guide*. Apart from his discussion in part two, Maimonides treats the issue of the cause of motion in the sublunar world toward the end of the first part of the *Guide*. Among the things that he explains are the various motions of the elements. Each has a natural motion of its own, earth and water toward the centre of the earth and air and fire toward the sphere of the moon. They are also moved, however, by external forces: the motion of the spheres. The spheres' rotation causes the elements to move in unnatural ways:

> Inasmuch as the fifth body as a whole is engaged perpetually in a circular motion, it thus engenders forced motion in the elements because of which they leave their places.[27]

This causes the elements to mix together, resulting in the existence of the composite things that come to be and pass away: the material beings below the lunar sphere. If left to their own devices, the elements would always return to their natural places. The motion of the heavens is also responsible for the existence of the forces that subsist in beings subject to generation and corruption. Maimonides puts the existence of these things down to the motion of the heavens in general and the soul of heaven:

> Heaven in virtue of its motion exerts influence over the other parts of the world and sends to every generated thing the forces that subsist in the latter. Accordingly, every motion existing in the world has as its first principle the motion of heaven, and every soul existing in the beings endowed with souls that are in the world has as its principle the soul of heaven.[28]

8.4.3 The Second Statement of the Spheres' Influences

The second explanation of the spheres' influence is attributed to "the philosophers" (*al-falāsifa*). Maimonides states that they posit a particular connection between the moon and the sublunar element water. He then points out that there is an obvious connection between the element fire and the sun, since the sun is the source of heat in the world, as is clear from the fact that there is heat when the sun is shining and cold when the sun does not shine. Maimonides then relates that after considering the belief of "the philosophers" together with the influence of the sun, he realized that there is a connection between each element and one of the four spheres. The connection is that each one of the spheres influences one of the elements:

> When I knew this, it occurred to me that each of the four spheres having stars
> have forces that overflow from them as a whole toward all the things subject to
> generation—these spheres being the cause of the latter—each sphere is also
> specially assigned to one of the four elements, the sphere being the principle
> from which the forces of that particular element exclusively derive and that in
> virtue of its motion causes the element to move in the motion of generation.[29]

The moon controls the motion of the water in the sublunar realm, the sun controls the motion of fire, the sphere of the fixed stars moves the air, and the sphere of the planets moves the earth. A characteristic of the four-sphere theory, then, is the notion that each of the spheres has a particular influence on a single one of the elements. The idea must be connected with the four-sphere theory, or it simply will not work. It is the philosophers who posit a correspondence between the moon and water who lead Maimonides to that view.[30]

Tying together the four spheres with the four elements in such a way is Maimonides' own innovation. It is an innovation about which he is completely open. However, as noted above, Maimonides disclaims any scientific originality in the *Guide*.[31] Instead, he instructs the reader to study other books in order to understand science; Maimonides himself adds nothing to them at all.

> My purpose in this treatise was not to compose something on natural science, or
> to make an epitome of notions pertaining to the divine science according to
> some doctrines, or to demonstrate what has been demonstrated in them. Nor
> was my purpose in this treatise to give a summary and epitomized description
> of the disposition of the spheres. For the books composed concerning these
> matters are adequate. If, however, they should turn out not to be adequate with
> regard to some subject, that which I say concerning this subject will not be
> superior to everything else that has been said about it.[32]

In light of Maimonides' disavowing any sound scientific innovation of his own, it is reasonable to think that he alerts the reader to be wary of the idea that there is a particular relationship between each sphere and an individual element when he stresses that it is his own innovation. He presents it as a logical consequence of the belief that the moon is intimately connected with water, a belief attributed to "the philosophers." So Maimonides' connection of the four spheres with the four elements seems to imply the worldview of those he refers to as "the philosophers." In that case, he may be alerting the reader to be wary of the general theories of "the philosophers."

Perhaps Maimonides intends to liken the second belief of the "philosophers" to the first, and therefore his own belief, so as to indicate to the unaware reader that the second statement is nothing more than an explanation of the first. Nevertheless, the second statement does not seem to conform to Maimonides' view of the spheres' influence. It is true that when outlining his own belief, Maimonides mentions that the light from heaven plays a role in the causative process. So the sun causes the motion of the element fire in the world, in the respect that it is generated by the sun. "All this takes place through the intermediary of the illumination and the darkness [on earth] resulting from the light in heaven and from heaven's motion around the earth."[33] However, even if it is granted that the sun has a particular connection with the element fire, it does not follow that each sphere has a special relationship to a single element. Maimonides only presents that as a consequence of the connection between the moon and water. So from the comment that the sun causes fire to move, one cannot conclude that Maimonides agrees with "the philosophers" who posit a connection between the moon and water.

An exhaustive account of Maimonides' sources is beyond the scope of this work. It is also unnecessary in order to make the point. However, it is necessary to consider the reasons given for the motion of the sublunar elements in order to distinguish what Maimonides would have considered to be true from the position he appears to adopt in the second part of the *Guide*.

8.4.4 "All the Philosophers": Possible Sources of the First Statement

Similar ideas to those expressed in part one of the *Guide* can be found in the writings of a philosopher whom Maimonides explicitly praises as an authority in connection with the issues currently under discussion, ibn Bāǧǧa, whom he calls the "excellent philosopher" (*al-faylasūf al-fāḍil*).[34] Otto Neugebauer writes that Maimonides mentions a treatise by ibn Bāǧǧa that argues in favor of the four-sphere system and that this legitimizes it in his eyes.[35] If this were so, then it would be easier to accept what Maimonides has to say about the four spheres at face value. In fact, Maimonides praises ibn Bāǧǧa for his refutation of the four-sphere system. True, Maimonides writes that he only shows it to be improbable rather than impossible, but he does say that the arguments ibn Bāǧǧa brings make the four-sphere system very unlikely.[36] Ibn Bāǧǧa presents ideas similar to those in the *Guide* but not similar to those Maimonides uses to explain the chariot's meaning. Maimonides was almost certainly aware of ibn Bāǧǧa's commentary on Aristotle's Meteorology. It is probably the work to which he is referring when he writes that ibn Bāǧǧa "expresses a doubt about whether Aristotle knew about the eccentricity of the sun and passes over it in silence."[37]

To recap, that each one of the spheres has a particular relationship with a single one of the elements is a position that Maimonides states that he understood from his own speculation. The idea that moved him to this position is that the moon moves the water. Therefore, the most crucial question for this discussion is the influence of the moon on the element water. However, ibn Bāǧǧa cannot be one of "the philosophers" who posit such a connection, since his explanation of water's motion is different. He says that the immediate cause of water's motion and particularly its mixture with other elements is illumination.[38] He states that "the stars are observable insofar as they have colours; they move the elements insofar as they are luminous or by some property related to it."[39] Ibn Bāǧǧa specifies the sun and the moon as causes of the motion of the elements, but this does not seem to be tied to the element water alone. What is causative is the light generated by the stars, including the moon. The reason the two major luminaries play the greatest role in this process is that they radiate more light than other stars.[40] In the sublunar realm, the elements' motions are all caused by the motion of fire, which is, in turn, caused by the motion of the spheres. Fire is given this prior role because it is the element closest to the sphere, so the sphere's motion is the proximate cause of fire's motion.[41]

8.4.5 The Identity of "the Philosophers": Possible Sources of the Second Statement

To whom does Maimonides refer when he talks of "the philosophers" who hold the second belief? Although the idea that the individuals of the superlunar spheres influenced those of the sublunar realm is not mentioned by ibn Bāǧǧa, it was a common belief at the time. Al-Kindī, who is considered the first of the philosophers and had great influence on Islamic philosophy as a whole, mentions that each star has a particular influence. He elaborates a theory that aims at explaining all particulars in the sublunar world on the basis of celestial forces proceeding from the heavenly bodies.[42] Among those on whom Kindī had an impact, a tenth-century group known as the Brethren of Purity (*Iḫwān al-Ṣafa'*) are particularly notable. The Brethren drew upon a number of sources besides Kindī for their ideas. They were also influenced by a Sabian culture that existed at the time, which would be significant for Maimonides' critical assessment of them.[43] There are fifty-two epistles of the Brethren of Purity. Although their authorship is disputed, they are usually thought to have been written by an Isma'ili group based in Baṣra and Baghdad.

The Brethren influenced a number of significant Jewish thinkers. This is important, since those Jewish thinkers often called them *ha-filosofim*, which is the equivalent Hebrew term for the Arabic that Maimonides uses when describing the second opinion, al-falāsifa. The doctrine that Maimonides attributes directly to "the philosophers" rather than to his own consideration of their ideas is that the moon is connected with and influences the element water. The Brethren of Purity also posit this connection.[44] If Maimonides adopts the term that Jewish writers who were influenced by the Iḫwān used in order to refer to them, some confusing issues become clear. If so, they may be the people he has in mind in the second statement.

An intriguing figure in this discussion is Josef ibn Ṣaddiq, author of The Microcosm. Maimonides' attitude toward him has been confused. In a letter to ibn Tibbon, there is a comment about ibn Ṣaddiq.[45] Maimonides writes that he has not read ibn Ṣaddiq's Microcosm but is aware of his learning. He then adds that ibn Ṣaddiq follows the ways of the Iḫwān al-Ṣafa'.[46] Thus, Maimonides dismisses ibn Ṣaddiq's ideas. Nevertheless, ibn Ṣaddiq appears to be distinguished from the other thinkers whom Maimonides spurns. The comment about ibn Ṣaddiq is ambiguous enough to mislead one translator into an interpretation in which Maimonides actively praises ibn Ṣaddiq.[47] As Pines points out, however, it is "an observation implying criticism. For the authors of the philosophic encyclopedia entitled the Epistles of the Brethren were held in but slight esteem by the rigorous Aristotelian philosophers."[48] Stroumsa argues that the reference is a negative one. She shows that Maimonides dismisses the Microcosm using words similar to 2 Kings 9:11.[49] There, in reference to a "madman," the statement "you know the fellow and how he talks" is made. Maimonides' reference to ibn Ṣaddiq is worded similarly, and Stroumsa argues that Maimonides means to associate ibn Ṣaddiq with the insult in that verse.[50] Maimonides may have couched his dismissal of ibn Ṣaddiq and the Brethren of Purity in ambiguous terms, because he uses them in the Guide in an apparently positive way. To dismiss them openly might make clear to a reader that any doctrines they hold are suspect and so would render problematic the entire section in which Maimonides uses their ideas.

In sum, there are two different beliefs attributed to the philosophers. The first, that the sublunar world is governed by forces deriving from the spheres, accords with those beliefs that Maimonides explains in the first part of the Guide and that seem to be his own. The second, that the moon has a particular influence over the element water, does not accord with the beliefs that Maimonides puts forward as his own. From his consideration of this second statement, Maimonides concludes that each of the four spheres corresponds to a single one of the elements. His account of the causality of the spheres in part one is closer to the belief of his contemporaries than that in part two, although his own explanation is brief. Since Maimonides does not seem to present the opinion of "the philosophers" when explaining his own view, his discussion of their position and the way in which he explains the consequences for the four-sphere theory can justifiably be understood as part of his explanation of Ezekiel rather than his own belief. The connections between individual spheres and individual elements is an idea that should be associated with the four-sphere theory. If it is true that Ezekiel numbers the spheres incorrectly, the idea of the sympathies of the spheres may also be a mistake. Then a more coherent picture of the worldview attributed to Ezekiel begins to emerge, and an explanation of why Maimonides considers it to be wrong arises. So the worldview that Maimonides attributes to Ezekiel is identifiable, and there are reasons it is wrong. He may well have wished to associate the four-sphere theory, and thereby Ezekiel, with ideas common in his time, ideas that can be found in the epistles of the Brethren of Purity and the works of their followers.

8.5   CONSEQUENCES OF ATTRIBUTING THE FOUR-SPHERE THEORY TO EZEKIEL

So far, I have discussed two mistakes already recognized in the literature: the four-sphere theory and the sound of the spheres. These two mistakes should not be considered isolated instances of errors but should rather be connected to each other. A third mistake is in the details of the connections between the spheres and the elements, which is a consequence of the four-sphere theory, and Maimonides may have wished to connect all of these errors to one another in a way that shows them to imply an entire worldview. There is an indication that this is exactly what he does when he mentions Pythagoras. It is also further evidence that the entire vision of the chariot is related to the Brethren of Purity's ideas.

8.5.1   Pythagoras and Ezekiel's Errors

The hypothesis presented here considerably aids in understanding this section of the *Guide*. The section containing Maimonides' exegesis of Ezekiel is full of explanations for why the number four is so important. It is as if this number underlies the constitution of the entire cosmos. Numerology and the correspondence of things sharing this number are an important theme. Maimonides refers to Pythagoras by name only once in the *Guide*, when discussing the harmonies of the spheres. He points out that Pythagoras is one of the philosophers who argues for the view that the spheres make a sound. So he associates him with one mistake made by Ezekiel. Although Pythagoras is highly regarded by many, being numbered among the "pillars of wisdom," use of methods associated with him is uncharacteristic for Maimonides.[51] It is, however, characteristic of the Brethren of Purity, for whom Pythagoras is among the greatest sages. Like him, they believed that the universe is built on numbers. They considered the number four to be of particular importance and thought that things were created in groups of four.[52] For Maimonides, Ezekiel agrees with Pythagoras on much more than the sound of the spheres; they share a common worldview, which includes that belief among others, the worldview of the Brethren of Purity. This explains the fascination with the number four in the *Guide* and why this section is so out of character for Maimonides. He does not himself accept the theories presented here but is using them to explain what he takes Ezekiel to be representing in the vision.

8.5.2 The Statement of the Sages

The epistles of the Brethren are full of astrological features. This leads to a further issue raised by the sympathies of the spheres. In between the two statements of the spheres' influence, Maimonides mentions a view of the sages that appears to be closer to the second statement, the one that seems to reflect the belief of the Brethren. They also hold that there is a connection between the individuals of the superlunar world and what happens below the sphere of the moon: "There is not a single herb below that has not a *mazzal* in the firmament that beats upon it and tells it to grow."[53] Since Maimonides attributes the mistake concerning the music of the spheres to the sages, it is possible that he also associates this belief with them. Certainly, the obvious meaning of this statement is that every individual thing in the sublunar sphere is governed by an individual of the superlunar sphere, so some of the sages are also included in this network. Some of the sages, the Pythagoreans, and the Brethren of Purity are associated with Ezekiel and with his mistakes.[54]

Pines notes that *mazzal* is usually a sign of the zodiac, but Maimonides argues that it can also mean "star."[55] Maimonides makes no effort to interpret the statement, so it is left ambiguous. Gad Freudenthal writes that this saying is a favorite of Jewish astrologers.[56] Although, given Maimonides' aversion to literalist readings of sacred texts, one should be wary of taking the quotations that he cites literally, his own explanations do seem to imply an astrological bent. Furthermore, Maimonides does not hesitate to state that there are many among "the good and pious of our nation" who accept astrological notions, so he is clearly aware of its widespread acceptance among Jews.[57] Maimonides contrasts their beliefs with those of the "perfect philosophers" who do not believe in astrology and talismans.[58]

Astrology and magical practices were common among the Jews of Maimonides' time. They are practices and beliefs that Maimonides considered idolatrous.[59] He is a staunch enemy of astrology and writes that an aim of the law is to uproot it along with other elements of idolatry.[60] In this context, it is important to distinguish idolatry as erroneous belief from practices of idolatry involving rituals carried out for the purpose of worshipping false gods. Maimonides explains that the law was given within a historical context in which idolatrous beliefs and practices prevailed and that much of its purpose is to combat them and to create a society in which worship is based on a true understanding of the nature of the universe and a nonidolatrous notion of God. Because Maimonides thinks that astrology, star worship, and magic are inextricably bound up with one another, astrology is an integral part of the worldview that the law combats. The law was given in order to combat idolatrous beliefs and practices typified by the Sabians. As Josef Stern writes, "the Sabian context for the Mosaic legislation was a pagan culture of star-worship built on, or presupposing, astrology which led in practice directly to magic. This is not only the way in which Maimonides believes idolatry and magic historically evolved, as he sketches it at the beginning of *MT 'Avodah Zarah.* The three are also one interconnected conceptual and psychological complex."[61]

Maimonides uses "Sabian" to refer to all types of idolatrous religious beliefs and practices. By such a term, he also refers to contemporaries he considers idolatrous. Besides being significant for Maimonides' historical Sabians, then, astrology is also an integral part of the worldview of popular religion. Maimonides' account of Sabianism combines "ingredients of Neoplatonism, astrology and popular religion. . . . He argues that the Sabian myths, entrenched by habit, familiarity and the power of the written word, have come to have a life of their own and that they are still very much alive in the imagination of the twelfth century."[62] What Maimonides considers idolatrous Sabian doctrine, includes the kind of belief that he attributes to Ezekiel.

8.5.3 The Relevance of Astrology to Maimonides' Exegesis of the Chariot

Although astrology is presented as a part of popular folk religion that must be opposed, it accords well with the four-sphere theory. By taking the four-sphere theory and all that it implies to be Maimonides' own position, Freudenthal is led to conclude that "in Maimonides' view medieval science indeed provided a rational basis for some of the fundamental claims of astrology."[63] According to Freudenthal, Maimonides endorses the theory of causality that is used by the astrologers. In his words, "Maimonides is keenly aware of the fact that this physical doctrine . . . is closely related to astrology." If the explanations of the four-sphere theory are taken to be his own opinions rather than explanations of Ezekiel, Maimonides is open to the objections that Freudenthal raises. Maimonides would himself be in danger of accepting astrology or at least notions connected with it. Freudenthal speculates that Maimonides may have been more influenced by astrological notions than he would care to admit, since rejection of astrology, he explains, is quite problematic for a medieval scientist. Freudenthal points out that there are two aspects to the scientific basis of astrology. The first is that the superlunar beings influence individual things in the sublunar world. The bodies of the planets are the efficient causes of events in the sublunar world, as they blend the elements. The formal cause is the active intellect. Its existence is necessitated by the fact that matter itself is totally passive and requires a cause in order to take on different shapes. The astrologers, however, attribute the formal causality to the planets.[64]

In support of his argument, Freudenthal uses Narboni, who comments that belief in the sympathy of the spheres opens up the possibility for astrology and consequently of talismanic practices.[65] The reason is that the individuals of the sublunar sphere are held to be governed by particular individuals of the superlunar world. That encourages people to attempt to control the individuals of the sublunar world by influencing those of the superlunar world. If the four-sphere theory implies the above relationship between the spheres and the elements and if that, in turn, opens up the possibility for astrology and practices connected with it, then any adoption of the four-sphere theory implies the possibility of astrological beliefs and practices.

Whether Maimonides attributes astrological notions to Ezekiel is still unclear. Maimonides is aware of the fact that there is a danger of moving from the four-sphere theory to astrology. However, his explanation of Ezekiel may be taken to mean that the prophet writes false opinions without himself believing them, for the reason that it would be impossible to influence the masses without adhering to their prior deeply held beliefs.[66] Ezekiel might then be taken to be imitating God's "wily graciousness" in using a ruse to draw people away from idolatry.[67] Alternatively, he could have attributed to Ezekiel a belief that, although similar to that of the astrologers, is not itself astrological. He may have explained the influence of the spheres on the sublunar world in such a way as to make it acceptable, as did Šāfiʿī (767–820) and Faḫr al-Dīn al-Rāzī (1149–1209).[68] This would involve positing a relationship between each individual sphere and an element that is purely physical, while formal causality would proceed from the intelligences. The sphere would then be nothing more than an instrument of God's causal influence on the sublunar world. It would not have any power of its own by which to influence the forms of the sublunar realm. Although Langermann understands the four-sphere theory to be Maimonides' own, he argues that Maimonides is not guilty of astrology, and therefore idolatry, for similar reasons.[69] He argues that Maimonides adopts the language of the astrologers without accepting their doctrines. He then argues that Maimonides limits the influence of the spheres to physical influences and thus avoids the notion that supports astrology: that the celestial bodies are capable of quasi-divine activities involving influencing the forms of the sublunar world. This saves Maimonides from the need to accept astrology. Langermann is therefore able to consider the passages in which Maimonides explains the meaning of Ezekiel's vision to be his own.

Langermann attempts to provide an alternative way of rescuing Maimonides from asserting doctrines that are false and potentially idolatrous. Nevertheless, his method does not account for all of the anomalies of the relevant passages.

It is possible that his solution should be considered part of the interpretation of Ezekiel. While that would save Ezekiel from the charge of idolatry, it would not alter the fact that the worldview with which Ezekiel is associated is close to that of idolaters. Maimonides would still have been critical of Ezekiel for having been mistaken, even if he considered his ideas acceptable in their rejection of astrology.

Freudenthal concludes that Maimonides does not accept astrology but that he is incapable of refuting it on scientific grounds. Consequently, Maimonides objects to it in *halakic* contexts but not in his philosophical writings. There is, therefore, a kind of embarrassed silence rather than a refutation of astrology in the *Guide*.[70] Maimonides seems to present the problem as an embarrassment that he would rather not speak about. However, Freudenthal does point out that Maimonides would not have felt the need to offer a detailed refutation of astrology, since it was not a part of the worldview of the *falāsifa*. If the doctrines implying astrology are attributed to Ezekiel rather than to Maimonides himself, the problem disappears. The reason Maimonides seems to advocate it in one place but not in others is not that he advocates certain doctrines but refuses to accept their consequences. Rather, it is that he advocates it in the context of his commentary on Ezekiel. Maimonides does not present two incompatible positions as if there were no incompatibility. One is his own and, perhaps more important, an explanation of part of scripture, while the other is one to which he objects and an explanation of another part of scripture.[71] The positions may be incompatible while Maimonides' own position remains consistent.

If the four-sphere system is taken to represent an exegesis of Ezekiel, rather than what Maimonides himself believes, the traditional understanding of Maimonides' attitude toward astrology is preserved, while seemingly contrary doctrines present in the *Guide* that appear to indicate otherwise are explained. In this way, it is possible to provide an account of Maimonides that seems to accord with the spirit of his work and his sources. Furthermore, identifying the ideas underlying it with the ideas of the Brethren of Purity helps in an assessment of exactly how Maimonides represented Ezekiel. Because Maimonides' explanations of the four-sphere theory may open up the possibility of astrology, Ezekiel is a representative of much of what is present in popular belief.

8.5.4   Reasons for Ezekiel's Mistakes

Earlier I mentioned two reasons offered to explain why Maimonides attributed errors to Ezekiel. If Ezekiel is to be associated with an entire worldview, they can both be considered correct, but neither tells the whole story. Rosenberg is correct to point out the historical context in which Ezekiel lived, since, in Maimonides' view, that would have influenced his beliefs. However, Harvey is also correct since Maimonides thinks it possible for an individual to break out of an idolatrous system alone, if they undergo the correct training. That is shown by Maimonides' explanation of how Abraham did so.[72] Furthermore, since Ezekiel lived after the law was revealed to Moses, there was a prescribed order he could have followed. Had he done so correctly, he would have rejected a false belief system.

Associating astrology with popular belief solves another problem. Throughout the *Guide*, Maimonides recognizes four sources of authority. The most important are primary intelligibles and sense evidence.[73] Maimonides also recognizes the authority of tradition and generally accepted opinions. However, in his *Letter on Astrology*, Maimonides neglects to mention that generally accepted opinions are authoritative, despite specifying the other three, so his works yet again seem inconsistent. In this case, the epistle's agenda explains the omission. Maimonides does not say that generally accepted opinions have a dialectical level of authority because of their widespread acceptance. If he wishes to combat the astrologers, he cannot give them support for their own doctrine. They would realize that astrology is widespread, even generally accepted. If Maimonides tells them that this makes them a source of authority, they will be able to use that fact as evidence, so he does not.[74]

A similar reason explains why Maimonides does not explain all that he associates with Ezekiel openly. Given that the statements of prophecy are authoritative, a reader may conclude that the beliefs behind Maimonides' explanation of the chariot are acceptable. Maimonides would not want to lend any authority to such ideas, so he does not openly attribute them to Ezekiel. In Maimonides' work, the mistakes of which Ezekiel is guilty are connected with an ancient worldview, some of which still remains in Maimonides' time. Astrology is a strong element of popular belief to which Maimonides is opposed. This explains why Ezekiel is thought to have made some mistakes and also why Maimonides' explanation of Ezekiel's mistakes is so well hidden. He would not wish to lend prophetic authority to the very people he is opposing.

8.5.5 Theological Consequences

I finish this chapter with comments about some theological consequences of Maimonides' rejection of astrology and the worldview that goes along with it. A couple of doctrines central to the law's view of creation are opposed to the ideas of the Brethren of Purity. Both are concerned with the limits Maimonides draws around the extent of human knowledge. Recall that the law teaches that there is no unified scientific view of the whole of creation.[75] One of the reasons for this is that the superlunar spheres are not understood. They are full of anomalies, indicating that they were probably particularized by a being who chose for them to take such an order. There seems to be no explanation for why the spheres move the way that they do, relative to one another, or that the kind of matter constituting the stars seems to be different from that of the spheres. Furthermore, their motions are disordered and unpredictable. Maimonides argues that their eccentricity might be evidence that creation does not proceed necessarily from God but that God creates through will.[76] So, while Aristotle and those who believe that the world proceeds from God of necessity have no basis to ask why the world exists, or how it exists in one way rather than others, followers of the law can attribute it to God's will.

> If the matter of all the spheres is one and the same, in virtue of what thing has any sphere been so particularized as to receive a nature other than the nature of any other sphere? How then is there to be found in that sphere a certain desire, different from the desire of that other sphere, that obliges one to move in this direction and the other to move in another direction? There must of necessity be something that particularizes.[77]

For the Brethren's beliefs to hold true, the cosmos must be an ordered whole with parts corresponding to and influencing one another in ways that the sages understand. The harmonies of the spheres depend on it. The heavenly bodies must be related to one another according to the rules of musical proportion. "The distances and the movements of the spheres and of their stars are also placed in relation to each other according to the laws of eminent proportion. These co-ordinated movements produce harmonious melodies, touching, symmetrical and sweet."[78] Furthermore, they say that the cosmos is ordered in a way that Maimonides specifically denies. To support their belief in the efficacy of magic and astrology, they need also to believe that there are links between what happens in the superlunar realm and what takes place in the sublunar realm. Both realms must follow the same proportions.

Maimonides would object to their position because it presumes that humans already know all about the superlunar spheres and that they follow the same rules and regulations as those that pertain on earth. Their view would also cut off a major piece of evidence in favor of the law's view of creation and would make it more difficult to affirm. Maimonides' explanation of the belief in the harmonies is different from that of the Brethren, though. He says that those who think that the spheres move, but the planets and stars do not, believe that the spheres make sounds. Nevertheless, the difference does not indicate that Maimonides' target was someone other than the Brethren of Purity. He takes his cue from a Talmudic discussion that explains the disagreement along the lines he uses in the *Guide*.[79] This is a further example of how he brings together the rabbinic tradition with his contemporary world and updates it into an idiom for his own time.

In Maimonides' view, God's will is the explanation of why the cosmos is and why it is the way it is. Aristotle and his followers have no answer to these questions, because they hold that the world is the way it is out of necessity. They would only become "perplexed" by seeking the purpose of existence. However, in a later chapter, Maimonides explains that the law's view does not enhance a believer's knowledge, since God's will is inscrutable in any case. So what is the difference between the two positions? In the later chapter, Maimonides emphasizes the gulf between God and people. God does not create for the benefit of humanity or of humans; God creates only because it is God's will to do so. Besides, people are only a minuscule part of creation. There is far more in heaven and earth than humans or than can be grasped by humans. Once human exsistence is "compared to that of the spheres, and all the more to that of the separate beings, it is very, very contemptible."[80] Maimonides encourages an attitude of pious reverence before the enormity of God's creation:

> It should not be believed that all the beings exist for the sake of the existence of humanity. On the contrary, all the other beings too have been intended for their own sakes and not for the sake of something else. Thus even according to our view, holding that the world has been produced in time, the quest for the final end of all the species of beings collapses. For we say that in virtue of his will he has brought into existence all the parts of the world, some of which have been intended for their own sakes, whereas others have been intended for the sake of some other thing that is intended for its own sake.[81]

This, too, is opposed to the theological views of the Brethren. They seem to think that God took pity on humanity because people are unable to understand the whole of creation and granted them a microcosm of the entire universe in the human body. Langermann explains how Maimonides uses the same analogy but strips it of the connotations that the Brethren gave to it.[82] He specifies that the analogy breaks down in three crucial ways. First, the relationship is not mutually beneficial. Whereas both aspects of the microcosm benefit from being in relationship with each other, the more noble part of the macrocosm derives no benefit from being in relation with the baser part. The influence occurs only one way, so the world's purpose is not to benefit the spheres. Moreover, it follows that events and actions in the lower realm do not influence the upper realms, and this, as explained, rules out magic and astrology. Second, the most noble part of the human body is located in its center. The heart rules the body and the farther a part of the body is from the heart, the baser it is. Of the macrocosm, the reverse is true. The more noble parts are located on the outside; closer to the center are the baser, turbid parts. Here is further reason to deny that humans are the purpose of God's creation; the inscrutable divine purpose does not create for the sake of humans but simply because it wills to do so. So once more, Maimonides' contemporaries make claims to knowledge that he tries to limit and to replace with a reverence for God and creation as a whole. By pointing out the limitations of one of the Brethren's analogies, Maimonides neutralizes it, eviscerating it of its astrological essence.

8.6 SUMMARY

Maimonides attributes some mistakes to Ezekiel. He does not state openly that they are mistakes but requires the reader to understand alone. Maimonides' explicit mention of Pythagoras connects the mistake regarding the spheres' sounds with the numerology, and so the mistakes can be seen together. Since Maimonides does not seem to put forward the views he attributes to Ezekiel when outlining his own opinion, and since it does not appear in the writings of ibn Bāǧǧa, whom Maimonides considers an authority on these matters, it is possible to conclude that the opinion is not his own. It is, however, mentioned by many others, including the Iḫwān al-Ṣafā'. Their position is part of a complete worldview that Maimonides opposes. In the light of this examination, the presence of the number four and its connection with the elements are not so confusing. That there is a particular relationship between each sphere and a single element can be considered to be another mistake that Maimonides holds Ezekiel to believe. It is not an idea with which he himself agrees. All of the mistakes should therefore be considered part of the same system that was supported by Ezekiel, Pythagoras, some sages, and "the philosophers." Maimonides cannot present this interpretation in an open way because of Talmudic stipulations. However, he would also not wish to point out openly that the four-sphere theory is potentially dangerous since it is connected with a false worldview.

CHAPTER 9

"A Kind of Conclusion"

Maimonides begins the final chapters of the *Guide* by stating that they serve as "a kind of conclusion," summing up the important aspects of the treatise as a whole.[1] Those final few chapters touch on a wide range of topics, but Maimonides states that they contain nothing more than those preceding them. One of the key points that he stresses in the closing chapters involves the nature of providence and worship. The goal of life is, he says, to achieve an ideal form of worship. Ultimately, in a messianic era, this is something that could be carried out by everyone.[2] The *Guide*'s purpose is to direct individual students toward that goal. It is not an easy goal, and although the *Guide* is designed to help, Maimonides can never make it easy. The students' task is to reach such a state, as far as humanly possible, and they have to work hard to do so. Likewise, they have to work hard to understand the *Guide*. It may be a focal point for their efforts, but it cannot replace that effort. Maimonides uses several methods to encourage the student to think and work through the issues independently. Accordingly, he finishes one of the concluding chapters with the following instruction:

> Bring your soul to understand this chapter, and direct your efforts to the multiplying of those times in which you are with God, or endeavoring to approach him, and to decreasing those times in which you are with other than he and in which you make no efforts to approach him. This guidance is sufficient in view of the purpose of this treatise.[3]

The conclusion I offer here is also only a kind of conclusion to the present work. Neither the conclusion nor the work as a whole is totally comprehensive. However, the method of reading the *Guide* that I argue for can be extended to other parts. I think it should be. I have tried to use a number of threads in order to offer an interpretive tool by which the *Guide* can be understood. As I pointed out in chapter 1 above, the way in which Maimonides tries to move students to think independently but also with the help of the *Guide* is by using pointers and allusions. He encourages students to read and think about all other worthwhile books. His *Guide* is just that, a guide; it is not supposed to stand alone. It functions as a companion both to the rabbinic tradition and to the Arabic philosophical tradition. Maimonides tries to help a student negotiate a path through both of these. Only by forging a way through both traditions can one be led away from the perplexity he describes in his introduction.[4]

More than a recognition that Maimonides aims to address pupils' needs is required to make sense of the *Guide* as a whole, though. The extent and the nature of disagreements surrounding its interpretation indicate as much. Of course, as a method for addressing pupils, dialectic is important, but the roles it plays on top of that must also be taken into account. Maimonides uses dialectic when he needs to examine competing opinions and come to a decision about which, if any, he will ultimately favor. One way in which the *Guide* is sometimes difficult to interpret arises because of this. Maimonides does not always state very clearly when he is examining a position in a dialectical manner, rather than expounding his own view. When he adopts this strategy to address the topic of creation, he makes it clear that is what he is doing. On this occasion, he takes each position to its logical conclusion. After having done so, he is in a position to judge those conclusions. Because he assents to certain doctrines of the law and because, after examining the competing positions, he now thinks that those doctrines are consistent with only one of them, he must assent to that one position. He argues for the law's view on the basis of further dialectical considerations, premises that are acceptable as they are supported by the prophetic tradition. In order for this method of argument to work, Maimonides needs to adhere to a single, coherent metaphysical vision. Only because his views cohere with one another can he assert creation ex nihilo on the basis of the law. The doctrines of the law as a whole are what is at stake.

So the prophetic tradition teaches creation and, as a corollary, God's knowledge of particulars. The philosophers reject the law's doctrine of creation and God's knowledge. That the two camps disagree seems to indicate a conflict between reason and revelation or between philosophy and prophecy. Many were hostile to philosophy because they thought it opposed to religion. They thought that philosophy encourages people to question religion and ultimately weakens their adherence. Because philosophers looked for intelligible reasons for the commandments, there is a danger that they could cause people to focus more on the reasons than on the commandments themselves. Performing the commandments might then be considered unimportant and even, in some situations, fall away altogether.

Maimonides' view is different. He sees religion and philosophy as mutually complementary. Observing the commandments is the first step on the way to developing the character traits that make proper worship of God possible. They are a stepping stone on the way to the true religious life, which is also the true philosophical life. The commandments induce reverence and piety by encouraging reflection. For example, while explaining the laws of *mezuzah*, he writes:

> Whenever one enters or leaves a home with the *mezuzah* on the doorpost, he will be confronted with the declaration of God's unity, blessed be the holy name, and will remember the love due to God, and will be aroused from his slumbers and his foolish absorption in temporal vanities. He will realize that nothing endures to all eternity save knowledge of the ruler of the universe. This thought will immediately restore him to his right senses and he will walk in the paths of righteousness. Our ancient teachers said "whoever has phylacteries on his head and arm, fringes on his garment, and a *mezuzah* on his door may be presumed not to sin, for he has many monitors, angels that save him from sinning. As it is said 'the angel of the lord encamps around those that fear him and delivers them.'"[5]

The purpose of the commandments, like the purpose of the *Guide*, is to develop proper worship in those who obey them. Proper worship comes after a process of character training and of philosophical reflection. For Maimonides, it opposes neither philosophy nor religion, and the assumption that there is a conflict between religion and philosophy is, in his view, unfounded. One cannot distinguish between them on the basis that religion begins with obedience whereas philosophy begins in wonder. Maimonides argues that they both lead to the same place: pious reverence. The commandments are supposed to lead the obedient to the sense of wonder that philosophy requires. Although commanded, they are commanded for a purpose beyond themselves, so one who obeys does not automatically fulfill them: "one who knows God finds grace in his sight not one who merely fasts and prays."[6] Since the *Guide* is performative and transformative, following the book's instructions by treating it as a *Guide* and companion leads to a sense of the mystery of God and creation. Both the rabbis and the philosophers exhort people to perfect themselves, to become Godlike, as far as is humanly possible.

What does becoming Godlike involve? Maimonides locates the "image of God" in the intellect.[7] So perfecting the speculative intellect would enable one to imitate God. Furthermore, God is immaterial, and the intellect is the only part of a human that is also immaterial. Of the four kinds of human perfections that Maimonides enumerates, he ranks knowledge of immaterial truths as the best, above possessions, bodily perfection, and perfect moral virtues. People ought to progress through perfecting their habits, character traits, and, finally, their intellects. Each of these tasks is a protracted process with numerous stages. When Maimonides explains why it is so difficult to acquire rational virtues, he says that there are five reasons. The third of them is that the preliminary studies take a long time. Few people have the patience to go through them step by step. The fourth reason is that people have natural constitutions and temperaments that do not allow for perfection without training. "It has been explained, or rather demonstrated, that the moral virtues are a preparation for the rational virtues, it being impossible to achieve true, rational acts [nuṭqiyāt]—I mean perfect apprehensions [maʿaqūlāt]—unless by a man whose character traits are thoroughly trained who is endowed with tranquility and quiet."[8]

That, at least, is the traditional take, but in recent decades, some have argued that it is too simplistic and that Maimonides holds an esoteric "skeptical" opinion. On this view, first advanced by Shlomo Pines, he denies that metaphysical knowledge is possible and so exalts ethical actions as the ultimate goal.[9] God and the intelligences are ineffable. Only God's actions in the world are open to investigation, so the way in which one imitates God can only be by imitating God's actions. Those actions are taken to be expressions of "loving-kindness," "judgment," and "righteousness."[10] Therefore, Maimonides aims to teach the perfect person that since metaphysical knowledge is impossible, and intellectual perfection is therefore impossible, the most one can hope for is to perfect one's ethical characteristics. This could be posed as a question of what Maimonides takes to be the proper form of worship. Political perfection, constituted of moral perfection and the perfect society, rather than intellectual perfection, is now considered the ultimate end, and the *Guide* teaches the careful reader that ethical actions, because they are an imitation of God's actions, constitute correct worship. To become Godlike is to act ethically.

Several responses have been offered to Pines, and there is no need to rehearse them all here.[11] More recently, though, Josef Stern has argued for an attenuated skepticism in which Maimonides holds that knowledge of God and the cosmos is impossible. Stern is certainly correct to say that Maimonides held God to be unknowable, but scholars are divided over whether he held that nothing can be known about the superlunar cosmos. Stern's arguments remove some of the problems with Pines's view, because in the attenuated sense, the skeptical interpretation of Maimonides does not now deny the possibility of knowledge but, rather, it denies the possibility of knowledge of God. Nothing about God's nature can be understood, but it can be known that God exists as the necessary existent even if the human intellect has no way of grasping what necessary existence is. Maimonides does not say that humans can know or understand God. He does argue that it is important to understand why God must be inscrutable to human reason, and this discussion is part of the study of metaphysics. Furthermore, he says that they can know that God is the necessary of existence and that, as such, God is perfect in an unlimited way.[12] Despite these constraints, however, Maimonides still considers intellectual perfection to be a worthy goal.[13]

The claim that Maimonides considers ethical or political perfection more exalted than intellectual perfection relies on opposing moral and intellectual virtues to each other. If the two are incompatible, imitating God cannot involve perfection of both kinds of virtues. In the words of David Shatz, it is a "highly esoteric" reading, and it claims that "Maimonides means the exact opposite of what he says."[14] The esotericism is fueled by the fact that Maimonides places intellectual perfection at the peak of humanity but also considers imitation of God to reside in ethical rather than intellectual activity. In order to bring the two together, Shatz distinguishes between the perfect person and the way of life of that person. The way of life is a consequence of the perfection. Although moral perfection is part of the training for intellectual perfection and therefore comes about first, it is posterior in importance and flows from ultimate perfection. Human perfection involves perfecting the human intellect as far as is humanly possible, not in possessing positive knowledge of God's essence, which is impossible for humans to know even in their perfected state. This involves learning about metaphysical ideas, discussions of the most general principles of being, such as the nature of universals and causes. Only thus can one contemplate the universals of the sublunar world. However, people are not disembodied intellects, and human perfection must involve perfecting all of the virtues, moral as well as intellectual. Moral virtues may not themselves be the final human end, but their importance cannot be minimized. Maimonides does not divide between one who is intellectually perfect and one who is morally perfect. Moral perfection is a stage on the way to intellectual perfection and would remain after perfection has been achieved. The human ideal is not isolation, because humans cannot continue to exist in total isolation from other humans. People are called to strive for a perfection in which the moral virtues remain, so morality is part of an entire human perfection rather than separated from ultimate perfection, even if they are not sufficient for ultimate perfection.[15]

What of the esotericism that results from the contradiction peculiar to the *Guide* and the rabbinic tradition? Maimonides states that the seventh cause of contradictions is one he uses, but he does not attribute it to any works by other philosophers. The seventh cause is one of the major reasons readers of the *Guide* have been moved to distinguish between Maimonides as philosopher and Maimonides as religious believer. I have argued that there is no warrant to search for a hidden philosophical or political meaning in the *Guide* that opposes Maimonides' exoteric teaching. The fact that one cannot understand how a position might be coherent does not mean that it is self-contradictory, and it certainly does not mean that the author of the position intended to contradict himself. Philosophical arguments are often difficult to follow; they use fine distinctions and subtle qualifications; they rely on the followers' commitment to understand, rather than to remain satisfied with apparent inconsistencies. Maimonides' beliefs are openly presented and coherent.

But this assertion is unsatisfactory unless the esotericism can be explained in another way. If his statements are to be taken seriously, there needs to be some accounting for the seventh contradiction; this is no less true than that if his statements are to be taken seriously, he should not be thought to hold a secret position on the eternity of the world. Maimonides uses the seventh cause for contradictions as another way to explain different parts of scripture. There are discussions that proceed on the basis of contradictory premises because the tradition, and indeed scripture itself, contains multiple, sometimes contradictory views. Therefore, the political interpretations that have Maimonides offering a secret philosophical doctrine, in line with that which he presents as Aristotle's, on the basis that he himself admits to contradicting himself, have no basis in the introduction to the *Guide*. Whether or not a reader today believes there to be an unbridgeable gap between religion and philosophy, there is no need to impose the division on Maimonides. Although it is important to recognize the difference between the community of the religious as a whole and the subset of philosophers within that community, one ought not to assimilate Maimonides' own opinions to those he opposes. Rather, the seventh contradiction is a product of Maimonides' need to present a number of different interpretations of the Bible and the rabbinic tradition.

NOTE ON REFERENCES

References to the *Guide for the Perplexed* begin with part and chapter numbers. Page and line numbers are then given to the Munk-Joël Arabic edition (M). This is followed by a reference to the page number in the Pines English translation (P) and the page number in the Schwarz Hebrew translation (S). Finally, the transliteration into Arabic characters published by Hossein Atay (A) is referred to by page and line numbers. For full details of these editions, see the bibliography. Quotations are taken from the Pines edition. My own translations could not compare to Pines's, but I have taken the liberty of changing some details. One of these changes is in the title of Maimonides' work. I use the more idiomatic *Guide for the Perplexed* rather than *Guide of the Perplexed* to avoid ambiguities involved in the latter construction.

NOTES

INTRODUCTION

1. Introduction; M3 (14–17); P7; S12; A11 (6–8).
2. The statement appears in some of the earliest sources with the number "forty-nine." It is better known in the form used by Abraham ibn Ezra, which I quote here. For an example, see his commentary on Num. 10: 29.

CHAPTER 1

1. Good biographies of Maimonides have appeared in recent years. See Joel Kraemer, *Maimonides: The Life and World of One of Civilization's Greatest Minds* (New York: Doubleday, 2008). The first part of Herbert Davidson's *Moses Maimonides: The Man and His Works* (Oxford: Oxford University Press, 2004) is dedicated to biographical details.
2. *Mishnah with Commentary by Maimonides*, Arabic text with Hebrew translation by Yosef Kafiḥ, 7 vols. (Jerusalem: Mossad Harav Kook, 1963–1968).
3. For an examination of the medieval discussion, see Menachem Kellner, *Dogma in Medieval Jewish Thought: From Maimonides to Abravanel* (Oxford: Oxford University Press, 1986); and Marc Shapiro, *The Limits of Orthodoxy* (Oxford: Oxford University Press, 2004).
4. For an account of the aims of MT, see Isadore Twersky, *Introduction to* The Code of Maimonides (New Haven, Conn.: Yale University Press, 1980), 61–81.
5. *Sefer ha-Madda'* (Jerusalem: Mossad Harav Kook, 1976).
6. An autograph of a fragment from a rough draft of the *Guide* was discovered as recently as 2004 by Ben Outhwaite and Freidrich Niessen. See their "A Newly Discovered Autograph Fragment of Maimonides' 'Guide for the Perplexed' from the Cairo Genizah," *Journal of Jewish Studies* 2 (2006): 287–297.

7. An example of Shneur Zalman's use of Maimonides can be seen in his exposition of ḥasidic thought, *Liqqutey Amarim* (London: Soncino, 1973), 6. Moshe Idel examines Maimonides' influence on some later kabbalistic thinkers in "Maimonides' 'Guide of the Perplexed' and the Kabbalah," *Jewish History* 18 (2004): 197–226. For Mendelssohn's debt to Maimonides, see Alexander Altmann, *Moses Mendelssohn: A Biographical Study* (London: Routledge and Kegan Paul, 1973), 12.

8. Menachem Kellner's *Maimonides on the Decline of the Generations and the Nature of Rabbinic Authority* (Albany: State University of New York Press, 1996) is a response to one such attempt to appropriate Maimonides, as the epilogue makes clear.

9. Daniel Lasker, "The Interpretation of Maimonides—Past and Present" [Heb.], *Alei Sefer* 19 (2001): 209–213.

10. Michael Shmidman, "On Maimonides' Conversion to Kabbalah," in *Studies in Medieval Jewish History and Literature*, ed. Isadore Twersky (Cambridge, Mass: Harvard University Press, 1984), 379–384.

11. See, for example, *The Zohar*, vol. 1, translated with a commentary by Daniel Matt (Stanford, Calif.: Stanford University Press, 2004), 119, n. 80.

12. See Menachem Kellner, *Maimonides' Confrontation with Mysticism* (Oxford: Littman Library of Jewish Civilization, 2006).

13. See Abraham Halkin and David Hartman, *Epistles of Maimonides: Crisis and Leadership* (Philadelphia: Jewish Publication Society, 1993), 211–292, for a translation of the "Epistle on Resurrection" and a commentary.

14. For an example, see Efodi's commentary on the *Guide* 1: 42, which is included in *More Nebuchim (Doctor Perplexorum)*, 2 vols., *ex versione Samuelis Tibbonidae cum commentariis Ephodaei, Schemtob, Ibn Crescas, nec non Don Isaci Abravanel adjectis summariis et indicibus* (Berlin: Adolf Cohn, 1875).

15. See Daniel Silver, *Maimonidean Criticism and the Maimonidean Controversy, 1180–1240* (Leiden: Brill, 1965), 16, for an account of the burning; and 109–135, for an examination of the controversy over resurrection.

16. Joseph Karo defends Maimonides from this attack. See R. J. Zwi Werblowsky, *Joseph Karo: Lawyer and Mystic* (Oxford: Oxford University Press, 1962), 31.

17. See Aryeh Motzkin, "On the Interpretation of Maimonides," *Independent Journal of Philosophy* 2 (1978): 42–44. For further details on the reception of the *Guide,* see Davidson, *Moses Maimonides,* 402–428.

18. See Warren Zev Harvey, "How Leo Strauss Straightjacketed Research on the *Guide* in the Twentieth Century" [Heb.], *Iyyun* 50 (2001): 388. Strauss points out that Maimonides was an adherent of the law and opposed those he called "the philosophers" in *Persecution and the Art of Writing* (Chicago: University of Chicago Press, 1988), 43. For an excellent account of Strauss's take on Arabic thought, see Joel Kraemer, "The Medieval Arabic

Enlightenment," in *The Cambridge Companion to Leo Strauss,* ed. Steven B. Smith (Cambridge, U.K.: Cambridge University Press, 2009), 137–170.

19. An example of this approach can be seen in Alvin Reines, "Maimonides' Concepts of Providence and Theodicy," *Hebrew Union College Annual* 43 (1972): 169–206.

20. Dimitri Gutas identifies Straussian interpretations of Arabic philosophy as one of the enlightenment relics of twentieth-century scholarship in "The Study of Arabic Philosophy in the Twentieth Century," *British Journal of Middle Eastern Studies* 29 (2002), 19.

21. Aviezer Ravitsky explores some similarities between the medieval commentators and modern scholars in "The Secrets of Maimonides: Between the Thirteenth and Twentieth Centuries," in *Studies in Maimonides,* ed. Isadore Twersky (Cambridge, Mass: Harvard University Press, 1990), 159–207.

22. See Menachem Kellner, "The Literary Character of the Mishneh Torah: On the Art of Writing in Maimonides' Halakhic Works," in *Me'ah She'arim: Studies in Medieval Jewish Spiritual Life,* ed. E. Fleischer et al. (Jerusalem: Magnes, 2001), 29–45.

23. There are many questions concerning the details of this relationship. An instance of the debate about the relationship between CM and the *Guide* is the question of the connection between the thirteen principles and the structure of the *Guide,* in which they are never mentioned. See, for example, Menachem Kellner, "Maimonides' Thirteen Principles and the Structure of the 'Guide of the Perplexed,'" *Journal of the History of Philosophy* 20 (1982): 76–84. A question raised about MT concerns the relationship between the fourteen books of MT and the fourteen classes of commandments in the *Guide.* Marvin Fox highlights this issue in *Interpreting Maimonides: Studies in Methodology, Metaphysics, and Moral Philosophy* (Chicago: University of Chicago Press, 1990), 14. Josef Stern's discussion of the commandment of circumcision attempts to explain the different classification of that duty in *Problems and Parables of Law: Maimonides and Nahmanides on Reasons for the Commandments (Ta'amei ha-Mitzvot)* (Albany: State University of New York Press, 1998), 87–107.

24. Shlomo Pines, "The Philosophic Purport of Halachic Works and the Purport of the Guide of the Perplexed," in *Maimonides and Philosophy,* ed. Shlomo Pines and Yirmiahu Yovel (Dordrecht: Martinus Nijhoff, 1986), 5.

25. For further on this, see Warren Zev Harvey, "The Mishneh Torah as a Key to the Secrets of the *Guide,*" in *Me'ah She'arim: Studies in Medieval Jewish Spiritual Life,* ed. E. Fleischer et al. (Jerusalem: Magnes, 2001), 11–28. In the *Guide,* Maimonides states that he uses the premise of eternity in MT not because he accepts it but because it is most appropriate; 1:71; M125 (23–27); P182; S192; A188 (19–22). This issue will be dealt with below in chapters 2 and 3.

26. Heidi Ravven, "Some Thoughts on What Spinoza Learned from Maimonides about the Prophetic Imagination: Part 1. Maimonides on Prophecy and the Imagination," *Journal of the History of Philosophy* 39 (2001): 193–214.

27. Lawrence Berman, "Maimonides, the Disciple of Alfarabi," *Israel Oriental Studies* 4 (1974): 154–178. For Alfarabi's text, see *Book of Letters*, Arabic text, ed. Muhsin Mahdi (Beirut: Dar el-Mashreq, 1969), 150–157.

28. See Alexander Marx, "Texts by and about Maimonides," *Jewish Quarterly Review* 25 (1934–35): 374–381.

29. See, for example, Shlomo Pines, "The Limitations of Human Knowledge according to al-Farabi, ibn Bajja, and Maimonides," in *Studies in Medieval Jewish History and Literature,* ed. Isadore Twersky (Cambridge, Mass.: Harvard University Press, 1979), 82–109, in which this principle is applied.

30. Alvin Reines, "Maimonides' True Belief concerning God," in *Maimonides and Philosophy,* ed. Shlomo Pines and Yirmiahu Yovel (Dordrecht: Martinus Nijhoff, 1986), 31.

31. For an account of Alfarabi's theory of demonstration, see Miriam Galston, "Al-Fārābī on Aristotle's Theory of Demonstration," in *Islamic Philosophy and Mysticism,* ed. Parviz Morewedge (New York: Caravan, 1981), 23–34. She points out that dialectical discussions are important precursors to demonstrations.

32. Hans Daiber has recently argued that Pines's hermeneutic presents a distorted picture of Alfarabi. He points out that those who argue on the basis of Maimonides' Farabian framework that Maimonides hides philosophical truths from the masses turn Maimonides into an unfaithful disciple of Alfarabi. "Das Fārābī-Bild des Maimonides: Ideentransfer als hermeneutischer Weg zu Maimonides' Philosophie," in *The Trias of Maimonides/Die Trias des Maimonides,* ed. Georges Tamer (Berlin: Walter de Gruyter, 2005), 119–209.

33. See, for example, Warren Zev Harvey, "Why Maimonides Was Not a Mutakallim," in *Perpectives on Maimonides,* ed. Joel Kraemer (Oxford: Oxford University Press, 1991), 104–114.

34. For an example of this, see Sandra Walker-Ramisch, "Between the Lines: Maimonides on Providence," *Studies in Religion* 21 (1992): 29–42. It is an application of Strauss's observation in *Persecution,* 83.

35. See section 1.3.3 below for more on the relevance of contradictions in the *Guide.* Leonard Kravitz applies this hermeneutic throughout his reading of the *Guide* in *The Hidden Doctrine of Maimonides' Guide for the Perplexed: Philosophical and Religious God-language in Tension* (Lewiston: Mellen, 1988). Again, this approach can be traced to Strauss, as is made clear by Joel Kraemer in "How (Not) to Read the *Guide of the Perplexed,*" *Jerusalem Studies in Arabic and Islam* 32 (2006): 381.

36. Kravitz, *Hidden Doctrine*, 25.
37. Many of Abraham Nuriel's papers have been collected in *Concealed and Revealed in Medieval Jewish Philosophy* [Heb.] (Jerusalem: Magnes, 2000). See also Warren Zev Harvey, "Nuriel's Method for Deciphering the Secrets of the *Guide*" [Heb.], *Da'at* 32–33 (1994): 67–71. Harvey points out the similarity between Nuriel's approach and Strauss's but also stresses that Nuriel disagrees with Strauss's assertion of an incompatibility between religion and philosophy.
38. 1: Introduction; M9 (28); P15; S19; A20 (22–23).
39. This point is made by Aviezer Ravitsky in "Creation or Eternity according to Maimonides" [Heb.], *Tarbiẓ* 35 (1966): 333–348. He responds to Nuriel's arguments concerning Maimonides' view of creation and also to his method in general.
40. Harvey, "Why Maimonides Was Not a Mutakallim," 111.
41. Joel Kraemer, "On the Philosophic Sciences in Maimonides' Treatise on the Art of Logic," in *Perspectives on Maimonides: Philosophical and Historical Studies*, ed. Joel Kraemer (Oxford: Oxford University Press, 1991), 102.
42. Joel Kraemer, "Maimonides' Use of (Aristotelian) Dialectic," in *Maimonides and the Sciences*, ed. Robert S. Cohen and Hillel Levine (Dordrecht: Kluwer Academic, 2000), 124.
43. Aristotle, *Topics* 100a31.
44. Maimonides recognizes four sources of authority for beliefs in general. Two of these, primary intelligibles and sense experience, he considers undoubtedly reliable, providing premises for demonstrative arguments. Maimonides mentions them in 1: 51; M75 (25); P112; S115; A120 (2). For his use of tradition as an authority, see 1:33; M48 (12); P71; S76; A77 (19). For generally accepted opinions, see 3:8; M312 (21); P434; S444; A491 (12). These are usually described as Maimonides' authorities on the basis of the "Treatise on Logic," chapter 8, in *Proceedings of the American Academy for Jewish Research* 34 (1966) [Heb. section]: 21–24. The relationship between that work and Maimonides' later thought is uncertain. Davidson, in *Moses Maimonides*, 314, has argued that the "Treatise" was not even written by Maimonides. Sarah Stroumsa suggests that it is a summary written by Maimonides of something by another philosopher; see *Maimonides in His World: Portrait of a Mediterranean Thinker* (Princeton, N.J., and Oxford: Princeton University Press, 2009), 127.
45. For an account of assent (*tasdīq*) on the basis of less than demonstrative premises in the Arabic tradition, see Deborah Black, *Logic and Aristotle's Rhetoric and Poetics in Medieval Arabic Philosophy* (Leiden: Brill, 1990), 94–102.
46. This supports Arthur Hyman's position in "Demonstrative, Dialectical and Sophistic Arguments," in *Moses Maimonides and His Time*, ed. Eric L. Ormsby (Washington: Catholic University of America Press, 1989), 51.

47. 1: Introduction; M1; P3–4; S5–8; A7–8.
48. Kraemer, "Maimonides' Use," 123.
49. 1: Introduction; M2 (11–12); P5; S10; A9 (12–13).
50. 1: Introduction; M2 (13–14); P5; S10; A9 (13–14). A adds a negative in square brackets resulting in the meaning "the purpose . . . is [not] the science of the law." Although this addition may seem to make the sentence accord with what follows in the Arabic text, it is not in other versions and is thus an unnecessary addition. Furthermore, it does not affect my argument as long as it is accepted that the purpose of the *Guide* includes dealing with some of the "science of the law in its true sense."
51. Menachem Kellner, "The Conception of the Torah as a Deductive Science in Medieval Jewish Thought," *Revue des Etudes Juives* 146 (1987): 270. See Kellner's essay for a number of convincing arguments.
52. 1: Introduction; M11 (2–6); P16; S20; A22 (8–12).
53. 1: Introduction; M9 (26–27); P15; S19; A20 (19–20).
54. 1: Introduction; M10 (3–4); P15; S19; A21 (2–3).
55. By practicing methods of withholding knowledge, Maimonides does not diverge from the philosophical tradition. See Gutas, *Avicenna and the Aristotelian Tradition: Introduction to Reading Avicenna's Philosophical Works* (Leiden: Brill, 1988), 225–236.
56. Aristotle, *Topics* 159a18–21.
57. See, for example, section 3.2 below.
58. 1: Introduction; M13 (13–14); P20; S24; A25 (18–19). Some manuscripts mistakenly include the sixth among those he uses. See Davidson, *Moses Maimonides*, 389.
59. 1: Introduction; M13 (9); P19; S23; A25 (14). S includes the seventh in this statement. It does not appear in the other editions, and there is no indication of why it is added. Lorberbaum follows S in "Changes in Maimonides' Approach to Aggadah" [Heb.], *Tarbiz* 78 (2008): 108.
60. In "Maimonides' Use," 123, Kraemer lists the "dialectical" process of learning as among the indications that the *Guide* is essentially a book of *kalām*.
61. 1: Introduction; M11 (19–26); P17; S21; A23 (6–12).
62. Aviezer Ravitsky labels this "educational philosophy" in "Maimonides: Esotericism and Educational Philosophy," in *The Cambridge Companion to Maimonides*, ed. Kenneth Seeskin (Cambridge: Cambridge University Press, 2005). See also Jose Faur's *Homo Mysticus: A Guide to Maimonides' Guide for the Perplexed* (Syracuse, N.Y.: Syracuse University Press, 1998). Faur imitates Maimonides' *Guide* by focusing less on what Maimonides might really have meant and more on how the student understands what is being said, as stated in the preface, xi.
63. 1: Introduction; M12 (7–12); P18; S22; A23 (22)–24 (3).

64. Lorberbaum stresses that what must be hidden is the fact of contradiction, not one of the positions consequent upon one of the sets of premises. He presents a close examination of the seventh contradiction in "On Contradictions, Rationality, Dialectics, and Esotericism in Maimonides's *Guide of the Perplexed,*" *Review of Metaphysics* 55 (2002): 722–735. His reading is thorough, but I disagree with some of his conclusions.

65. Lorberbaum, "On Contradictions," 724.

66. Lorberbaum translates *qawlat,* here rendered "dicta," as "conviction." "On Contradictions," 725.

67. Lorberbaum, "On Contradictions," 726.

68. Lorberbaum, "On Contradictions," 743–748. Lorberbaum argues this point more extensively in "The Men of Knowledge and the Sages Are Drawn, as It Were, toward This Purpose by the Divine Will (*The Guide of the Perplexed,* Introduction): On Maimonides' Conception of Parables" [Heb.], *Tarbiz* 71 (2001): 87–132. See Kenneth Seeskin, *Searching for a Distant God: The Legacy of Maimonides* (New York: Oxford University Press, 2000), 177–187.

69. Lorberbaum, "On Contradictions," 734.

70. 1:34; M43 (26); P65; S70; A71 (10).

71. Fox, *Interpreting Maimonides,* 80.

72. Ibid., 83.

73. Ibid., 84.

74. David Blumenthal, "Maimonides: Prayer, Worship, and Mysticism," in *Approaches to Judaism in Medieval Times,* vol. 3, ed. David Blumenthal (Atlanta: Scholars, 1988), 7.

75. Y. Tzvi Langermann, *Yemenite Midrash: Philosophical Commentaries on the Torah* (San Francisco: Harper Collins, 1996), xviii.

76. In this sense, I believe that they read the *Guide* in the way that Maimonides hoped it would be read, as I explained above in the introduction.

77. Davidson, *Moses Maimonides,* 399.

78. Lorberbaum points to this fact in "On Contradictions," 714 n.

79. This is emphasized by Sara Klein-Braslavy in *Maimonides' Interpretation of the Story of Creation* [Heb.] (Jerusalem: Aḥvah, 1978), 52. See also James Arthur Diamond, *Maimonides and the Hermeneutics of Concealment: Deciphering Scripture and Midrash in the Guide of the Perplexed* (Albany: State University of New York Press, 2002), 5. Davidson also discusses the exegetical aim of the *Guide* in *Moses Maimonides,* 334–350. Shalom Rosenberg's "On Biblical Exegesis in the *Guide*" [Heb.], *Jerusalem Studies in Jewish Thought* 1 (1981): 85–157, is an important discussion of this matter.

80. 1: Introduction; M2 (6); P5; S9; A9 (6).

81. 1: Introduction; M2 (19–22); P5–6; S11; A10 (4–7).

82. 1: Introduction; M2 (24–25); P6; S11; A10 (10–11).

83. 1: Introduction; M2 (27–29); P6; S11; A10 (13–14).
84. 1: Introduction; M5 (23–26); P9; S15; A14 (18–20). See Lorberbaum, "The Men of Knowledge."
85. For further on this issue, see section 7.1 below.
86. 1:35; M54 (20–26); S84; P80; A86 (15–21).
87. See, for example, section 2.3.
88. This would not be a problem if Maimonides assents to contradictions simultaneously, as Fox holds. If, as I argue, dialectical assent is assent to a coherent position given because of dialectical premises, the inconsistency requires explanation. It can be explained, since Maimonides' purpose is not just to make truth available to the worthy, a truth they could find elsewhere in any case, but also to explain scripture.
89. This may be why Maimonides does not rule out the possibility that contradictions in prophetic books occur because of the seventh cause: "Whether contradictions due to the seventh cause are to be found in the books of the prophets is a matter for speculative study [*naẓar*] and investigation [*baḥt*]. Statements about this should not be a matter of conjecture [*ǧuzuf*]." 1: Introduction; M13 (6–8); P19; S23; A25 (11–13).

CHAPTER 2

1. Aristotle, *Topics* 101a, 30–37, including the following quotation.
2. Kraemer includes creation among the "false questions" that are raised about the *Guide* because scholars fail to pay attention to Maimonides' use of dialectic. See Kraemer, "Maimonides' Use," 123.
3. 2:13; M197 (6); P282; S298; A310 (10).
4. 2:13; M196 (6); P281; S297; A309 (3).
5. 2:13; M197 (12); P282; S299; A310 (16).
6. Falaquera is an example of a Jewish philosopher who believed Plato's view to be the true position of the law, as Raphael Jospe explains in *Torah and Sophia: The Life and Thought of Shem Tov ibn Falaquera* (Cincinnati: Hebrew Union College Press, 1988), 28.
7. 2:13; M198 (8–18); P284; S300; A311 (20)–312 (5).
8. It might not be immediately obvious why the past eternity of the world implies that it is necessary. I will explore this issue further in section 3.1 below.
9. 2:15; M202 (3–4); P289; S305; A316 (21–22).
10. See section 1.2.4 above.
11. 2:16; M204 (18–20); P293; S309; A320 (5–6).
12. 2:23; M224 (30); P321; S335; A348 (7).
13. 2:14; M200 (17); P287; S303; A314 (20).
14. 2:17; M207 (17–19); P297; S313; A324 (1–2).
15. 2:17; M207 (13–14); P297; S313; A323 (19–20).

16. On the question of the posteternity of the world, Maimonides departs from Ġazālī, although they agree about creation. See the latter's *The Incoherence of the Philosophers*, Arabic text and English translation by Michael Marmura (Provo, Utah: Brigham Young University Press, 2000), 47–55. See below for further on Maimonides' view. Kenneth Seeskin explains Maimonides' presentation and critique of the Aristotelian arguments in *Maimonides on the Origin of the World* (Cambridge, U.K.: Cambridge University Press, 2005), 60–95.

17. 2:17; M205 (14–17); P295; S310; A321 (11–13).

18. 2:17; M207 (24–27); P298; S313; A324 (7–9). I quote in Arabic transliteration rather than in Judeo-Arabic so that the statement is open to all who read Arabic.

19. Jonathan Malino, "Aristotle on Eternity: Does Maimonides Have a Reply?" in *Maimonides and Philosophy*, ed. Shlomo Pines and Yirmiahu Yovel (Dordrecht: Martinus Nijhoff, 1986), 59. My understanding of the critique accords with Seeskin's in *Maimonides on the Origin*. Furthermore, the reason time is so heavily involved in these comments is that Maimonides is using an analogy to make his point. Pointing out the temporal nature of the critique does not invalidate the critique as a whole; it merely draws attention to the analogy's limitations, which are inevitable in any analogy.

20. This translation is reflected in S. It is also supported by ibn Tibbon 2, 49b; and *Les Guides des Égarés*, 3 vols., translated by Salomon Munk (Paris: A. Franck, 1856–66), 2:136. However, Kafiḥ's translation is in accord with that of Pines; *Moreh Ha-nebukim*, Arabic text with Hebrew translation by Yosef Kafiḥ, 3 vols. (Jerusalem: Mossad Harav Kook, 1972), 3:324.

21. Andrew Gluck argues that Maimonides' view is esoteric inasmuch as it is not in agreement with the plain meaning of scripture in "Maimonides' Arguments for Creation 'Ex Nihilo' in the 'Guide of the Perplexed,'" *Medieval Philosophy and Theology* 7 (1998): 253.

22. This is the stance taken by Malino. He therefore argues that the scriptural view is that of creation ex nihilo and is to be rejected in favor of Aristotle's view. See Jonathan Malino, "Scientific Cosmology and Creation," in *Creation and the End of Days: Judaism and Scientific Cosmology*, ed. David Novak and Norbert Samuelson (Lanham, Md.: University Press of America, 1986), 157–183.

23. P298.

24. 2:30; M245 (6–15); P349; S361–362; A379 (4–13).

25. 2:25; M230 (3–4); P329; S342; A355 (8–9).

26. Alfred Ivry argues that Maimonides esoterically accepts a fourth position, which is a kind of creation from some preexisting matter. He distinguishes this from the opinion of Plato, however, by arguing that the matter that the law posits is not something that warrants being called a "thing" at all. Ivry believes that Maimonides must have understood the opinion of the law in this manner, since he could not have countenanced the belief that

something can be created from nothing. That would be contrary to one of his basic logical principles, "the law of identity," which, Ivry says, Maimonides must accept holds of creation as well as everything created. Alfred Ivry, "Maimonides on Creation" [Heb.], *Jerusalem Studies in Jewish Thought* 9 (1990): 122. However, it is no easier to think of Maimonides accepting that the world comes to be from such an entity as the one Ivry posits than it is to think of him believing in creation ex nihilo. Of course, Ivry is right to point out that creation from absolute nonexistence is an idea that cannot be conceived. At one point, Maimonides even appears to liken it to certain Mu'atazilite doctrines that are "violently rebutted by speculation." 3:15; M332 (10); P460; S469; A520 (21). However, what he is saying there is that he sides with the philosophers generally but disagrees with them inasmuch as he argues that creation out of nothing is possible while they hold that it is impossible. There is disagreement about creation; because it can be supposed or denied, both options are possible, as far as the intellect can tell. Unlike some *kalām* opinions, however, it cannot be imagined. Creation out of nothing cannot be imagined because "nothing" cannot be imagined. Maimonides is stressing that the fact that it cannot be imagined does not make it impossible, just as being able to imagine a thing's existence does not make that thing possible. Neither intellect nor imagination can stretch as far as conceiving creation from absolute nonexistence, but it remains possible.

27. See Herbert Davidson, "Maimonides' Secret Position on Creation," in *Studies in Medieval Jewish History and Literature,* ed. Isadore Twersky (Cambridge, Mass: Harvard University Press, 1979), 21.

28. 2:13; M199 (3–6); P285; S301; A312 (20–23).

29. 2:25; M229 (23–25); P328; S342; A354 (20–21).

30. See section 1.3.1 above.

31. Tamar Rudavsky has recently argued that the tension in the Platonic view shows that it is the opinion that Maimonides ultimately holds; Plato's view is Maimonides' true, esoteric opinion. She points out that it satisfies the criteria of both the law and Aristotle. On the one hand, it accords with the Aristotelian understanding of time, which Maimonides adopts, and so is scientifically respectable; on the other, it accords with the law and so is religiously respectable. Rudavsky is right to connect the views on creation with other doctrines that the law as a whole teaches. However, she does not distinguish between the law's view and the external sense of scripture and so presents a different solution from that advanced here. Furthermore, the notion that Maimonides held an esoteric position that reflects his true opinion is based, at least in part, on an interpretation of the seventh cause of contradictions that Maimonides enumerates in his introduction. Since I offer an alternative reading of that cause for contradictions in later chapters of this book, it is a position that, if my reading is convincing, is untenable, so there is no warrant to search for an esoteric meaning in the first place.

32. Davidson suggests that Maimonides may have "expressed himself carelessly"; *Moses Maimonides*, 369.

33. See Erik Olsson, *Against Coherence: Truth, Probability, and Justification* (Oxford: Clarendon, 2005).

34. For more on this issue, see section 3.1 below.

35. 2:25; M229 (10); P327; S341; A354 (4–5).

36. 2:25; M355 (5); P329; S342; A230 (11).

37. 2:25; M229 (22); P328; S342; A354 (19).

38. 2:25; M229 (25–26);P328; S342; A354 (21)–355 (2).

39. Stroumsa, *Maimonides in His World*, 149. Kraemer also links the reference to the magical aspect of Isma'ili doctrine in "Moses Maimonides: An Intellectual Portrait," in *The Cambridge Companion to Maimonides*, ed. Kenneth Seeskin (Cambridge, U.K.: Cambridge University Press, 2005), 25. I will say more about this in later chapters in which I consider Ezekiel's vision.

40. Ġazālī also proceeds to criticize another method of interpretation commonly used by Isma'ili writers, in which letters are said to stand for particular things, and collections of multiple things appearing in a text are said to correspond to a collection of things with the same number in the world. Ġazālī, *Faḍā'iḥ al-Bāṭiniyya* (Beirut: Al-Maktabah al-'Aṣri'yah, 2000), 59–71. Such interpretations do appear in the *Guide* and, again, in the chapters below about Ezekiel, I will investigate the matter further.

41. See section 8.5 below for more on this matter.

CHAPTER 3

1. 2:19; M211 (7–9); P302; S318; A328 (16–18).

2. 2: Introduction; M166 (1–3); P236; S251; A251 (1–3).

3. Maimonides lists these issues in 2:25; M230 (5–13); P329; S343; A355 (11–19). See section 3.3 for more.

4. One notable source might be Ġazālī. See Muammer İskenderoğlu, *Fakhr al-Dīn al-Rāzī and Thomas Aquinas on the Question of the Eternity of the World* (Leiden: Brill, 2002), 47–51.

5. This position is strong throughout Aristotle's corpus. See Simo Knuuttila, *Modalities in Medieval Philosophy* (London: Routledge, 1993), 1–44.

6. 2:1; M172 (18–19); P248; S263; A278 (1–2).

7. For further explanation, see Alvin Plantinga, "De Re et de Dicto," *Nous* 3 (1969): 235–258.

8. 2:21; M220 (3); P315; S328; A341 (4).

9. It might be eternal either because of the nature of the world or because of the nature of God.

10. 1:71; M124 (30); P181; S192; A187 (20).

11. 1:71; M124 (15–16); P180; S191; A187 (6–7).

12. See section 1.2.4 above.

13. 2: Introduction; M165–169; P235–241; S249–257; A235–273. A includes some of the editor's comments, as well as Tabrizi's commentary. For more on the commentary and a Hebrew translation, see Maurice-Ruben Hayoun, "Moses Maimonides und Muhammad al-Tabrisi," *Trumah* 5 (1996): 206–245. Šem Toḇ writes that not all of these have the force of demonstrated principles.
14. See section 1.3.1 above.
15. 2: Introduction; M168 (30); P240; S257; A273 (9–10).
16. 2: Introduction; M165 (11–12); P235; S249; A243 (1–2).
17. For more on these demonstrations, see Josef Stern, "Maimonides' Demonstrations: Principles and Practice," *Medieval Philosophy and Theology* 10 (2001): 47–84.
18. 2:2; M175 (15–17); P252; S267; A281 (14–16). Another clear expression of this position is found in 1:71; M125 (16–17); P181; S191; A188 (13).
19. Kenneth Seeskin pointed out to me that Aquinas follows the same strategy. He seems to assume creation in the first two of his "five ways," but the third requires eternity, because it uses the "principle of plenitude" as a premise: in infinite time, all possibilities will become actual, so the world's nonexistence must at some point come about. ST 1a, 2, 3. *Summa Theologiæ Vol. 2: Existence and Nature of God* (1a, 2–11) (Cambridge: Cambridge University Press, 2006).
20. These kinds of arguments became popular in Arabic philosophy as a whole. The "first of the philosophers," al-Kindī, used them throughout his writings. See Peter Adamson, *Al-Kindī* (New York: Oxford University Press, 2007), 37.
21. 3:25; M365 (24–26); P503; S509; A570 (14–15).
22. 3:13; M326 (29); P453; S463; A512 (19).
23. 3:25; M365 (30)–366 (5); P503; S509; A570 (20)–571 (3).
24. 3:13; M324 (21–24); P449; S461; A509 (16–19).
25. As may be expected, Maimonides' true view on miracles is disputed. For an overview of the different positions, see Hannah Kasher, "Biblical Miracles and the Universality of Natural Laws: Maimonides' Three Methods of Harmonization," *Journal of Jewish Thought and Philosophy* 8 (1998): 25–29. There is a more recent account by Y. Tzvi Langermann, "Maimonides and Miracles: The Growth of a (Dis)belief," *Jewish History* 18 (2004): 147–172. Langermann argues that miracles show science to be uncertain.
26. That miracles authenticate the message of a prophet is a common belief in Islam. See Blake Dutton, "Al-Ghazālī on Possibility and the Critique of Causality," *Medieval Philosophy and Theology* 10 (2001): 24.
27. See, for example, MT Foundations 10:1.
28. For more, see Lawrence Kaplan, "Maimonides on the Miraculous Element in Prophecy," *Harvard Theological Review* 70 (1977): 233–256.

29. That God's direct role in prophecy is only preventative is explained by Abrabanel, Maimonides, *More Nebuchim* 86b. See Alexander Altmann, "Maimonides and Thomas Aquinas: Natural or Divine Prophecy?" *AJS Review* 3 (1978): 6. This means that prophetic knowledge is not essentially supernatural. What is supernatural is its not occurring in certain circumstances.

30. 2:29; M243 (6–8); P344; S358; A376 (7–9). Maimonides accepts the eternity *a parte post* of the world, since it leads to the view that the "laws of nature" are permanent and cannot be changed. The world and its laws operate according to their natural laws forever. See Roslyn Weiss, "Maimonides on the End of the World," *Maimonidean Studies* 3 (1992–93): 216–218. Miracles change the nature of an individual thing, but they presumably do not give that thing an "unnatural" nature. Maimonides uses Solomon as his main biblical witness for this view. On Maimonides' view of Solomon's metaphysical knowledge, see Sara Klein-Braslavy, "King Solomon and Metaphysical Esotericism in Maimonides," *Maimonidean Studies* 1 (1990) : 57–86.

31. For further consideration, see section 6.3.2 below.

32. See Peter Adamson, "On Knowledge of Particulars," *Proceedings of the Aristotelian Society* 105 (2005): 273–294, for a detailed explanation.

33. 3:13; M326 (18); P452; S463; A512 (7–8).

34. I address the difference between divine and human knowledge in greater detail in chapter 6 below.

35. 3:21; M351 (16–20); P485; S493; A548 (11–15).

CHAPTER 4

1. Peter Eli Gordon, "The Erotics of Negative Theology," *Jewish Studies Quarterly* 2 (1995): 7. The kabbalists' position is perhaps more complicated than appears at first sight, as witnessed by Naḥmanides' famous defense of Maimonides against the attacks of some anthropomorphists. See David Berger, "How Did Naḥmanides Propose to Resolve the Maimonidean Controversy?" in *Me'ah She'arim: Studies in Medieval Jewish Spiritual Life*, ed. E. Fleischer et al. (Jerusalem: Magnes, 2001), 135–146. Naḥmanides himself is sometimes thought to have been an anthropomorphist. See, for example, Martin Cohen, "Reflections on the Text and Context of the Disputation of Barcelona," *Hebrew Union College Annual* 35 (1964): 157–192.

2. Franz Rosenzweig, *The Star of Redemption,* translated by William Hallo (London: Routledge and Kegan Paul, 1971), 23.

3. See sections 5.3 and 6.4 below.

4. A helpful collection of articles about the reception of Maimonides in Jewish thought has recently been published: James T. Robinson, ed., *The*

Cultures of Maimonideanism: New Approaches to the History of Jewish Thought (Leiden: Brill, 2009).

5. Harry Wolfson, "Crescas on the Problem of Divine Attributes," in *Studies in the History and Philosophy of Religion*, 2 vols., ed. Isadore Twersky and George H. Williams (Cambridge, Mass.: Harvard University Press, 1973–1977), 2:269.

6. Wolfson offers a response to Guttmann's critique of his position in "Maimonides on Negative Attributes," in *Studies in the History and Philosophy of Religion*, 2 vols., ed. Isadore Twersky and George H. Williams (Cambridge, Mass.: Harvard University Press, 1973–1977), 2:227–228.

7. Ehud Benor, "Meaning and Reference in Maimonides' Negative Theology," *Harvard Theological Review* 88 (1995): 353.

8. For an account of some limitations of Wolfson's approach, see Charles Manekin, "Belief, Certainty and Divine Attributes in the Guide of the Perplexed," *Maimonidean Studies* 1 (1990): 131. Manekin argues that Maimonides' negative theology is more "optimistic" than it is usually thought to be, a position supported in this chapter.

9. It is worth noting that many neglect the opening chapters of this section. For example, Solomon ben Moses begins his commentary on chapter 50 with the following statement: "here begin the chapters on attributes." Ms. CUL Add. 672, folio 39r. Mauro Zonta reports that Solomon was in close contact with Christian thinkers, including Aquinas's teacher, and that he drew on those sources in his commentary. See Mauro Zonta, *Hebrew Scholasticism in the Fifteenth Century: A History and Source Book* (Dordrecht: Springer, 2006), 3. Perhaps a focus on the more obviously philosophical sections of the *Guide*, as opposed to its exegetical parts, is responsible for some common misconceptions. For more on the medieval misunderstanding, see Seymour Feldman, "A Scholastic Misinterpretation of Maimonides' Doctrine of Divine Attributes," *Journal of Jewish Studies* 20 (1968): 23–39.

10. Harry Wolfson considers the identity of those whom Maimonides refutes in *Repercussions of the Kalam in Jewish Philosophy* (Cambridge, Mass.: Harvard University Press, 1979), 73–74. He notes that the position discussed below is attributed to "some people of speculation." He does not specify who exactly they are but points out that Maimonides uses the same formula when refuting those who attribute modes (*aḥwāl*) to God. Wolfson argues that Maimonides' allusion in that case is to Abū Hāšim. The formula was also used by later Ash'arites to mean modes as well as attributes.

11. 1:56; M89 (7); P130; S137; A138 (4–5).

12. 1:56; M89 (12); P131; S138; A138 (9).

13. 1:56; M89 (14–16); P131; S138; A138 (12–13).

14. Maimonides uses the term *amphibolous* in an unusual manner. Most refer to this kind of predication as "equivocation." Such thinkers often use *taškīk* to refer to a kind of systematic ambiguity. See Harry Wolfson, "The Amphibolous Terms in Aristotle, Arabic Philosophy and Maimonides," in *Studies in the History and Philosophy of Religion*, 2 vols., ed. Isadore Twersky and George H. Williams (Cambridge, Mass.: Harvard University Press, 1973–1977), 1:468. For further discussion, see section 5.3 below.

15. 1:56; M89 (17–21); P131; S138; A138 (14–17).

16. 1:60; M99 (11–12); P145; S153; A151 (16).

17. For an account of Maimonides' view of idolatry as a mistake, see Moshe Halbertal and Avishai Margalit, *Idolatry*, translated by Naomi Goldblum (Cambridge, Mass.: Harvard University Press, 1992), 109–112.

18. Harry Wolfson suggests why Maimonides divided the attributes in such a way in "The Aristotelian Predicables and Maimonides' Division of Attributes," in *Studies in the History and Philosophy of Religion*, 2 vols., ed. Isadore Twersky and George H. Williams (Cambridge, Mass.: Harvard University Press, 1973–1977), 2:192.

19. 1:52; M77 (21); P114; S118; A122 (11).

20. 1:52; M77 (25); P115; S119; A122 (15).

21. 1:52; M78 (2); P115; S119; A122 (20).

22. 1:52; M79 (7); P117; S121; A124 (14).

23. MT, *Foundations*, 1:2–3.

24. 1:52; M79 (21); P117; S122; A125 (17).

25. 1:52; M80 (11); P118; S123; A126 (3).

26. 1:52; M80 (14–15); P118; S123; A126 (6). For a modern explanation of this kind of essential attribute, see Peter Geach, *God and the Soul* (London: Routledge and Kegan Paul, 1969), 71–72.

27. 1:52; M80 (16) ;P118; S123; A126 (7).

28. Things made are the only examples of attributes of action that Maimonides uses.

29. For an account of Maimonides' explanation, see Hyman, "From What Is One and Simple Only What Is One and Simple Can Come to Be," in *Neoplatonism and Jewish Thought*, ed. Lenn E. Goodman (Albany: State University of New York Press, 1991), 117. Hyman focuses on the idea that a being acting through will can create a plurality. This indicates that the world is a plurality. However, elsewhere, Maimonides solves the difficulty by arguing that a simple God can create the world because the world is actually a single unit rather than a plurality. 1:72; M129 (27–29); P187; S198; A193 (21–23). He uses this idea in an argument for God's unity in 2:1; M174 (4); P250; S265; A280 (1–2). A consideration of this seeming inconsistency is beyond the scope of the present work.

30. Oliver Leaman is therefore correct when arguing that it is necessary to bear in mind that there is no similarity between divine attributes of action and human attributes of action. *Moses Maimonides* (London: Routledge, 1990), 27.

31. 1:52; M80 (16); P118; S123; A126 (8).

32. Leaman, *Moses Maimonides*, 29.

33. 1:55; M87 (19–20); P128; S135–136; A136 (6–7).

34. 1:58; M92 (4); P135; S144; A141 (20).

35. 1:58; M92 (11); P135; S144; A142 (3). Kenneth Seeskin notes this in "Sanctity and Silence: The Religious Significance of Maimonides' Negative Theology," *American Catholic Philosophical Quarterly* 76 (2002): 14.

36. 1:58; M91 (17–18); P134; S143; A141 (4–5).

37. 1:58; M91 (29); P135; S143; A141 (16).

38. 1:59; M94 (28); P139; S148; A145 (12).

39. 1:58; M93 (4–6); P136; S145; A143 (6–7).

40. 1:26; M38 (3); P56; S62; A62 (16).

41. 1:59; M95 (1); P139; S148; A145 (14).

42. 1:52; M80 (27); P119; S124; A126 (18).

43. The rabbinic statement is also used in this way by the Karaite al-Qirqisānī. See Daniel Frank, *Search Scripture Well: Karaite Exegesis and the Origins of the Jewish Bible Commentary in the Islamic East* (Leiden: Brill, 2004), 11. For a discussion of Maimonides' theory of the relationship between words and things, see Josef Stern, "Maimonides on Language and the Science of Language," in *Maimonides and the Sciences*, ed. Robert S. Cohen and Hillel Levine (Dordrecht: Kluwer, 2000), 189–197.

44. 1:53; M82 (12–13); P121; S126; A128 (17–18).

45. 1:46; M66 (11); P98; S100; A105 (5–6). This is one of the prophets' great innovations. It indicates the positive role of the intellect. See Warren Zev Harvey, "'Great Is the Power': On Guide of the Perplexed I 46" [Heb.], *Da'at* 37 (1996): 60.

46. 1:46; M67 (28); P100; S103; A107 (11–12).

47. 1:46; M67 (9–10); P99; S102; A106 (10–11).

48. 3:28; M373 (12); P512; S518; A581 (15).

49. The distinction is explained in this way by Howard Kreisel in *Maimonides' Political Thought: Studies in Ethics, Law and the Human Ideal* (Albany: State University of New York Press, 1999), 196.

50. See also 1:35; M54 (7–20); P80; S76; A86 (2–14), where God's incorporeality and absolute otherness are included.

51. Richard Frank, "Knowledge and *Taqlīd*," *Journal of the American Oriental Society* 109 (1989): 37.

52. See Manekin, "Belief, Certainty and Divine Attributes," 119–129.

53. 1:53; M81 (13); P120; S125; A127 (12).

54. 1:53; M81 (14); P120; S125; A127 (13).

CHAPTER 5

1. For a detailed description of Maimonides' explanation of divine unity as both uniqueness and indivisibility, see Harry Wolfson, "Maimonides on the Unity and Incorporeality of God," in *Studies in the History and Philosophy of Religion,* 2 vols., ed. Isadore Twersky and George H. Williams (Cambridge, Mass.: Harvard University Press, 1973–1977), 2:433–456.
2. 1:57; M90 (12); P132; S140; A139 (11–12).
3. 1:57; M90 (16–18); P132; S141; A139 (15–17).
4. 1:57; M91 (9); P133; S142; A140 (15–16).
5. I mentioned these above in section 4.3.
6. 1:57; M90 (3); P132; S139; A139 (2). A has *'ārid lil-mawǧūd.*
7. See Richard Walzer, *Al-Farabi on the Perfect State: Abū Naṣr al-Fārābī's Mabādi' Ārā' Ahl al-Madīna al-Fāḍila* (Oxford: Clarendon, 1985), 56.
8. See Alexander Altmann, "Essence and Existence in Maimonides," in *Maimonides: A Collection of Critical Essays,* ed. Joseph A. Buijs (Notre Dame, Ind.: University of Notre Dame Press, 1988), 148–165.
9. See Fazlur Rahman,' "Essence and Existence in Avicenna," *Medieval and Renaissance Studies* 4 (1958): 1–16, and "Essence and Existence in Ibn Sīnā: The Myth and the Reality," *Hamdard Islamicus* 4 (1981): 3–14.
10. Ġazālī was critical of Avicenna's view. Crescas may have included him in this list, since he was not familiar with all of Ġazālī's work. He certainly did know his *Intentions of the Philosophers,* and he seems to have erroneously taken it to represent Ġazālī's own opinion, as Harry Wolfson explains in *Crescas' Critique of Aristotle* (Cambridge, Mass.: Harvard University Press, 1971), 11. The same view of Ġazālī was held by many in the Latin tradition, as Steven Harvey explains in "Why Did Fourteenth Century Jews Turn to al-Ghazali's Account of Natural Science?" *Jewish Quarterly Review* 91 (2001): 362.
11. Ḥasdai Crescas, *Or Hashem* (Jerusalem: Sifre Ramot, 1990), 1.3.1. Crescas offers two arguments here. See Wolfson, "Crescas on the Problem."
12. The main source for these ideas is the work of Barry Miller, particularly the books *A Most Unlikely God: A Philosophical Enquiry into the Nature of God* (Notre Dame, Ind.: University of Notre Dame Press, 1996) and *The Fullness of Being: A New Paradigm for Existence* (Notre Dame, Ind.: University of Notre Dame Press, 2002). Although Miller takes himself to be opposing Maimonides, I argue that their respective positions are more similar than he thinks. His criticisms may be fair for most interpretations of Maimonides. For further support of similar views, see William Vallicella, *A Paradigm Theory of Existence: Ontotheology Vindicated* (Dordrecht: Kluwer, 2002).
13. 3:18; M343 (9); P474; S483; A536 (8). For the purposes of this chapter, there is no need to enter into a detailed discussion of the history of how universals were understood. Avicenna's explanation is treated by Michael

Marmura in *Probing in Islamic Philosophy: Studies in the Philosophies of Ibn Sīnā, al-Ghazālī and Other Major Muslim Thinkers* (New York: Global Academic, 2005), 61–70.

14. There might be some basis for the view that Maimonides thought that things exist before they receive existence if he were to be associated with some early Kalām thinkers who appeared to hold exactly that. However, both Alfarabi and Avicenna opposed their view, and Maimonides would certainly have taken one of their positions on the matter. Which one he adopted makes no difference to the argument of this chapter. For an account of the views on the relationship between "thing" and "existent" prior to Maimonides, see Robert Wisnovsky, *Avicenna's Metaphysics in Context* (London: Duckworth, 2003), 145–160; and Richard Frank, "The Non-Existent and the Possible in Classical Ash'arite Teaching," *Mideo* 24 (2000): 1–37.

15. Averroes likens the relationship of being to all other things to that of genus to species. It is not a real genus, though, since there is nothing to distinguish it from others. See *The Incoherence of the Incoherence*, translated with an introduction and notes by Simon van den Bergh (London: Luzac, 1954), 179.

16. It is interesting to note the difference between Maimonides' scale and that of some other Jewish thinkers. For example, Halevi posits a fifth level above that of regular humans, which is the Jew. According to this theory, a Jew is distinguished from other humans by possessing the capacity for prophecy. See Menachem Kellner, *Maimonides on Judaism and the Jewish People* (Albany: State University of New York Press, 1991), 1–7, for various approaches to this question.

17. Many pieces have been written on human perfection in Maimonides. See, for example, Menachem Kellner, *Maimonides on Human Perfection* (Atlanta: Scholars Press, 1990).

18. See section 7.3.4 below.

19. Howard Kreisel points out that in Maimonides' view, a perfect human intellect is superior to the intelligences in "The Place of Man on the Hierarchy of Existence in the Philosophy of Ibn Gabirol and Maimonides," in *Alei Shefer: Studies in the Literature of Jewish Thought*, ed. M. Ḥallamish (Ramat-Gan: Bar-Ilan University Press, 1990), 103.

20. 1:57; M90 (5); P133; S139; A139 (4).

21. 1:57; M90 (7); P132; S140; A139 (6). The Avicennan argument for God's existence—a version of which is present in Maimonides' third demonstration for God's existence, as explained by Stern in "Maimonides' Demonstrations," 66—is clearly in the background of Maimonides' comments here. Šem Toḇ outlines the argument when explaining Maimonides' meaning, 1:116a Maimonides, *More Nebuchim*. Toby Mayer explains Avicenna's demonstration for the existence of a necessary being in "Ibn Sīnā'a 'Burhān al Ṣiddiqīn,'" *Journal of Islamic Studies* 12 (2001): 18–39.

22. See section 5.1 above.
23. 1:56; M89 (14–16); P131; S138; A138 (1213).
24. Avicenna, *The Metaphysics of The Healing*, trans. Michael E. Marmura (Provo, Utah: Brigham Young University Press, 2005), 284.
25. 3:10; M317 (10); P440; S451; A498 (14).
26. See Oliver Leaman, *Evil and Suffering in Medieval Jewish Philosophy* (Cambridge, U.K.: Cambridge University Press, 1995).
27. Miller uses this example in *A Most Unlikely God*, 8.
28. See section 4.3.1 above.
29. Another way to think of this might be as the change from one substance to another, when the specific difference is altered.
30. 3:20; M349 (26); P483; S491; A546 (5).
31. Maimonides insists on this point as explained in section 5.1 above.
32. 1:57; M90 (10–11); P133; S141; A139 (9–10).
33. 1:58; M91 (12–13); P134; S142; A140 (19–20).
34. 1:56; M89 (15); P131; S138; A138 (12).
35. David Burrell, *Aquinas: God and Action* (London: Routledge and Kegan Paul, 1979), 8–10.
36. ST, 1a, 13, 6. Burrell explains how this distinction enables analogical predication in *Aquinas*, 55–67.
37. ST, 1a, 13, 4.
38. Avicenna is one such example. In *Talking about God and Talking about Creation: Avicenna's and Thomas Aquinas' Positions* (Leiden: Brill, 2005), Rahim Acar explains how Avicenna's position might be developed so that *taškīk* could be used to describe the relationship between terms used of God and created beings. Avicenna does not apply the word in that particular way, though.
39. Harry Wolfson, "Maimonides and Gersonides on Divine Attributes as Ambiguous Terms," in *Studies in the History and Philosophy of Religion*, 2 vols., ed. Isadore Twersky and George H. Williams (Cambridge, Mass.: Cambridge University Press, 1973–1977), 2:240.
40. See section 4.3.1 above. He does use it this way in the "Treatise on Logic."
41. The difference is correctly identified in Seeskin, *Searching for a Distant God*, 47.

CHAPTER 6

1. For example, Alfred Ivry denies that the principles of Maimonides' thought allow him to posit divine knowledge of particulars. Consequently, Ivry argues that Maimonides' doing so is merely a concession to the masses in "Providence, Divine Omniscience, and Possibility: The Case of Maimonides," in *Maimonides: A Collection of Critical Essays*, ed. Joseph A. Buijs (Notre Dame, Ind.: University of Notre Dame Press, 1988), 185–187.

Ehud Benor argues that Maimonides believes that God knows particulars in *Worship of the Heart: A Study of Maimonides' Philosophy of Religion* (Albany: State University of New York Press, 1995), 131–153.

2. 3:21; M351 (10); P485; S493; A548 (5).

3. For the limitations of the analogy, see below.

4. For a similar explanation, see Averroes' *The Book of the Decisive Treatise and Epistle Dedicatory*, translated with introduction and notes by Charles Butterworth (Provo, Utah: Brigham Young University Press, 2001), 38–42. See Charles Manekin, "Maimonides on Divine Knowledge: Moses of Narbonne's Averroist Reading," *American Catholic Philosophical Quarterly* 76 (2002): 51–74, for more on the similarity. I am in agreement with this excellent article in that it takes Maimonides' explicit claims about God's knowledge seriously.

5. 3:21; M350 (14–17, 29); P484; S492; A547 (2–5, 16–17).

6. 3:21; M350 (26–27); P484; S492; A547 (14).

7. Maimonides' use of a water clock is probably not accidental. The water clock is an example of objects created by demonstrative, perfectly accurate knowledge. It works exactly as its maker intends because it is built along the lines of geometrical proofs. See, for example, Galen, *Selected Works*, translated by Peter Singer (Oxford: Oxford University Press, 1997), 132. Al-Ġazālī uses a water clock to illustrate the way the cosmos follows its creator's orders. See Frank Griffel, *Al-Ghazālī's Philosophical Theology* (New York: Oxford University Press, 2009), 238.

8. Aristotle, Meta., 981a25. These were rendered "speculative knowledge" (*ma'arifah al-naẓiriyah*) and "practical knowledge" (*ma'arifah al-'amaliyyah*) by Isḥāq ibn Ḥunayn. His translation is included in Averroes' *Tafsīr Mā Ba'd Aṭ-Ṭabī'at*, vol. 1 (Beirut: Imprimerie Catholique, 1938), 11, line 3.

9. Avicenna points out that it is superior because apprehension through the intellect rather than through the senses is the true fulfillment of the intellect. See Avicenna, *Metaphysics*, 298.

10. It is important to keep in mind that this is an analogy, and as such, it is not the same as that of which it is an analogy. The important point is that it is similar in the way in which it is supposed to be enlightening, not in all respects. Maimonides states that God is the formal, final, and efficient cause of the universe. 1:69; M115 (20); P167; S178; A175 (10–11). The artificer's knowledge is only the formal cause of the clock. The artificer himself is the efficient cause. The final cause, however, is external to the craftsman.

11. The same claim is made in relation to Maimonides' referring to God as an intellect in the first part of the *Guide*, which is an issue I consider below in the appendix to this chapter.

12. For a clear and forceful statement of this view, see Alexander Broadie, "Maimonides and Divine Knowledge," in *Of Scholars, Savants, and Their Texts: Studies in Philosophy and Religious Thought*, ed. Ruth Link-Salinger

(New York: Peter Lang, 1989). I will briefly consider some other arguments below in the chapter appendix.

13. 3:20; M348 (24–25); P482; S490; A544 (13).

14. 3:20; M348 (30); P482; S490; A544 (18).

15. The analogy of the water clock appears in chapter 21, which I will return to in section 6.3.3 below.

16. Maimonides' presents his thoughts on evil and providence as intimately connected with his exegesis of the book of Job. See Robert Eisen, *The Book of Job in Medieval Jewish Philosophy* (New York: Oxford University Press, 2004), 43–77.

17. 3:19; M347 (3–5); P479; S488; A542 (5–7).

18. Earlier in the *Guide*, Maimonides mentions that those who have not studied and understood books about the intellect have great difficulty understanding what is said about the divine intellect. 1:68; M112 (20–22); P163; S173; A171 (15–17).

19. 3:19; M346 (9–11); P478; S487; A541 (1–3).

20. 2:20; M218 (2–3); P312; S326; A338 (9–10).

21. 3:19; M346 (21); P479; S487; A541 (14).

22. That Maimonides is aware that a system can cater to the generality of existence without considering every individual is clear from his justification of the Mosaic law. He argues that the presence of anomalies in the law does not show it to be deficient, since it is intended to benefit the generality of people and cannot be suitably adjusted to every individual case. See Miriam Galston, "The Purpose of the Law according to Maimonides," *Jewish Quarterly Review* 69 (1978): 32.

23. 3:17; M340 (16–17); P471; S480; A532 (10–11). I plan to discuss the difference between God's knowledge and God's providence in a separate study. Briefly, when writing about God's knowledge, Maimonides is making a theological point. He is concerned with differentiating God's knowledge from human knowledge and preserving our total ignorance of God. Because "knowledge" is used by way of absolute equivocation, it is illegitimate to say that God cannot know disordered particulars simply because humans cannot know them. That would be an anthropomorphism. When writing about providence, however, Maimonides is usually concerned with the order of the created universe.

24. 3:19; M347 (13–16); P480; S488; A542 (15–17).

25. See section 3.3 above.

26. 3:20; M347 (19–21); P480; S488; A543 (2–4).

27. 3:20; M347 (21); P480; S488; A54 3(4). P has "a Law." In note 3, S points out that the phrase *ma'šar al-mutaša'irīn* encompasses those who believe in a law other than the Torah. On Maimonides' use of the word *šarī'a*, see Joel Kraemer, "Naturalism and Universalism in Maimonides' Political and Religious Thought," in *Me'ah She'arim: Studies in Medieval Jewish Spiritual Life,* ed. E. Fleischman et al. (Jerusalem: Magnes, 2001), 52.

28. 3:20; M348 (4–5); P481; S489; A543 (14–15). There is a puzzle that Maimonides does not deal with: Does God know the various alternatives that could result from a free human choice? His general approach, distinguishing between God's knowledge and human knowledge so radically that humans can understand nothing of divine knowledge, seems to render the question impossible to answer. Since God's knowledge is of such a different kind, one cannot impose such dichotomies between actual events and nonactual events on God's knowledge. Nevertheless, it seems as if Maimonides does indeed make a rather robust claim about the matter when he writes "that which never exists is not an object of God's knowledge." My own suspicion is that here he is referring to classes of things. So, for example, God does not know "elephants with wings" if such a thing never exists, but God does know "elephants." This interpretation would fit his statement that God creates everything that can be created. There he is clearly talking about kinds of things rather than every single possible accidental feature that may or may not attach to an individual, such as "sitting at time x" or "standing at time x." 3:25; M368 (1); P506; S511; A573 (14).

29. See chapter 3 above.

30. See section 5.2.4 above.

31. 3:20; M348 (18); P481; S489; A544 (7).

32. See section 5.3 above.

33. 3:20; M348 (29); P482; S490; A544 (18).

34. This seeming oversight is pointed out by Charles Manekin in *On Maimonides* (Belmont, Calif.: Thomson Wadsworth, 2005), 73. He does not offer an explanation.

35. 3:20; M349 (2–4); P482; S490; A544 (20–22). An objection may be raised on the basis of MT *Hilḳot Teśuḅah*: "we can know without doubt that man's deeds are in his own hands and God does not drive him to do them or decree that he should do them. It is not only because of our tradition that we know this to be so but by means of clear scientific proof." However, there is no conflict here. As Louis Jacobs explains, "what is proved is that man has free will, not that free will is compatible with divine omniscience." *Jewish Ethics, Philosophy and Mysticism* (New York: Behrman House, 1969), 92. Maimonides makes the same statement in the *Guide* when he says that human liberty is a fundamental principle of the law and that he understands from the Torah rather than speculation that God knows free human actions. 3:20; M349 (3); P482; S490; A544 (21). The earlier statement might be a more confident affirmation of freedom but not of its compatibility with God's knowledge. Some have argued that Maimonides was a determinist and that his belief in human freedom was an exoteric position. The most extensive response to this position is Josef Stern, "Maimonides' Conceptions of Freedom and the Sense of Shame," in

Freedom and Moral Responsibility: General and Jewish Perspectives, ed. Charles Manekin (Bethesda: University Press of Maryland, 1997).

36. See section 5.2.2 above.

37. An important principle is that things are known in the manner of the knower.

38. This use of "eternal" is to be distinguished from the way in which it is often used in Maimonidean scholarship, in which it usually refers to the past eternity of the world.

39. 2:30; M245 (26)–246 (2); P350; S363; A380 (6–9).

40. What exactly this idea amounts to is contested. Norman Kretzmann and Eleonore Stump offer one explanation in "Eternity," *Journal of Philosophy* 78 (1981): 429–458. John Marenbon offers alternatives in "Eternity," in *The Cambridge Companion to Medieval Philosophy,* ed. A. S. McGrade (Cambridge: Cambridge University Press, 2003), 51–60.

41. Benor, *Worship of the Heart,* 148. See also p. 151: "It is a view that offers an interpretation of Maimonides, which, to me at least, seems coherent."

42. 3:19; M345 (5–7); P477; S485; A539 (2–4). This is another clear statement that perfections exist in God. See section 4.4 above. An objection may be raised on the basis of Pines's translation, which has "good things" rather than "perfections." He translates in accordance with what appears in the body of the text in the Munk edition: ḥayrāt. The version I have used is mentioned by Munk as an alternative and is used by Kafiḥ, *Moreh,* 3:520. I have chosen to use that version for a number of reasons. First, Munk himself translates "perfections" in his rendering of the *Guide* into French, *Les Guides,* 3:141. Second, ibn Tibbon translates "perfections" (*šlemuyot*), 2:35b. Third, Maimonides attributes perfections to God in the first part of the *Guide.* Reading the same word here preserves the consistency of the text. Finally, "perfections" conveys the sense of absolute perfections, which is the assertion that Maimonides is making here. The perfections are not limited by being attached to things, as "good things" may be thought to indicate.

43. See Wolfson, "Maimonides and Gersonides," 236.

44. Ibid., 237.

45. 1:68; M112 (13–15); P163; S173: A17 (9–11).

46. An obvious candidate for the works Maimonides is referring to is Aristotle's *De Anima,* 431a1. Aryeh Kosman argues that Aristotle's consideration of God's thought in the Metaphysics is also about thought itself in "Metaphysics' Λ9: Divine Thought," in *Aristotle's Metaphysics Lambda: Symposium Aristotelicum,* ed. Michael Frede and David Charles (Oxford: Oxford University Press, 2000), 307.

47. 1:68; M114 (8–12); P165; S176; A173 (8–11).

48. Shlomo Pines, "Translator's Introduction: The Philosophical Sources of the Guide of the Perplexed," in Maimonides, *The Guide of the Perplexed,* translated by Shlomo Pines (Chicago: Chicago University Press, 1963), xcvii.

49. Pines, "Translator's Introduction," xcviii. Perhaps p. lxxix implies that he accepts the doctrine of intellect, since Pines says there that it is unorthodox, and if Maimonides is trying to hide an opinion, it would presumably be the unorthodox view. It is worth noting that Pines expanded this view later in his career and wrote that there are no fewer than four different concepts of God present in the *Guide.* See Pines, "The Philosophic Purport," 13. For an elucidation of the meaning of the different concepts and their consequences for a reading of the *Guide,* see Harvey, "How Leo Strauss," 390–395.

50. Shoey Raz, "Metaphysics and the Account of the Chariot: Maimonides and Isḥaq Ibnul Laṭif" [Heb.], in *Maimonides and Mysticism,* ed. A. Elqayam and D. Schwartz (Ramat Gan: Bar-Ilan University Press, 2009), 144.

51. Alexander Even-Chen, "God's Positive Attributes in Maimonides' Philosophy" [Heb.], *Da'at* 63 (2008): 34.

52. See Reines, "Maimonides' True Belief," 30.

53. Hannah Kasher, "Self-Cognizing Intellect and Negative Attributes in Maimonides' Theology," *Harvard Theological Review* 87 (1994): 466. This is similar to Fox's position described above.

54. Her main strategy is one I find unconvincing. She assimilates attributes of action to negative attributes and argues that to call God intellect is to express an attribute of action. Nevertheless, because she focuses on the "looseness of expression" that Maimonides says must be used when referring to God's attributes, this interpretation might also be put down to the fifth, rather than the seventh, cause of contradictions. See Diana Lobel, "'Silence Is Praise to You': Maimonides on Negative Theology, Looseness of Expression, and Religious Experience," *American Catholic Philosophical Quarterly* 76 (2002): n. 68.

55. Benor's argument is anticipated by Kellner in *Maimonides on Human Perfection,* 59–60.

56. Benor, "Meaning and Reference," 353.

57. Ibid., 357.

58. Ibid., 339.

59. See Avicenna, Meta. 8, 6.

60. See Griffel, *Al-Ghazālī's Philosophical Theology,* 253.

61. See Davidson, *Alfarabi, Avicenna, and Averroes on Intellect: Their Cosmologies, Theories of Active Intellect, and Theories of Human Intellect* (New York: Oxford University Press, 1992), 75, for more on Avicenna.

62. 1:68; M114 (15–16); P166; S176; A174 (1–2).

63. See section 1.3.2 above.

CHAPTER 7

1. I follow traditional interpretations. Jose Faur rejects them but does not enter into detail to explain what he takes Maimonides to mean. See Faur, *Homo Mysticus*, 18.

2. Maimonides identifies three different types of readers of scripture. The first two types take scripture literally; one accepts it, while the other rejects it. The third type interprets scripture in the light of philosophical truth. Such a reader would make the effort to understand Ezekiel's meaning. See CM, 4:200–203.

3. See section 1.3.4 above.

4. For an account of the Talmudic story of the orchard and rabbinic receptions, see Alon Goshen Gottstein, "Four Entered Paradise Revisited," *Harvard Theological Review* 88 (1995): 69–133.

5. See, for example, 3: Introduction; M298 (3); P415; S428; A463 (4).

6. Maimonides makes this identification throughout his literary career. See Twersky, *Introduction*, 366.

7. Mishnah Ḥagiga 3:2.

8. See section 1.3.1 above.

9. The Talmud extends this prohibition to the other two. However, the use of the singular implies that it should be limited to the last secret. See BT tractate Ḥagiga, 11a.

10. 1:33; M48 (24–25); P72; S77; A78 (7).

11. 1: Introduction; M10 (28–29); P16; S20; A22 (46).

12. This may be learned out of the verse that Maimonides cites in support of his action. He states that "it is time to do something for the Lord, and so on." The rest of the verse reads, "for they have infringed the law." Maimonides states that the Israelites were in possession of the truth but that their current spiritual state has led to its decline, in 1:71; M121 (9–10); P175; S185; A183 (5–6). These ideas are similar to the rabbinic notion that the law was lost "because of our sins." On this idea in rabbinic literature, see David Weiss-Halivni, *Peshat and Derash* (New York: Oxford University Press, 1991), 137. Maimonides states the second reason in 3: Introduction; M297 (22–23); P416; S427; A464 (6–7).

13. BT *Megilla*, 3a.

14. 3:7; M309 (17–18); P430; S440; A486 (13).

15. 3: Introduction; M298 (3–8); P416; S428; A464 (18)–465 (3).

16. 1: Introduction; M8 (3–5); S17; P12; A18 (1–3).

17. To illustrate his point, Maimonides mentions Jacob's dream of a ladder as an example. He thereby points out that this is an important image. It also has connections with the vision of the chariot. For a treatment of the connections, see Diamond, *Maimonides and the Hermeneutics*, 118–119.

18. 3:7; M309 (16–17); P430; S440; A486 (12).

19. See section 1.3.4 above.

20. 2:2; M176 (1–2); P253; S268; A282 (6–7).
21. 2:2; M176 (3–8); P253; S268; A282 (8–13).
22. Similar comments are commonly used by authors in order to gain respectability for their work by referring to prior authorities. Nevertheless, I believe that Maimonides' comment is to be taken seriously and that doing so reveals some "secrets" of the *Guide*. Elsewhere, he refuses to refer to his sources, since they may make his ideas less respectable in the eyes of some. Nevertheless, in doing so, he openly states that his sources are such that they may lead someone to view them negatively. See CM 4:372. Furthermore, he was not given to false modesty.
23. 2:2; M176 (16–17); P253; S268; A282 (20–22).
24. 2:2; M176 (24–26); P254; S269; A283 (4–6).
25. A number of Maimonides' medieval commentators wrote on his understanding of the vision of the chariot. There is only one chapter of Abrabanel's commentary, but in addition to this, he wrote twenty-eight objections (*ta'anot*) to Maimonides' interpretation. These are printed at the end of the edition without page numbers, so I refer to them by objection number. He also considers it in his biblical commentary. There is a consensus among these commentators on the broad nature of the meaning behind the parable: that it describes the makeup of the cosmos. Shalom Rosenberg mentions that Kimḥi disagreed with the others over what the beasts and the wheels mentioned in the vision stand for in Rosenberg, "On Biblical Exegesis," 144. For an alternative explanation that ignores this signpost, see David Bakan, *Maimonides on Prophecy: A Commentary on Selected Chapters of the Guide of the Perplexed* (Northvale, N.J.: Aronson, 1991), 199–278.
26. 3:5; M305 (16); P425; S436; A479 (3).
27. 3:5; M306 (10); P426; S437; A480 (15).
28. Isaac Husik echoes this but does not discuss the details of Maimonides' commentary in *A History of Mediaeval Jewish Philosophy* (New York: Atheneum, 1974), 304.
29. This translation is taken from the Jewish Publication Society.
30. 3:7; M307 (21–23); P428; S438; A483 (1–3).
31. This is similar to Judah Halevi's assertion that scripture only records famous events in *Kitāb al-Radd wa-'l-dalīl fī'l-dīn al-Dhalīl*, edited by David Baneth (Jerusalem: Magnes, 1977), 136.
32. 3:7; M307 (3–4); P428; S438; A483 (4–5).
33. 2:47; M291 (20–22); P408; S421; A454 (12–14).
34. Maimonides, *More Nebuchim* 2:12a.
35. 3:7; M308 (24–26); P429; S439; A485 (5–7).
36. Avicenna considers the rainbow in part 2, chap. 3 of *Al-Shifā': La Physique V–Les Métaux et la Météorologie*, ed. Ibrahim Madkour (Cairo: Organisation Générale des Imprimeries Gouvernementaies, 1964).

37. Asher Crescas offers an alternative interpretation of the rainbow, Maimonides *More Nebuchim* 3:11b. He writes that it is varied like the glory of God, which is seen by the prophets, following BT Ḥagiga 14a and 16b. That would mean that it represents the active intellect. He also writes that the colors do not really exist in a rainbow, like the details of a vision that exist only in the imagination. Avicenna writes that he does not know why the colors come about. See *Al-Shifā': La Physique* 55 (14).

38. He states that the material cause is rain, 48b.

39. Howard Kreisel, *Prophecy: The History of an Idea in Medieval Jewish Philosophy* (Dordrecht, London: Kluwer, 2001), 250.

40. Ibid., 255.

41. Avicenna also distinguishes prophetic knowledge from philosophers' knowledge by attributing it to a strength of intuition. See Fazlur Rahman, *Avicenna's Psychology*, English translation of *Kitāb al-Najāt*, book 2, chapter VI (London: Oxford University Press, 1952), 36. There is an examination of what Avicenna means by *ḥads* in Gutas, *Avicenna*, 159–176.

42. 3:1; M298 (29); P417; S429; A466 (7).

43. 3:1; M299 (1); P417; S429; A466 (8).

44. See section 7.1, above.

45. 417n. He follows a number of other commentators on this point. See S429n for references.

46. 3:6; M307 (10–11); P426; S438; A482 (12–13).

47. 2:45; M285 (17); P401; S413; A444 (7).

48. 2:35; M259 (10); P367; S382; A402 (9). Abrabanel mentions that there are two manuscript traditions, one of which uses "amphibolous" (*sippuk*) and the other of which uses "equivocal" (*šituf*), Maimonides, *More Nebuchim* 96a. Abrabanel argues that Maimonides must have used "equivocal," since that is more suited to his account. Given Maimonides' definition of amphiboly, Abrabanel appears to be wrong. However, his comment may well be influenced by the fact that Maimonides' use of the term *taškīk* is unusual. He uses it to express a use of words usually termed "equivocal." See section 5.3 above.

49. See Fox, *Interpreting Maimonides*, 77.

50. See Kreisel, *Prophecy*, 172–181 and 189–190 for the differences in Maimonides' earlier works, 230–239 and 247–248 for the differences as they are expressed in the *Guide*.

51. See Alvin Reines, "Maimonides' Concept of Mosaic Prophecy," *Hebrew Union College Annual* 40–41 (1969–1970): 327–329. He explains that Moses' prophecy is superior because it does not involve bodily faculties.

52. 3: Introduction; M297 (27); P416; S428; A464 (12).

53. The section of the *Guide* that is expressly dedicated to explaining prophecy is in the second part, from chapter 32.

54. 1: Introduction; M9 (26–27); P15; S19; A20 (19–20).

55. 3:2; M299 (6–7); P417; S429; A466 (12–13).

56. *Foundations*, 3:1.
57. 2:18; M210 (16); P301; S317; A327 (20–21). He also states that there must be either eighteen or more spheres. 1:72; M128 (3–4); P185; S196; A191 (15–17).
58. 2:9; M187 (5); P268; S284; A297 (1–2).
59. 2:9; M187 (10); P268; S285; A297 (7). R. P. Lorch, "The Astronomy of Jābir Ibn-Aflah," *Centaurus* 19 (1975): 90. Lorch mentions the refutation of the four-sphere theory but points out that it is unclear whether Maimonides had read the work or knew it only by hearsay.
60. See section 7.6.3 below.
61. 3:1; M298 (19–20); P417; S428; A465 (13–14).
62. 3:1; M298 (28); P417; S429; A466 (6).
63. 2:6; M184 (18); P265; S281; A293 (15). This is another meaning in addition to that given above, that "cherub" can refer to the imagination.
64. Benor, *Worship of the Heart*, 140. For an explanation of this position in Avicenna, see Michael Marmura, "Some Aspects of Avicenna's Theory of God's Knowledge of Particulars," *Journal of the American Oriental Society* 82 (1969): 311.
65. 3:2; M299 (9); P418; S429; A467 (1).
66. 2:10; M189 (19–23); P272; S288; A300 (11–15).
67. 3:2; M299 (25); P418; S430; A468 (3–4).
68. Rectilinear motion is discussed below.
69. 3:2; M300 (9–10); P419; S430; A468 (16–17).
70. 2:10; M189 (5–6); P271; S287; A299 (21–22).
71. 3:2; M299 (12); P418; S430; A467 (3).
72. See 7.3.3.
73. This is suggested by both Efodi and Šem Toḇ, 3:4a.
74. 1:43; M63 (24)–64 (2); P94; S97; A101 (6–11).
75. 1:49; M74 (12–14); P110; S112; A118 (3–5).
76. 1:49; M74 (14–15); P110; S112; A118 (5–6).
77. 1:49; M74 (20–22); P110; S112; A118 (11–13).
78. 2:10; M189 (2–4); P271; S287; A299 (17–19). See Maimonides' explanation there. In 2:4; M177 (18)–178 (19); P255–256; S270–271; A283 (21)–285 (8), he posits different causes for the motion of the sphere in the name of Aristotle: soul or nature, mental representation, intellect, and desire. It is possible that the desire can be considered equivalent to the causality of the separate intellect. Nevertheless, there is at least a shift in emphasis. On Crescas's and Šem Toḇ's interpretation, the final causes of the beasts' motions are indicated by Ezekiel's explanation that the wings and faces of the beasts are separated from above.
79. This point is clear from part of Maimonides' first argument for God's existence. See 2:1; M170 (17); P244; S260; A275 (10).
80. This particular objection is mentioned as part of the eighteenth.

81. See section 8.3 below for more on this.
82. He supports this with reference to a Talmudic story that appears in a slightly different form in the Talmud. Ibn Tibbon pointed out the change. See Klein-Braslavy, *Maimonides' Interpretation,* 188.
83. The point was drawn to the attention of modern scholars by Charles Touati in "Le Problème de l'Inerrance Prophetique dans la Théologie Juive du Moyen Age," *Revue de l'Histoire des Religions* 174 (1968): 180–181. It has also been discussed by Rosenberg in "On Biblical Exegesis," 145–147; and Harvey in "How to Begin to Study *The Guide of the Perplexed,* I, 1," *Da`at* 21 (1988); 21–23. Their views will be discussed below.
84. Maimonides, *More Nebuchim* 2:34b.
85. Objection 4.
86. Objection 20.
87. One other occasion is when he discusses the meaning of the beasts' wings. See above.
88. 2:9; M187 (16); P269; S285; A297 (13–14).
89. 2:22; M223 (20–21); P319; S333; A346 (11).
90. 3:7; M308 (2); P428; S439; A483 (11).
91. 3:2; M301 (10–13); P420; S431; A471 (1–4).
92. 3:4; M305 (1–6); P424; S435–436; A478 (3–9). Maimonides dedicates this chapter to a discussion of Jonathan's interpretation. He writes that it is acceptable but that he disagrees with it. Jonathan interprets the wheels as the heavens. Maimonides' disagreements do not affect the argument presented here.
93. 1:28; M40 (22–23); P60; S97; A66 (14–15).
94. Kafiḥ notes that it is a pointer toward 1:64 and 1:70.
95. Michelle Levine, "Maimonides' Philosophical Exegesis of the Nobles' Vision (Exodus 24): A Guide for the Pursuit of Knowledge," *Torah U-Madda Journal* 11 (2002–2003): 61–106.
96. Ibid., 70.
97. Ibid., 72–73. Levine connects prime matter to Ezekiel's vision. She connects it with the throne of glory, which will be discussed below.
98. 3:2; M301 (16–17); P420; S432; A471 (7).
99. 1:72; M127 (19); P184; S195; A191 (2–3).
100. 3:2; M301 (22–23); P420; S432; A471 (14).
101. 3:2; M301 (28)–302 (1); P421; S432; A472 (7).
102. 3:2; M302 (14–16); P421; S432; A473 (7–9).
103. For more on this issue, see section 8.4 below.
104. 3:3; M303 (25–27); P423; S434; A475 (15–16).
105. 2:10; M188 (20–21); P270; S286; A299 (5–7).
106. Narboni and Crescas relate this to the four faces. The faces may also indicate the four effects that the sphere has on the world, as well as being a

reference to the fact that they are all different in species. Maimonides states that there are four forces proceeding from the spheres toward the sublunar world. They influence the four levels of the soul, as well as the four elements. 2:10; M189 (15–17); P271; S288; A300 (8–10).

107. 3:7; M307 (27)–308 (16); P428; S439; A483 (8)–484 (11).
108. 2:22; M223 (17–18); P319; S333; A346 (7–8).
109. 3:2; M302 (23–25); P422; S433; A474 (1–4).
110. 3:7; M309 (10–12); P430; S440; A486 (5–7).
111. 3:7; M309 (2–3); P429; S440; 485 (11–12).
112. 3:7; M308 (9–10); P429; S439; A484 (5).
113. S439n.
114. Klein-Braslavy, *Maimonides' Interpretation*, 186.
115. See Amnon Shiloah, *The Epistle on Music of the Ikhwan Al-Safa* (Tel-Aviv: Tel Aviv University Press, 1978), 35.
116. 1:9; M23 (18–19); P34; S44; A40 (7–8).
117. David Blumenthal, "Ezekiel's Vision Seen through the Eyes of a Philosophic Mystic," *Proceedings of the American Academy of Religion* 47 (1979): 420.
118. It is stated that God's glory may be the "created light" in 1:64; M107 (25); P156; S165; A164 (14). The created light is what the prophets see, as stated in 1:21; M32 (16–17); P48; S57; A54 (6). It is particularly related to Moses' vision, which is essentially intellectual, as noted above.
119. 1:28; M40 (14); P61; S67; A66 (7).
120. Levine, "Maimonides' Philosophical Exegesis," 69.
121. Aristotle, *De Anima*, 429a20.
122. *Pitron Torah* (Jerusalem: Magnes, 1978), 106.
123. MT *Hilkot Tešuḇā* 8: 7.
124. If this is indeed Narboni's meaning, he may also have taken the idea from the Brethren of Purity, whom I will say more about in chapter 8. They talk about "the simple [things] that are there, delighting in the world of the spirits which is above the sphere, whose substances are more noble than those of the world of the spheres. This is the world of souls and the dwelling-place whose delight is entirely repose and perfume in the various degrees of paradise as God most high has pronounced in the Qur'ān." "Epistle on Music" 152 (22–23), Shiloah, *The Epistle on Music*, 37.

CHAPTER 8

1. See 1:17; M29 (7); P43; S51; A49 (5), where Maimonides states that ancient philosophers of other nations also presented their ideas in riddles (*yalġazūn*).
2. E.g., *Mishna Megilla*, 4:8.
3. Maimonides reiterates this time and again. He uses the parable of the *pardes* in 1:32.

4. Scholem makes this point in a number of places. See, for example, Gershom Scholem, *Jewish Gnosticism, Merkabah Mysticism, and Talmudic Tradition* (New York: Jewish Theological Seminary of America, 1965), 14.

5. The practice of weeping is one such example. See Moshe Idel, *Kabbalah: New Perspectives* (New Haven, Conn.: Yale University Press, 1988), 76–88.

6. See section 7.1 above.

7. MT, *Foundations*, 2:11.

8. Ibid., 4:10.

9. If Kraemer is right that astronomy is key to understanding the *Guide*'s secrets more so than other preparatory sciences, the reason would be that it is key to understanding these features of Ezekiel's vision. See Kraemer, "How (Not) to Read."

10. 2:8; M186 (7); P267; S283; A295 (16). See section 8.5.1 below for more on Pythagoras.

11. Chapters 2 and 3 of this book are examples of how Maimonides puts this into practice.

12. See section 7.1 above.

13. As argued above, the conclusion is also supported by certain verses in Ezekiel. See section 7.4.7 above. However, another possible interpretation is that Maimonides intends to explain what leads people to posit the music of the spheres in order to disassociate the idea from the Mosaic account of the cosmos. When describing the meaning of Genesis, through hints and allusions, Maimonides states that it teaches that the stars are situated within the sphere rather than on its surface, "as the vulgar imagine." 2:30; M247 (21–23); P352; S365; A383 (7–9). For an explanation of Maimonides' understanding of this part of the creation story, see Klein-Braslavy, *Maimonides' Interpretation of the Story*, 187. However, were that the only point of the chapter, there would be no need to write it in a "hidden" manner.

14. Rosenberg, "On Biblical Exegesis," 146–151.

15. Ibid., 150. On the notion of science's progress in Maimonides, see Kellner, *Maimonides on the Decline*, 76–78.

16. 1:34; M50 (23–25); P75; S79; A80 (18–19).

17. "How to Begin," 22.

18. 3:5; M306 (16–22); P426; S437; A481 (6–11).

19. 3:5; M306 (10); P426; S437; A480 (15).

20. Šem Toḇ mentions this difficulty but thinks that Maimonides successfully avoids inconsistency, Maimonides, *More Nebuchim* 3:9b. He argues that knowledge of the sublunar sphere is preceded by knowledge of mathematics, which is involved in study of the superlunar spheres. Hence, in this sense, the beasts can be seen to be preparatory to the study of the wheels.

21. Harvey points out that there are others who Maimonides believes were mistaken for the same reason: the nobles of Israel, Elisha ben Abuyah (Aḥer), and Aristotle. See "How to Begin," 22.

22. Harvey argues that another reason Maimonides attributes mistakes to Ezekiel is that he wishes to show that scripture should not be used as a source for scientific knowledge. Ibid., 22.

23. He would not be the only Jewish thinker to do so. See, for example, Horovitz, *Der Mikrokosmos der Josef Ibn Ṣaddiḳ* (Breslau: Schatzky, 1903), vi–vii. Ibn Ṣaddiq will be considered below when I argue that those he was influenced by are in the background of this section of the *Guide*.

24. For example, Joel Kraemer explains Maimonides' multiple uses of the word *šarīʿa* in 2:40 in "Naturalism and Universalism," 52.

25. If, however, this is not the case, and there is no distinction to be made between two sets of philosophers here, it does not affect my argument as a whole. The important point is that Maimonides disagrees with the second statement made by the philosophers, not whether the first is considered to be true or false.

26. 2:10; M187 (29–30)–188 (1); P269; S286; A298 (4–6).

27. 1:72; M128 (21–22); P186; S196; A192 (9–11).

28. 1:72; M129 (13–16); P186–187; S197; A193 (6–9).

29. 2:10; M188 (18–21); P270; S286; A299 (3–7). Falaquera quotes Avicenna's argument that there are scientists who argue that the heat of the element fire derives from the motion of the sphere. However, in Falaquera's opinion, that is an incorrect doctrine. *Moreh ha-Moreh* [Heb.], ed. Yair Shiffman (Jerusalem: Graphit, 2001), 250 (10–18). Falaquera was influenced by the Iḥwān, so his interpretation of Maimonides on this point may well be affected by their beliefs.

30. Contrast Gad Freudenthal, who argues that positing the connections in question even in a nine-sphere system is a logical consequence of the connections between the sun and the moon. "Maimonides' Stance on Astrology in Context: Cosmology, Physics, Medicine, and Providence," in *Moses Maimonides*, ed. Fred Rosner and Samuel S. Kottek (Northvale, N.J.: Aronson, 1993), 78.

31. See section 7.1 above.

32. 2:2; M176 (3–8); P253; S268; A282 (8–13).

33. 1:72; M129 (20–21); P187; S198; A193 (13–14).

34. 2:9; M187 (11); P268; S285; A297 (8). See Paul Lettinck, *Aristotle's Meteorology and Its Reception in the Arab World with an Edition and Translation of Ibn Suwar's Treatise on Meteorological Phenomena and of Ibn Bājja's Commentary on the Meteorology* (Leiden: Brill, 1999).

35. Otto Neugebauer, "The Astronomy of Maimonides and Its Sources," *Hebrew Union College Annual* 2 (1949), 334.

36. 2:9; M187 (14); P269; S285; A297 (10–11).

37. 2:24; M228 (9–10); P326; S339; A352 (21–22). For the reference in Ibn Bāǧǧa, see Lettinck, *Aristotle's Meteorology*, 399.

38. Ibid., 394–397.

39. Ibid., 401.
40. When explaining why astrological notions are unacceptable, Langermann objects to the notion that the sun's heat is what causes heat in fire, because the sun is not thought to be hotter than any of the other stars. However, if the cause of motion is supposed to be illumination rather than heat, the problem does not arise, since the sun is the brightest of stars. See Y. Tzvi Langermann, "Some Issues relating to Astronomy in the Thought of Maimonides" [Heb.], *Da'at* 37 (1996): 112.
41. For an account of the sublunar waters according to Aristotle and later commentators, see Lettinck, *Aristotle's Meteorology*, 120–155.
42. For an account of al-Kindī's view, see Adamson, *Al-Kindī*, 181–189. As Adamson explains, Kindī actually presents two different theories in different works. His later view is closer to the four-sphere theory.
43. For details of this influence, see Yves Marquet, "Sabeens et Ihwan al-Safa'," *Studia Islamica* 24 (1966): 35–109; 25 (1966): 77–109.
44. "Risāla fī Kayafiyyat Aḥwāl al-Rūḥaniyyīn" (Epistle XLIX), in *Rasā'il Ikhwān al-Ṣafā' wa Khillān al-Wafā*, ed. Buṭruṣ al-Bustānī (Beirut: Dār Ṣadir, 1957), 4:223.
45. Sarah Stroumsa suggests that he is mentioned because ibn Tibbon probably asked about the works with which he was familiar in a previous letter to Maimonides. "Note on Maimonides' Attitude to Joseph Ibn Ṣaddiq," *Jerusalem Studies in Jewish Thought* 9 (1990): 33.
46. Another manuscript version has "those who believe in attributes." This confusion may well be down to scribal error caused by the similarity between the words *ṣafa'* and *ṣifāt* ("attributes"). See Stroumsa, "Note on Maimonides' Attitude," 35.
47. *Letters of Maimonides*, trans. and ed. Leon Stitskin (New York: Yeshiva University Press, 1977), 135. Kraemer also takes the reference to be positive in "Moses Maimonides," 13.
48. Pines, "Translator's Introduction," lx.
49. Stroumsa, "Note on Maimonides' Attitude," 37.
50. Ibid., 38.
51. For a list of the pillars, see Ilai Alon, "Socrates in Arabic Philosophy," in *A Companion to Socrates*, ed. Sara Ahbel-Rappe and Rachana Kamtekar (Chichester, U.K.: Wiley-Blackwell, 2009), 324. Y. Tzvi Langermann notes how strange Maimonides' playing with the number four is in "Maimonides' Repudiation of Astrology," *Maimonidean Studies* 2 (1991): 144–145. Langermann describes "Maimonides' self-proclaimed discovery of an additional and highly significant correspondence" as "striking." He also comments on the "striking similarity" of some of the language that Maimonides uses in this section and that of the Iḫwān al-Ṣafa'. He argues that Maimonides avoids the problems arising from an association with the ideas of the Brethren of Purity while using the same language.

52. Ian Richard Netton, *Muslim Neoplatonists: An Introduction to the Thought of the Brethren of Purity (Ikhwān al-Ṣafā')* (London: Allen and Unwin, 1982), 11.

53. 2:10; M188 (2–3); P269; S286; A298 (7–8).

54. For an account of how the music of the spheres may be connected with astrology, a point discussed below, see N. M. Swerdlow, "Ptolemy's Harmonics and the Tones of the Universe in the Canobic Inscription," *Studies in the History of the Exact Sciences*, ed. Charles Burnett et al. (Leiden: Brill, 2004).

55. 269 n. 3.

56. Freudenthal, "Maimonides' Stance," 80.

57. CM *'Aḇodah Zarah*, 4:7.

58. Dov Schwarz suggests that one of the imperfect philosophers may be Abraham ibn Ezra, who wrote much about astrology. *Astral Magic in Medieval Jewish Thought* [Heb.] (Tel Aviv: Aḥva, 1999), 104. Ibn Ezra was also influenced by the Brethren of Purity.

59. The Cairo Genizah contains many amulets and incantations that can easily be dated to around Maimonides' time. See Gideon Bohak, "Greek, Coptic, and Jewish Magic in the Cairo Genizah," *Bulletin of the American Society of Papyrologists* 36 (1999): 27–44. There is also a chapter on Jewish astrology in Joshua Trachtenberg, *Jewish Magic and Superstition: A Study in Folk Religion* (New York: Atheneum, 1979), 249–259.

60. See Leon Stitskin, "Maimonides' Unbending Opposition to Astrology," *Tradition* 13 (1972): 131–142. Some articles raising difficulties for this view will be dealt with below.

61. Stern, *Problems and Parables*, 119. For an account of how Maimonides explains the historical rise of idolatry, see David Hartman, *Torah and Philosophic Quest* (Philadelphia: Jewish Publication Society of America, 1977), 54–57.

62. Stern, *Problems and Parables*, 111.

63. Freudenthal, "Maimonides' Stance," 77.

64. Ibid., 79.

65. Ibid., 81.

66. This is a strategy that Maimonides attributes to the sages. See Marc Shapiro, "Maimonidean Halachah and Superstition," *Maimonidean Studies* 4 (2000), 66.

67. Maimonides uses the term *talaṭṭuf* to refer to this idea. In the Qur'ān, different words are used to describe similar ideas.

68. Fathalla Kholeif, *A Study on Fakhr al-Dīn Al-Rāzī and His Controversies in Transoxiana* (Beirut: Dar El-Machreq, 1966), 149. On some similarities between Maimonides and Rāzī, see Langermann, "Criticism of Authority in the Writings of Moses Maimonides and Fakhr al-Din al-Razi," *Early Science and Medicine* 7 (2002): 255–274.

69. Langermann, "Maimonides' Repudiation," 147.
70. Freudenthal, "Maimonides' Stance," 87.
71. The account of the beginning should be interpreted closer to the lines of Maimonides' description of the cosmos in part one of the *Guide*. See, for example, Maimonides' comment on the elements' motions when explaining the Mosaic version in 2:30; M249 (3–6); P354; S367; A385 (9–11). Sara Klein-Braslavy offers an extensive interpretation of Maimonides' exegesis in *Maimonides' Interpretation of the Story*, 63–266. She also considers other aspects of the account in *Maimonides' Interpretation of the Adam Stories in Genesis: A Study in Maimonides' Anthropology* [Heb.] (Jerusalem: Daf-Ḥen, 1986).
72. Hartman, *Torah and Philosophic Quest*, 57–59.
73. See chapter 1, n. 44, above.
74. This question is raised by Ralph Lerner in "Maimonides' Letter on Astrology," *History of Religions* 8 (1968): 145. Marc Shapiro writes that he does not know why Maimonides omits the fourth source of authority; see Shapiro, "Maimonidean Halachah," 67n. Herbert Davidson questions the authenticity of Maimonides' authorship of this epistle in *Moses Maimonides*, 494–496.
75. See section 3.3 above.
76. There is scholarly disagreement over whether Maimonides believed that an explanation is ultimately possible. I agree with Langermann's view that he considered scientific knowledge to be advancing and that he was not certain that a solution will never be found. See Y. Tzvi Langermann, "My Truest Perplexities," *Aleph* 8 (2008): 301–317. The whole of that issue of *Aleph* is dedicated to the question, and alternative views are offered there.
77. 2:19; M217 (14–17); P311; S325; A337 (15–18).
78. "Epistle on Music," chapter 13, 168 (8–9). Shiloah, *The Epistle on Music*, 56.
79. BT *Pesaḥim*, 94b.
80. 3:13; M328 (17–18); P455; S465; A515 (7–8).
81. 3:13; M326 (18–23); P452; S463; A512 (7–12).
82. Langermann, "Maimonides' Repudiation," 145.

CHAPTER 9

1. 3:51; M454 (19); P618; S655; A718 (7).
2. It may be that Maimonides never thought such a state could be actualized, but he certainly thought that humans ought to consider it their goal. See Aviezer Ravitsky, "'To the Utmost of Human Capacity': Maimonides on the Days of the Messiah," in *Perspectives on Maimonides: Philosophical and Historical Studies*, ed. Kraemer (Oxford: Oxford University Press, 1991), 221–256.

3. 3:51; M463 (14–17); P628; S666; A732 (3–6).

4. See section 1.3.4, above.

5. MT Laws of the *Mezuzah*, 6:13.

6. 1:54; M84 (2–3); P123; S130; A131 (1–2).

7. 1:1; M15 (15); P23; S31; A28 (9).

8. 1:34; M52 (6–9); P77; S80; A82 (15–18).

9. For Pines's argument, see "The Limitations of Human Knowledge."

10. 3:53; M466 (5); P632; S668; A736 (9).

11. For two examples, see Langermann, "Some Issues relating to Astronomy," 16; and Herbert Davidson, "Maimonides on Metaphysical Knowledge," *Maimonidean Studies* 3 (1992–1993): 49–103. Thérèse-Anne Druart dismisses Pines's claims about Alfarabi in "Al-Farabi and Emanationism," in *Studies in Medieval Philosophy*, ed. John F. Wippel (Washington: Catholic University of America Press, 1987), 23 n. 5.

12. Stern agrees that Maimonides thinks that God's existence can be demonstrated but that humans cannot know anything about God's nature. See Stern, "Maimonides' Demonstrations." Even this is rejected by Warren Zev Harvey in "Maimonides' First Commandment, Physics and Doubt," in *Hazon Nahum: Studies in Jewish Law, Thought and History*, ed. Yaakov Elman and Jeffrey S. Gurock (New York: Yeshiva University Press, 1997).

13. See Josef Stern, "Maimonides' Epistemology," in *The Cambridge Companion to Maimonides*, ed. Kenneth Seeskin (Cambridge, U.K.: Cambridge University Press, 2005), esp. 127–129.

14. David Shatz, "Maimonides' Moral Theory," *in The Cambridge Companion to Maimonides*, ed. Kenneth Seeskin (Cambridge, U.K.: Cambridge University Press, 2005), 186.

15. Maimonides' position is not unusual. Al-Kindī also writes only of making one's actions like God's. Adamson, *Al-Kindī*, 157. This does not render striving for intellectual perfection worthless or any less of an aim. For Kindī, it remains the case that one must perfect the intellect to become near to God.

BIBLIOGRAPHY

Acar, Rahim. *Talking about God and Talking about Creation: Avicenna's and Thomas Aquinas' Positions.* Leiden: Brill, 2005.

Adamson, Peter. *Al-Kindī.* New York: Oxford University Press, 2007.

——. "On Knowledge of Particulars." *Proceedings of the Aristotelian Society* 105 (2005): 273–294.

Alfarabi. *Book of Letters*, Arabic text, ed. Muhsin Mahdi. Beirut: Dar el-Mashreq, 1969.

Alon, Ilai. "Socrates in Arabic Philosophy." In *A Companion to Socrates,* ed. Sara Ahbel-Rappe and Rachana Kamtekar, 317–336. Chichester, U.K.: Wiley-Blackwell, 2009.

Altmann, Alexander. "Essence and Existence in Maimonides." In *Maimonides: A Collection of Critical Essays,* ed. Joseph A. Buijs, 148–165. Notre Dame, Ind.: University of Notre Dame Press, 1988.

——. "Maimonides and Thomas Aquinas: Natural or Divine Prophecy?" *AJS Review* 3 (1978): 1–19.

——. *Moses Mendelssohn: A Biographical Study.* London: Routledge and Kegan Paul, 1973.

Aquinas. *Summa Theologiæ Volume 2: Existence and Nature of God,* trans. Timothy McDermott. Cambridge, U.K.: Cambridge University Press, 2006.

——. *Summa Theologiæ Volume 3: Knowing and Naming God,* ed. Herbert McCabe (Cambridge, U.K.: Cambridge University Press, 2006).

Aristotle. *On the Soul, Parva Naturalia, On Breath,* with an English translation by W. S. Hett. Cambridge, Mass.: Harvard University Press, 1964.

——. *Posterior Analytics and Topica.* Translated by Hugh Tredennick and E. S. Forster. Cambridge, Mass.: Harvard University Press, 1966.

Averroes. *The Book of the Decisive Treatise and Epistle Dedicatory,* translated with introduction and notes by Charles Butterworth. Provo, Utah: Brigham Young University Press, 2001.

———. *The Incoherence of the Incoherence,* translated with an introduction and notes by Simon van den Bergh. London: Luzac, 1954.

———. *Tafsīr Mā Ba'd Aṭ-Ṭabī'at,* vol. 1. Beirut: Imprimerie Catholique, 1938.

Avicenna. *Al-Shifā': La Physique V—Les Métaux et la Météorologie,* edited by Ivrahim Madkour. Cairo: Organisation Générale des Imprimeries Gouvernementales, 1964.

———. *The Metaphysics of* The Healing, *trans.* Michael E. Marmura. Provo, Utah: Brigham Young University Press, 2005.

Bakan, David. *Maimonides on Prophecy: A Commentary on Selected Chapters of the Guide of the Perplexed.* Northvale, N.J.: Aronson, 1991.

Ben Moses, Solomon. Commentary on Maimonides' Guide for the Perplexed. Ms. CUL Add. 672.

Benor, Ehud. "Meaning and Reference in Maimonides' Negative Theology." *Harvard Theological Review* 88 (1995): 339–360.

———. *Worship of the Heart: A Study of Maimonides' Philosophy of Religion.* Albany: State University of New York Press, 1995.

Berger, David. "How Did Naḥmanides Propose to Resolve the Maimonidean Controversy?" In *Me'ah She'arim: Studies in Medieval Jewish Spiritual Life,* ed. E. Fleischer et al., 135–146. Jerusalem: Magnes, 2001.

Berman, Lawrence. "Maimonides, the Disciple of Alfarabi." *Israel Oriental Studies* 4 (1974): 154–178.

Black, Deborah. *Logic and Aristotle's Rhetoric and Poetics in Medieval Arabic Philosophy.* Leiden: Brill, 1990.

Blumenthal, David. "Ezekiel's Vision Seen through the Eyes of a Philosophic Mystic." *Proceedings of the American Academy of Religion* 47 (1979): 417–427.

———. "Maimonides: Prayer, Worship, and Mysticism." In *Approaches to Judaism in Medieval Times,* vol. 3, ed. David Blumenthal, 1–16 . Atlanta: Scholars, 1988.

Bohak, Gideon. "Greek, Coptic, and Jewish Magic in the Cairo Genizah." *Bulletin of the American Society of Papyrologists* 36 (1999): 27–44.

Brethren of Purity. *Rasā'il Ikhwān al-Ṣafā' wa-Khillān al-Wafā,* 4 vols., ed. Buṭruṣ al-Bustānī. Beirut: Dār Ṣadir, 1957.

Broadie, Alexander. "Maimonides and Divine Knowledge." In *Of Scholars, Savants, and Their Texts: Studies in Philosophy and Religious Thought,* ed. Ruth Link-Salinger, 47–55. New York: Peter Lang, 1989.

Burrell, David. *Aquinas: God and Action.* London: Routledge and Kegan Paul, 1979.

Cohen, Martin. "Reflections on the Text and Context of the Disputation of Barcelona." *Hebrew Union College Annual* 35 (1964): 157–192.

Crescas, Ḥasdai. *Or Hashem.* Jerusalem: Sifre Ramot, 1990.

Daiber, Hans. "Das Fārābī-Bild des Maimonides: Ideentransfer als hermeneutischer Weg zu Maimonides' Philosophie." In *The Trias of Maimonides/Die Trias des Maimonides,* ed. Georges Tamer, 119–209. Berlin: Walter de Gruyter, 2005.

Davidson, Herbert. *Alfarabi, Avicenna, and Averroes on Intellect: Their Cosmologies, Theories of Active Intellect, and Theories of Human Intellect.* New York: Oxford University Press, 1992.

———. "Maimonides on Metaphysical Knowledge." *Maimonidean Studies* 3 (1992–1993): 49–103.

———. "Maimonides' Secret Position on Creation." In *Studies in Medieval Jewish History and Literature,* ed. Isadore Twersky, 16–40. Cambridge, Mass: Harvard University Press, 1979.

———. *Moses Maimonides: The Man and His Works.* Oxford: Oxford University Press, 2004.

Diamond, James Arthur. *Maimonides and the Hermeneutics of Concealment: Deciphering Scripture and Midrash in the Guide of the Perplexed.* Albany: State University of New York Press, 2002.

Druart, Thérèse-Anne. "Al-Farabi and Emanationism." In *Studies in Medieval Philosophy,* ed. John F. Wippel, 23–43. Washington: Catholic University of America Press, 1987.

Dutton, Blake. "Al-Ghazālī on Possibility and the Critique of Causality." *Medieval Philosophy and Theology* 10 (2001): 23–46.

Eisen, Robert. *The Book of Job in Medieval Jewish Philosophy.* New York: Oxford University Press, 2004.

Even-Chen, Alexander. "God's Positive Attributes in Maimonides' Philosophy" [Heb.]. *Da'at* 63 (2008): 19–45.

Falaquera, Shem-Tob ibn. *Moreh ha-Moreh* [Heb.], ed. Yair Shiffman. Jerusalem: Graphit, 2001.

Faur, Jose. *Homo Mysticus: A Guide to Maimonides' Guide for the Perplexed.* Syracuse, N.Y.: Syracuse University Press, 1998.

Feldman, Seymour. "A Scholastic Misinterpretation of Maimonides' Doctrine of Divine Attributes." *Journal of Jewish Studies* 20 (1968): 23–39.

Fox, Marvin. *Interpreting Maimonides: Studies in Methodology, Metaphysics, and Moral Philosophy.* Chicago: University of Chicago Press, 1990.

Frank, Daniel. *Search Scripture Well: Karaite Exegesis and the Origins of the Jewish Bible Commentary in the Islamic East.* Leiden: Brill, 2004.

Frank, Richard. "Knowledge and *Taqlīd.*" *Journal of the American Oriental Society* 109 (1989): 37–68.

———. "The Non-Existent and the Possible in Classical Ash'arite Teaching." *Mideo* 24 (2000): 1–37.

Freudenthal, Gad. "Maimonides' Stance on Astrology in Context: Cosmology, Physics, Medicine, and Providence." In *Moses Maimonides: Physician, Scientist, and Philosophy,* ed. Fred Rosner and Samuel S. Kottek, 77–90. Northvale, N.J.: Aronson, 1993.

Galen. *Selected Works,* translated by Peter Singer. Oxford: Oxford University Press, 1997.

Galston, Miriam. "Al-Fārābī on Aristotle's Theory of Demonstration." In *Islamic Philosophy and Mysticism*, ed. Parviz Morewedge, 23–34. New York: Caravan, 1981.

———. "The Purpose of the Law according to Maimonides." *Jewish Quarterly Review* 69 (1978): 27–51.

al-Ġazālī. *Faḍā'iḥ al-Bāṭiniyya*. Beirut: Al-Maktabah al-'Aṣri'yah, 2000.

———. *The Incoherence of the Philosophers*, Arabic text and English translation by Michael Marmura. Provo, Utah: Brigham Young University Press, 2000.

Geach, Peter. *God and the Soul*. London: Routledge and Kegan Paul, 1969.

Gluck, Andrew. "Maimonides' Arguments for Creation 'Ex Nihilo' in the 'Guide of the Perplexed.'" *Medieval Philosophy and Theology* 7 (1998): 221–254.

Gordon, Peter Eli. "The Erotics of Negative Theology." *Jewish Studies Quarterly* 2 (1995): 1–38.

Gottstein, Alon Goshen. "Four Entered Paradise Revisited." *Harvard Theological Review* 88 (1995): 69–133.

Griffel, Frank. *Al-Ghazālī's Philosophical Theology*. New York: Oxford University Press, 2009.

Gutas, Dimitri. *Avicenna and the Aristotelian Tradition: Introduction to Reading Avicenna's Philosophical Works*. Leiden: Brill, 1988.

———. "The Study of Arabic Philosophy in the Twentieth Century." *British Journal of Middle Eastern Studies* 29 (2002): 5–25.

Halbertal, Moshe, and Avishai Margalit. *Idolatry*, translated by Naomi Goldblum. Cambridge, Mass.: Harvard University Press, 1992.

Halevi, Judah. *Kitāb al-Radd wa-'l-Dalīl fī'l-Dīn al-Dhalīl*, ed. David Baneth. Jerusalem: Magnes, 1977.

Halkin, Abraham, and David Hartman. *Epistles of Maimonides: Crisis and Leadership*. Philadelphia: Jewish Publication Society, 1993.

Hartman, David. *Torah and Philosophic Quest*. Philadelphia: Jewish Publication Society of America, 1977.

Harvey, Steven. "Why Did Fourteenth Century Jews Turn to al-Ghazali's Account of Natural Science?" *Jewish Quarterly Review* 91 (2001): 359–376.

Harvey, Warren Zev. "'Great Is the Power': On Guide of the Perplexed I 46" [Heb.]. *Da'at* 37 (1996): 53–61.

———. "How Leo Strauss Straightjacketed Research on the *Guide* in the Twentieth Century" [Heb.]. *Iyyun* 50 (2001): 387–396.

———. "How to Begin to Study *The Guide of the Perplexed*, I, 1" [Heb.] *Da'at* 21 (1988): 5–23.

———. "Maimonides' First Commandment, Physics and Doubt." In *Hazon Nahum: Studies in Jewish Law, Thought and History*, ed. Yaakov Elman and Jeffrey S. Gurock, 149–162. New York: Yeshiva University Press, 1997.

———. "The Mishneh Torah as a Key to the Secrets of the *Guide*." In *Me'ah She'arim: Studies in Medieval Jewish Spiritual Life*, ed. E. Fleischer et al., 11–28. Jerusalem: Magnes, 2001.

———. "Nuriel's Method for Deciphering the Secrets of the *Guide*" [Heb.]. *Da'at* 32–33 (1994): 67–71.

———. "Why Maimonides Was Not a Mutakallim." In *Perpectives on Maimonides*, ed. Joel Kraemer, 104–114. Oxford: Oxford University Press, 1991.

Hayoun, Maurice-Ruben. "Moses Maimonides und Muhammad al-Tabrisi." *Trumah* 5 (1996): 201–245.

Horovitz, Saul. *Der Mikrokosmos des Josef Ibn Ṣaddiḳ.* Breslau: Schatzky, 1903.

Husik, Isaac. *A History of Mediaeval Jewish Philosophy.* New York: Atheneum, 1974 [1916].

Hyman, Arthur. "Demonstrative, Dialectical and Sophistic Arguments." In *Moses Maimonides and His Time,* ed. Eric L. Ormsby, 35–51. Washington: Catholic University of America Press, 1989.

———. "From What Is One and Simple Only What Is One and Simple Can Come to Be." In *Neoplatonism and Jewish Thought,* ed. Lenn E. Goodman, 111–135. Albany: State University of New York Press, 1991.

Idel, Moshe. *Kabbalah: New Perspectives.* New Haven, Conn.: Yale University Press, 1988.

———. "Maimonides' 'Guide of the Perplexed' and the Kabbalah." *Jewish History* 18 (2004): 197–226.

İskenderoğlu, Muammer. *Fakhr al-Dīn al-Rāzī and Thomas Aquinas on the Question of the Eternity of the World* (Leiden: Brill, 2002).

Ivry, Alfred. "Maimonides on Creation" [Heb.]. *Jerusalem Studies in Jewish Thought* 9 (1990): 115–137.

———. "Providence, Divine Omniscience, and Possibility: The Case of Maimonides." In *Maimonides: A Collection of Critical Essays,* ed. Joseph A. Buijs, 175–191. Notre Dame, Ind.: University of Notre Dame Press, 1988.

Jacobs, Louis. *Jewish Ethics, Philosophy and Mysticism.* New York: Behrman House, 1969.

Jospe, Raphael. *Torah and Sophia: The Life and Thought of Shem Tov ibn Falaquera.* Cincinnati: Hebrew Union College Press, 1988.

Kaplan, Lawrence. "Maimonides on the Miraculous Element in Prophecy." *Harvard Theological Review* 70 (1977): 233–256.

Kasher, Hannah. "Biblical Miracles and the Universality of Natural Laws: Maimonides' Three Methods of Harmonization." *Journal of Jewish Thought and Philosophy* 8 (1998): 25–52.

———. "Self-Cognizing Intellect and Negative Attributes in Maimonides' Theology." *Harvard Theological Review* 87 (1994): 461–472.

Kellner, Menachem. "The Conception of the Torah as a Deductive Science in Medieval Jewish Thought." *Revue des Etudes Juives* 146 (1987): 265–279.

———. *Dogma in Medieval Jewish Thought: From Maimonides to Abravanel.* Oxford: Oxford University Press, 1986.

———. "The Literary Character of the Mishneh Torah: On the Art of Writing in Maimonides' Halakhic Works." In *Me'ah She'arim: Studies in Medieval Jewish Spiritual Life,* ed. E. Fleischer et al., 29–45. Jerusalem: Magnes, 2001.

——— . *Maimonides' Confrontation with Mysticism.* Oxford: Littman Library of Jewish Civilization, 2006.

——— . "Maimonides' Thirteen Principles and the Structure of the 'Guide of the Perplexed.'" *Journal of the History of Philosophy* 20 (1982): 76–84.

——— . *Maimonides on the Decline of the Generations and the Nature of Rabbinic Authority.* Albany: State University of New York Press, 1996.

——— . *Maimonides on Human Perfection.* Atlanta: Scholars Press, 1990.

——— . *Maimonides on Judaism and the Jewish People.* Albany: State University of New York Press, 1991.

Kholeif, Fathalla. *A Study on Fakhr al-Dīn Al-Rāzī and His Controversies in Transoxiana.* Beirut: Dar El-Machreq, 1966.

Klein-Braslavy, Sara. "King Solomon and Metaphysical Esotericism in Maimonides." *Maimonidean Studies* 1 (1990): 57–86.

——— . *Maimonides' Interpretation of the Adam Stories in Genesis: A Study in Maimonides' Anthropology* [Heb.]. Jerusalem: Daf-Ḥen, 1986.

——— . *Maimonides' Interpretation of the Story of Creation* [Heb.]. Jerusalem: Aḥvah, 1978.

Knuuttila, Simo. *Modalities in Medieval Philosophy.* London: Routledge, 1993.

Kosman, Aryeh. "Metaphysics' Λ9: Divine Thought." In *Aristotle's Metaphysics Lambda: Symposium Aristotelicum,* ed. Michael Frede and David Charles, 307–326. Oxford: Oxford University Press, 2000.

Kraemer, Joel. "How (Not) to Read the Guide of the Perplexed." *Jerusalem Studies in Arabic and Islam* 32 (2006): 350–409.

——— . *Maimonides: The Life and World of One of Civilization's Greatest Minds.* New York: Doubleday, 2008.

——— . "Maimonides' Use of (Aristotelian) Dialectic." In *Maimonides and the Sciences,* ed. Robert S. Cohen and Hillel Levine, 111–130. Dordrecht: Kluwer Academic, 2000.

——— . "The Medieval Arabic Enlightenment." In *The Cambridge Companion to Leo Strauss,* ed. Steven B. Smith, 137–170. Cambridge, U.K.: Cambridge University Press, 2009.

——— . "Moses Maimonides: An Intellectual Portrait." In *The Cambridge Companion to Maimonides,* ed. Kenneth Seeskin, 10–57. Cambridge, U.K.: Cambridge University Press, 2005.

——— . "Naturalism and Universalism in Maimonides' Political and Religious Thought." In *Me'ah She'arim: Studies in Medieval Jewish Spiritual Life,* ed. E. Fleischer et al., 47–81. Jerusalem: Magnes, 2001.

——— . "On the Philosophic Sciences in Maimonides' Treatise on the Art of Logic." In *Perspectives on Maimonides: Philosophical and Historical Studies,* ed. Joel Kraemer, 77–104. Oxford: Oxford University Press, 1991.

Kravitz, Leonard. *The Hidden Doctrine of Maimonides' Guide for the Perplexed: Philosophical and Religious God-language in Tension.* Lewiston: Mellen, 1988.

Kreisel, Howard. *Prophecy: The History of an Idea in Medieval Jewish Philosophy.* Dordrecht, London: Kluwer, 2001.

——. *Maimonides' Political Thought: Studies in Ethics, Law and the Human Ideal.* Albany: State University of New York Press, 1999.

——. "The Place of Man on the Hierarchy of Existence in the Philosophy of Ibn Gabirol and Maimonides." In *Alei Shefer: Studies in the Literature of Jewish Thought,* ed. M. Ḥallamish, 95–107. Ramat-Gan: Bar-Ilan University Press, 1990.

Kretzmann, Norman, and Eleonore Stump. "Eternity." *Journal of Philosophy* 78 (1981): 429–458.

Langermann, Y. Tzvi. "Criticism of Authority in the Writings of Moses Maimonides and Fakhr al-Din al-Razi." *Early Science and Medicine* 7 (2002): 255–274.

——. "Maimonides and Miracles: The Growth of a (Dis)belief." *Jewish History* 18 (2004): 147–172.

——. "Maimonides' Repudiation of Astrology." *Maimonidean Studies* 2 (1991): 123–158.

——. "My Truest Perplexities." *Aleph* 8 (2008): 301–317.

——. "Some Issues relating to Astronomy in the Thought of Moses Maimonides" [Heb.]. *Da'at* 37 (1996): 107–118.

——. *Yemenite Midrash: Philosophical Commentaries on the Torah.* San Francisco: Harper Collins, 1996.

Lasker, Daniel. "The Interpretation of Maimonides—Past and Present" [Heb.]. *Alei Sefer* 19 (2001): 209–213.

Leaman, Oliver. *Evil and Suffering in Medieval Jewish Philosophy.* Cambridge, U.K.: Cambridge University Press, 1995.

——. *Moses Maimonides.* London: Routledge, 1990.

Lerner, Ralph. "Maimonides' Letter on Astrology." *History of Religions* 8 (1968): 143–158.

Lettinck, Paul. *Aristotle's Meteorology and Its Reception in the Arab World with an Edition and Translation of Ibn Suwar's Treatise on Meteorological Phenomena and of Ibn Bājja's Commentary on the Meteorology.* Leiden: Brill, 1999.

Levine, Michelle. "Maimonides' Philosophical Exegesis of the Nobles' Vision (Exodus 24): A Guide for the Pursuit of Knowledge." *Torah U-Madda Journal* 11 (2002–2003): 61–106.

Lobel, Diana. "'Silence Is Praise to You': Maimonides on Negative Theology, Looseness of Expression, and Religious Experience." *American Catholic Philosophical Quarterly* 76 (2002): 25–49.

Lorberbaum, Yair. "Changes in Maimonides' Approach to Aggadah" [Heb.]. *Tarbiẓ* 78 (2008): 81–122.

——. "The Men of Knowledge and the Sages Are Drawn, as It Were, toward This Purpose by the Divine Will (*The Guide of the Perplexed,* Introduction): On Maimonides' Conception of Parables" [Heb.]. *Tarbiẓ* 71 (2001): 87–132.

———. "On Contradictions, Rationality, Dialectics, and Esotericism in Maimonides's *Guide of the Perplexed.*" *Review of Metaphysics* 55 (2002): 711–750.

Lorch, R. P. "The Astronomy of Jābir Ibn-Aflah." *Centaurus* 19 (1975): 85–107.

Maimonides. *Dalālat al-Ḥā'irīn,* ed. Joel Kraemer and Salomon Munk. Jerusalem: Azrieli, 1929.

———. *Delâletü'l-Hâirîn: Filozof Mûsâ ibn Meymûn el-Kurtubî,* ed. Hüseyin Atay. Ankara: Ankara University Divinity Faculty, 1974.

———. *The Guide of the Perplexed,* translated by Shlomo Pines. Chicago: Chicago University Press, 1963.

———. *The Guide of the Perplexed,* 2 vols., Hebrew translation from the Arabic, with annotations, appendices, and indices by Michael Schwarz. Tel Aviv: Tel Aviv University Press, 2002.

———. *Les Guides des Égarés,* 3 vols., translated by Salomon Munk. Paris: A. Franck, 1856–1866.

———. *Letters of Maimonides,* trans. and ed. Leon Stitskin. New York: Yeshiva University Press, 1977.

———. *Mishnah with Commentary by Maimonides,* Arabic text with Hebrew translation by Yosef Kafiḥ, 7 vols. (Jerusalem: Mossad Harav Kook, 1963–1968).

———. *Moreh Ha-nebukim,* Arabic text with Hebrew translation by Yosef Kafiḥ, 3 vols. Jerusalem: Mossad Harav Kook, 1972.

———. *More Nebuchim (Doctor Perplexorum),* 2 vols., *ex versione Samuelis Tibbonidae cum commentariis Ephodaei, Schemtob, Ibn Crescas, nec non Don Isaci Abravanel adjectis summariis et indicibus.* Berlin: Adolf Cohn *Verlag und Antiquariat,* 1875.

———. *Sefer ha-Madda'.* Jerusalem: Mossad Harav Kook, 1976.

———. "Treatise on Logic." In *Proceedings of the American Academy for Jewish Research* 34 (1966) [Heb. section]: 1–136.

Malino, Jonathan. "Aristotle on Eternity: Does Maimonides Have a Reply?" In *Maimonides and Philosophy,* ed. Shlomo Pines and Yirmiahu Yovel, 52–64. Dordrecht: Martinus Nijhoff, 1986.

———. "Scientific Cosmology and Creation." In *Creation and the End of Days: Judaism and Scientific Cosmology,* ed. David Novak and Norbert Samuelson, 157–183. Lanham, Md.: University Press of America, 1986.

Manekin, Charles. "Belief, Certainty and Divine Attributes in the Guide of the Perplexed." *Maimonidean Studies* 1 (1990): 117–141.

———. "Maimonides on Divine Knowledge: Moses of Narbonne's Averroist Reading." *American Catholic Philosophical Quarterly* 76 (2002): 51–74.

———. *On Maimonides.* Belmont, Calif.: Thomson Wadsworth, 2005.

Marenbon, John. "Eternity." In *The Cambridge Companion to Medieval Philosophy,* ed. A. S. McGrade, 51–72. Cambridge: Cambridge Univeristy Press, 2003.

Marmura, Michael. *Probing in Islamic Philosophy: Studies in the Philosophies of Ibn Sīnā, al-Ghazālī and Other Major Muslim Thinkers.* New York: Global Academic, 2005.

———. "Some Aspects of Avicenna's Theory of God's Knowledge of Particulars." *Journal of the American Oriental Society* 82 (1969): 299–312.

Marquet, Yves. "Sabeens et Ihwan al-Safa'." *Studia Islamica* 24 (1966): 35–109; 25 (1966): 77–109.

Marx, Alexander. "Texts by and about Maimonides." *Jewish Quarterly Review* 25 (1934–35): 371–428.

Mayer, Toby. "Ibn Sīnā'a 'Burhān al-Ṣiddiqīn.'" *Journal of Islamic Studies* 12 (2001): 18–39.

Miller, Barry. *The Fullness of Being: A New Paradigm for Existence.* Notre Dame, Ind.: University of Notre Dame Press, 2002.

———. *A Most Unlikely God: A Philosophical Enquiry into the Nature of God.* Notre Dame, Ind.: University of Notre Dame Press, 1996.

Motzkin, Aryeh. "On the Interpretation of Maimonides." *Independent Journal of Philosophy* 2 (1978): 39–46.

Netton, Ian Richard. *Muslim Neoplatonists: An Introduction to the Thought of the Brethren of Purity (Ikhwān al-Ṣafā').* London: Allen and Unwin, 1982.

Neuegebauer, Otto. "The Astronomy of Maimonides and Its Sources." *Hebrew Union College Annual* 2 (1949): 321–364.

Nuriel, Abraham. *Concealed and Revealed in Medieval Jewish Philosophy* [Heb.]. Jerusalem: Magnes, 2000.

Olsson, Erik. *Against Coherence: Truth, Probability, and Justification.* Oxford: Clarendon, 2005.

Outhwaite, Ben, and Freidrich Niessen. "A Newly Discovered Autograph Fragment of Maimonides' 'Guide for the Perplexed' from the Cairo Genizah." *Journal of Jewish Studies* 2 (2006): 287–297.

Pines, Shlomo. "The Limitations of Human Knowledge according to al-Farabi, ibn Bajja, and Maimonides." In *Studies in Medieval Jewish History and Literature,* ed. Isadore Twersky, 82–109. Cambridge, Mass.: Harvard University Press, 1979.

———. "The Philosophic Purport of Halachic Works and the Purport of the Guide of the Perplexed." In *Maimonides and Philosophy,* ed. Shlomo Pines and Yirmiahu Yovel, 1–14. Dordrecht: Martinus Nijhoff, 1986.

———. "Translator's Introduction: The Philosophical Sources of the Guide of the Perplexed." In Maimonides, *The Guide of the Perplexed,* translated by Shlomo Pines, lvii–cxxxiv. Chicago: Chicago University Press, 1963.

Pitron Torah: A Collection of Midrashim and Interpretations, ed. Ephraim E. Urbach. Jerusalem: Magnes, 1978.

Plantinga, Alvin. "De Re et de Dicto." *Nous* 3 (1969): 235–258.

Rahman, Fazlur, ed. *Avicenna's Psychology,* English translation of *Kitāb al-Najāt,* book 2, chapter VI. London: Oxford University Press, 1952.

———. "Essence and Existence in Avicenna." *Medieval and Renaissance Studies* 4 (1958):1–16.

———. "Essence and Existence in Ibn Sīnā: The Myth and the Reality." *Hamdard Islamicus* 4 (1981): 3–14.

Ravitzky, Aviezer. "Creation or Eternity according to Maimonides." [Heb.] *Tarbiẓ* 35 (1966): 333–348.

———. "Maimonides: Esotericism and Educational Philosophy." In *The Cambridge Companion to Maimonides,* ed. Kenneth Seeskin, 300–323. Cambridge, U.K.: Cambridge University Press, 2005.

———. "The Secrets of Maimonides: Between the Thirteenth and Twentieth Centuries." In *Studies in Maimonides,* ed. Isadore Twersky, 159–207. Cambridge, Mass: Harvard University Press, 1990.

———. "'To the Utmost of Human Capacity': Maimonides on the Days of the Messiah." In *Perspectives on Maimonides: Philosophical and Historical Studies.* ed. Joel Kraemer, 221–256. Oxford: Oxford University Press, 1991.

Ravven, Heidi. "Some Thoughts on What Spinoza Learned from Maimonides about the Prophetic Imagination: Part 1. Maimonides on Prophecy and the Imagination." *Journal of the History of Philosophy* 39 (2001): 193–214.

Raz, Shoey. "Metaphysics and the Account of the Chariot: Maimonides and Isḥaq Ibnul Laṭif" [Heb.]. In *Maimonides and Mysticism,* ed. A. Elqayam and D. Schwartz, 133–164. Ramat Gan: Bar-Ilan University Press, 2009.

Reines, Alvin. "Maimonides' Concept of Mosaic Prophecy." *Hebrew Union College Annual* 40–41 (1969–1970): 325–361.

———. "Maimonides' Concepts of Providence and Theodicy." *Hebrew Union College Annual* 43 (1972): 169–206.

———. "Maimonides' True Belief concerning God." In *Maimonides and Philosophy,* ed. Shlomo Pines and Yirmiahu Yovel, 24–25. Dordrecht: Martinus Nijhoff, 1986.

Robinson, James T., ed. *The Cultures of Maimonideanism: New Approaches to the History of Jewish Thought.* Leiden: Brill, 2009.

Rosenberg, Shalom. "On Biblical Exegesis in the *Guide*" [Heb.] *Jerusalem Studies in Jewish Thought* 1 (1981): 85–157.

Rosenzweig, Franz. *The Star of Redemption,* translated by William Hallo. London: Routledge and Kegan Paul, 1971.

Rudavsky, Tamar. *Maimonides.* Chichester, U.K.: Wiley-Blackwell, 2010.

Scholem, Gershom. *Jewish Gnosticism, Merkabah Mysticism, and Talmudic Tradition.* New York: Jewish Theological Seminary of America, 1965.

Schwarz, Dov. *Astral Magic in Medieval Jewish Thought* [Heb.]. Tel Aviv: Aḥva, 1999.

Seeskin, Kenneth. *Maimonides on the Origin of the World.* Cambridge, U.K.: Cambridge University Press, 2005.

———. "Sanctity and Silence: The Religious Significance of Maimonides' Negative Theology." *American Catholic Philosophical Quarterly* 76 (2002): 7–24.

———. *Searching for a Distant God: The Legacy of Maimonides.* New York: Oxford University Press, 2000.

Shapiro, Marc. *The Limits of Orthodoxy.* Oxford: Oxford University Press, 2004.

————. "Maimonidean Halachah and Superstition." *Maimonidean Studies* 4 (2000): 61–108.

Shatz, David. "Maimonides' Moral Theory." In *The Cambridge Companion to Maimonides,* ed. Kenneth Seeskin, 167–192. Cambridge, U.K.: Cambridge University Press, 2005.

Shiloah, Amnon. *The Epistle on Music of the Ikhwan Al-Safa.* Tel-Aviv: Tel Aviv University Press, 1978.

Shmidman, Michael. "On Maimonides' Conversion to Kabbalah." In *Studies in Medieval Jewish History and Literature,* ed. Isadore Twersky, 379–384. Cambridge, Mass: Harvard University Press, 1984.

Shneur Zalman of Liadi. *Liqqutey Amarim.* London: Soncino, 1973.

Silver, Daniel. *Maimonidean Criticism and the Maimonidean Controversy, 1180–1240.* Leiden: Brill, 1965.

Stern, Josef. "Maimonides' Conceptions of Freedom and the Sense of Shame." In *Freedom and Moral Responsibility: General and Jewish Perspectives,* ed. Charles Manekin, 217–266. Bethesda: University Press of Maryland, 1997.

————. "Maimonides' Demonstrations: Principles and Practice." *Medieval Philosophy and Theology* 10 (2001): 47–84.

————. "Maimonides' Epistemology." In *The Cambridge Companion to Maimonides,* ed. Kenneth Seeskin, 105–133. Cambridge, U.K.: Cambridge University Press, 2005.

————. "Maimonides on Language and the Science of Language." In *Maimonides and the Sciences,* ed. Robert S. Cohen and Hillel Levine, 173–226. Dordrecht: Kluwer, 2000.

————. *Problems and Parables of Law: Maimonides and Nahmanides on Reasons for the Commandments (Ta'amei ha-Mitzvot).* Albany: State University of New York Press, 1998.

Stitskin, Leon. "Maimonides' Unbending Opposition to Astrology." *Tradition* 13 (1972): 131–142.

Strauss, Leo. *Persecution and the Art of Writing.* Chicago: University of Chicago Press, 1988.

Stroumsa, Sarah. *Maimonides in His World: Portrait of a Mediterranean Thinker.* Princeton, N.J., and Oxford: Princeton University Press, 2009.

————. "Note on Maimonides' Attitude to Joseph Ibn Ṣaddiq." *Jerusalem Studies in Jewish Thought* 9 (1990): 210–215.

Swerdlow, N. M. "Ptolemy's Harmonics and the Tones of the Universe in the Canobic Inscription." In *Studies in the History of the Exact Sciences,* ed. Charles Burnett et al., 137–180. Leiden: Brill, 2004.

Touati, Charles. "Le Problème de l'Inerrance Prophetique dans la Théologie Juive du Moyen Age." *Revue de l'Histoire des Religions* 174 (1968): 169–187.

Trachtenberg, Joshua. *Jewish Magic and Superstition: A Study in Folk Religion.* New York: Atheneum, 1979.

Twersky, Isadore. *Introduction to* The Code of Maimonides. New Haven, Conn.: Yale University Press, 1980.

Vallicella, William. *A Paradigm Theory of Existence: Ontotheology Vindicated.* Dordrecht: Kluwer, 2002.

Walker-Ramisch, Sandra. "Between the Lines: Maimonides on Providence." *Studies in Religion* 21 (1992): 29–42.

Walzer, Richard. *Al-Farabi on the Perfect State: Abū Naṣr al-Fārābī's Mabādi' Ārā' Ahl al-Madīna al-Fāḍila.* Oxford: Clarendon, 1985).

Weiss, Roslyn. "Maimonides on the End of the World." *Maimonidean Studies* 3 (1992–93): 195–218.

Weiss-Halivni, David. *Peshat and Derash.* New York: Oxford University Press, 1991.

Werblowsky R. J. Zwi. *Joseph Karo: Lawyer and Mystic.* Oxford: Oxford University Press, 1962.

Wisnovsky, Robert. *Avicenna's Metaphysics in Context.* London: Duckworth, 2003.

Wolfson, Harry. "The Amphibolous Terms in Aristotle, Arabic Philosophy and Maimonides." In *Studies in the History and Philosophy of Religion,* vol. 1, ed. Isadore Twersky and George H. Williams, 455–477. Cambridge, Mass.: Harvard University Press, 1973.

———. "The Aristotelian Predicables and Maimonides' Division of Attributes." In *Studies in the History and Philosophy of Religion,* vol. 2, ed. Isadore Twersky and George H. Williams, 161–194. Cambridge, Mass.: Harvard University Press, 1977.

———. *Crescas' Critique of Aristotle.* Cambridge, Mass.: Harvard University Press, 1971 [1929].

———. "Crescas on the Problem of Divine Attributes." In *Studies in the History and Philosophy of Religion,* vol. 2, ed. Isadore Twersky and George H. Williams, 247–337. Cambridge, Mass.: Harvard University Press, 1977.

———. "Maimonides and Gersonides on Divine Attributes as Ambiguous Terms." In *Studies in the History and Philosophy of Religion,* vol. 2, ed. Isadore Twersky and George H. Williams, 231–246. Cambridge, Mass.: Harvard University Press, 1977.

———. "Maimonides on Negative Attributes." In *Studies in the History and Philosophy of Religion,* vol. 2, ed. Isadore Twersky and George H. Williams, 195–230. Cambridge, Mass.: Harvard University Press, 1977.

———. "Maimonides on the Unity and Incorporeality of God." In *Studies in the History and Philosophy of Religion,* vol. 2, ed. Isadore Twersky and George H. Williams, 433–457. Cambridge, Mass.: Harvard University Press, 1977.

———. *Repercussions of the Kalam in Jewish Philosophy.* Cambridge, Mass.: Harvard University Press, 1979.

The Zohar, vol. 1, translated with a commentary by Daniel Matt. Stanford, Calif.: Stanford University Press, 2004.

Zonta, Mauro. *Hebrew Scholasticism in the Fifteenth Century: A History and Source Book.* Dordrecht: Springer, 2006.

INDEX

Abrabanel, Isaac, 123–124, 134, 138, 175 n.29, 188 n.25, 189 n.48
Abraham (Patriarch), 29, 36, 151
Account of the Beginning, 107–108, 110, 135–136, 197 n.71
Account of the Chariot,
  as metaphysics, 24, 107, 135–136
  as Ezekiel's vision, 24–25, 107, 110
  in the Rabbinic tradition, 134–135
  see also Secrets of the Torah
Active intellect, 113, 115, 131–132, 149, 189 n.37 (see also Intelligences)
Afterlife, 7, 132
Ahl al-Bāṭin. See Isma'ili
Akiba, Rabbi, 134
Alfarabi, 9–10, 70, 166 n.32
Amphiboly (taškīk), 58, 83, 116, 177 n.14, 189 n.48
Anagram as a method of Exegesis, 115
Analogy, 82–83
Aquinas, Thomas, 55, 82–83, 174 n.19
Aristotle, 14, 47–48, 109, 112, 124, 128, 136, 143, 153, 185 n.46
  on dialectic, 26–27
  see also creation
Ash'arites, 176 n.10
Assent (taṣdīq), 12, 17, 19, 24, 27–29, 36, 66, 156
Astrology, 147–151
Astronomy, 2, 143–144, 193 n.9, 195 n.40

Averroes, 70
Avicenna, 70–71, 73, 77, 103, 113–114, 180 n.14

Being. See existence
Benor, Ehud, 56, 97, 102–103, 104
Berman, Lawrence, 9
Blumenthal, David, 18
Brethren of Purity, 144–147, 150, 151–154, 192 n.124, 195 n.51

Cherub, 128, 190 n.63
Coherence, 19, 27, 156
Commandments, 156–159, 165 n.23
Contradictions,
  fifth cause of, 15, 104, 186 n.54
  seventh cause of, 16, 18, 20–25, 49, 105, 159–160, 170 n.89, 186 n.54
Cosmology, 124, 128
Creation,
  as dialectically proven, 17, 26–29
  as attributed to Aristotle, 28–33, 35
  as attributed to Plato, 34–39, 52–53
  as literally stated in Genesis, 31–34, 38–40
  the view of the law on, 28, 36–40
  see also divine knowledge
Crescas, Asher, 189 n.37, 190 n.78, 191 n.106
Crescas, Ḥasdai, 70–71, 73

Daiber, Hans, 166 n.32
Davidson, Herbert, 20

Definition, 57, 58, 59, 67, 77–81, 96
Demonstration 9–12, 17–19, 28,
    52–53, 92, 128, 132, 167 n.44
  absence of for creation, 29, 31, 34,
    36, 39
  of God's existence, 43, 47–49
Determinism, 96, 184 n.28
Dialectic 3, 9–20, 27–29, 36, 37, 43, 47,
    49, 53, 54, 57–58, 151, 156, 170
    n.88. See also Creation
Dilemmatic argument, 29, 49
Divine attributes, 18–19, 23, 57–61,
    69, 78, 83. See also negative
    theology
Divine knowledge, 19–20
  as causative, 85–88, 95–97, 103
  as equivocal, 89, 93–95, 104

Efodi, 164 n.14
Elements, 124–28, 130–131, 135,
    140–146, 149, 192 n.106, 197 n.71
Elisha ben Abuya, 193 n. 21
Equivocation 56–58, 76–77, 82–83, 85,
    89, 93–96, 98–99, 104, 177
    n.14, 183 n.23, 189n.48
Esotericism, 2–4, 7, 11, 13, 15–21,
    26–27, 85, 89, 133, 137,
    158–160
  and dialectic, 9–17
Eternity,
  as divine attribute, 96–97
  implications of, 35, 38, 40, 43–47, 93
  of world, 8, 18, 33, 36, 48, 160,
    175 n.30
  see also creation
Ethics, 157–159
Even-Chen, Alexander, 102
Exegesis,
  of Ezekiel, 106–133
  as purpose of the Guide, 4, 20–25, 65
Existence, 69–82
  as bound, 73–74
  as contingent, 70–71, 75–76
  distinguished from accidents, 71–73
  and divine simplicity, 75, 82–83
  hierarchy of, 74, 80
  as necessary, 69, 75–82
  and perfection, 77, 81–82
  purpose of, 52, 153
  unbounded existence, 79–82

Ezekiel (prophet), 4, 24–25, 102, 106
  mistakes of, 111, 136–146
Falaquera, Šem Tob ibn, 170 n.6,
    194 n.29
Al-falāsifa, 10, 141, 145, 150 (see also
    the philosophers)
Fāṭimid, 41
Faur, José, 168 n.62, 187 n.1
Fifth body, 141
Firmament, 123, 124, 130–131, 147
Fiqh, 9, 13
Foundations of the law, 35, 39–40,
    49–53
Fox, Marvin, 18, 170 n.88, 186 n.53
Freedom,
  divine freedom (see God)
  human freedom (see determinism)
Freudenthal, Gad, 147–149, 194 n.30

Galen, 182 n.7
al-Ġazālī, 41, 103, 171 n.16, 179 n.10
Gersonides, 55, 83, 98–99
God,
  existence of, 17, 47–49
  freedom of, 36, 39, 41, 43, 45–46,
    52, 104
  as intellect, 100–105
  knowledge of particulars, 19, 50–53,
    90–97
  modes in, 176 n.10
  and perfections, 19, 76, 81–82,
    97–99
  purpose in, 38–40, 43, 50–51
  as a simple unity, 55, 56–57, 58, 60,
    66, 69–70, 76, 79–82, 101–105,
    157
  in the vision of the Chariot, 130
  See also divine attributes and divine
    knowledge
Gutas, Dimitri, 165 n.25
Guttmann, Julius, 56

Halakah, 6, 50, 150, 183 n.22
Halevi, Judah, 180 n.16, 188 n.31
Harvey, Warren Zev, 11, 138–139, 151
Heavens,
  as cause, 128, 141, 143–146
  motion of, 8, 44, 48, 110, 119–122,
    135
  souls of, 119, 122, 141

Heḳalot literature, 135
Hints, as exegesis, evidence of
    philosophical esotericism, 122
Hoter ben Šelomo, 131
Husik, Isaac, 188 n.28

Ibn Aflāḥ, Ǧābir, 117
Ibn Baǧǧa, 143–144, 154
Ibn Ezra, Abraham, 163 n.2, 196 n.58
Ibn Judah, Joseph, 13
Ibn Ṣaddīq, Joseph, 145
Ibn Šem Toḇ, Šem Toḇ ben Joseph ben
    Šem Toḇ, 112, 123
Ibn Tibbon, Samuel, 9–10, 145, 185
    n.42, 191 n.82, 195 n.45
Idolatry, 59, 138, 148–151. See also
    Astrology
Imagination, 112, 114–116, 148
Immortality. See Afterlife
Infinite, 48, 56, 78
Intellect, 21, 30, 51, 84, 86, 93,
    174 n.19
    as image of God, 157
    limits of human, 17, 19, 40, 50, 52,
        151–154, 197 n.76
    see also God
Intelligences, 91, 102–103, 109–111,
    122, 128–130, 132, 149, 158
Intuition, 20, 114, 116
Isaiah (prophet), 114–116, 121
Isḥāq ibn Ḥunayn, 182 n.8
Isma'ili, 40–41, 144, 173 n.40
Ivry, Alfred, 171–172 n.26, 181 n.1

Jacob (patriarch), 187 n.17
Jacobs, Louis, 184 n.35
Job, 183 n.63
Jonathan ben Uzziel, 108, 125, 131
Judeo-Arabic, 6

Kabbalah, 6, 55, 175 n.1
Kafiḥ, Yosef, 171 n.20, 185 n.42
Kalām, 179 n.14. See also Dialectic
Karo, Joseph, 164 n.16
Kasher, Hannah, 102
al-Kindī, 144, 198 n.15
Klein-Braslavy, Sara, 130
Kosman, Aryeh, 185 n.46
Kraemer, Joel, 11, 13, 193 n.9
Kravitz, Leonard, 10

Langermann, Y. Tzvi, 18, 149, 153,
    195 n.40
Language, 64, 67, 78, 82–83
    God and, 54–57, 63–64, 76–77, 82,
        96, 102
Leaman, Oliver, 178 n.30
Levine, Michelle, 126, 131
Lobel, Diana, 102
Logic, 2
Lorberbaum, Yair, 16–18, 169 n.64
Luzzattto, Samuel David, 7

Maimonides,
    works (other than the Guide),
        Commentary on the Mishnah
            (Kitāb al-Siraǧ), 5, 187 n.2,
            188 n.22
        Letter on Astrology, 151
        Letter to ibn Tibbon, 9–10, 145
        Letter on Resurrection, 6
        Mishneh Torah, 6, 117, 135, 148,
            165 n.23
        Treatise on Logic, 167 n.48
    converted to Kabbalah, 6
    critique of those who posit attributes
        in God, 57–59, 61, 78
    equivocates between logical and
        metaphysical necessity?,
        44–46
    on evil, 77, 90
    Guide as dialogic teaching, 13–15,
        54, 155–156
    as heretic, 6–7, 55
    on Israel's spiritual decline, 187 n.12
    justification of for writing the
        Guide, 107–108
    life of, 5
    on misuse of dialectic, 11, 49
    relationship between different works
        of, 7–9
    on science of the law, 13, 23–24
    Thirteen Principles of, 165 n.23
    on uncertainty, 29
    use of rhetoric, 13, 90–91
    on worship of God, 148, 155,
        157–158
    See also specific topics
Malino, Jonathan, 31
Manekin, Charles, 176 n.8, 182 n. 29,
    184 n.3

Mathematics, 2, 913 n.20
Mendelssohn, Moses, 6
Merkaḅah. See Account of the Chariot
Messiah, 155
Metaphysics, 1, 2, 13, 23–24, 107, 135,
    158, 159. See also Science
Mezuzah, 157
Microcosm, 153. See also Ibn Ṣaddīq
Miller, Barry, 179 n.12. See also
    Existence
Miracles, 35, 40–41, 50–53, 100, 174
    n.25, 175 n.30
Moses (prophet) 26, 28, 29, 36, 50,
    114, 116, 151
Motion, 127–128. See also Heavens
Mysticism, 106, 157 (see also kabbalah)
    intellectual, 18
    merkaḅah, 135
Muʿatazilite, 172 n.26
Munk, Salomon, 171 n.20, 185 n.42
Music of the spheres, 123–124, 130,
    136–137, 146, 152

Naḥmanides, 175 n.1
Narboni, 114, 132, 149, 191 n.106
Necessity, 35, 37–38, 39, 43–47,
    50, 152
Negative theology, 62–64
    consistent with God's perfection,
    76–82, 97–100. See also
    Perfection
    extent of, 55–57
Neugebauer, Otto, 143
Numerology, 146
Nuriel, Abraham, 11

Onkelos, 125–126
Oral communication, 13–15, 54, 107

Perfection,
    divine, 19, 64–67, 78–79, 84, 89, 94,
    95, 96 (see also existence)
    human, 74, 102, 132, 157–159
The philosophers, 9, 53, 86, 90–92,
    100, 103, 140–145, 147,
    156–157 (see also al-falasifa)
Physics. See Science
Pines, Shlomo, 31–32, 33, 115, 145,
    147, 185 n.42, 186 n.49
    and esotericism, 8, 101, 105

on Maimonides on human
    perfection, 158
Plato, 123, 171 n.26. See also Creation
Prophecy, 110
    in the vision of the chariot, 11–116
    as a miracle, 50–51
    as a natural phenomenon, 50,
    113–114
    implications for God's
    knowledge, 52–53
Providence, 18, 23, 90–91, 119, 155,
    183 n.23
Pythagoras, 123, 136, 146–147, 154

al-Qirqisānī, Jacob, 178 n.43

Ravven, Heidi, 8
Raz, Shoey, 102
Rāzī, Fahr al-Dīn, 149
Reines, Alvin, 102
Relation, 58–60,
    between essence and accident,
    72–73
    between essence and existence,
    74–75
    between God and creatures, 61
Resurrection, 6–7
Rosenberg, Shalom, 138, 139, 150
Rosenzweig, Franz, 55
Rudavsky, Tamar, 172 n.31

Sabian, 144, 147
Šāfiʿī, Muḥammad ibn Idrīs, 149
Sages (of Talmud and Midrash), 23, 33,
    35, 97, 115, 120, 134, 136,
    147, 154
Scholem, Gershom, 135
Science, 13, 23–24, 27, 52, 87, 107,
    114, 139, 142, 148, 168 n.50
    divine, 1, 110, 135
Secrets of the Torah, 4, 22–23,
    106–110, 114, 122, 132,
    134–136
Seeskin, Kenneth, 17,
Senses (as evidence), 30, 51, 94, 96,
    151, 167 n.44
Separate intellects. See Intelligences
Shatz, David, 159
Shneur Zalman of Liadi, 6
Solomon ben Moses, 176 n.9

Soul, of sublunar creatures, 124, 128, 132, 135, 141, 192 n.124
Spheres. see Heavens
Stern, Josef, 148, 158
Strauss, Leo, 7, 9
Stroumsa, Sarah, 40, 145

Talmud, 6, 106, 130, 134–135, 136, 152, 187 n. 9, 191 n. 82
Time (see also creation)
  as measure of motion, 44
  not applicable to God, 60, 92, 96, 97
Tradition (taqlīd), 12, 29, 37, 66, 151

Unity,
  of God, 69–70, 75–76, 79–82
  of world, 177 n. 29
Universals, 52, 87, 88, 91, 93, 96, 159

Virtue, 157–159

Wolfson, Harry, 55–56, 98
World to come. See afterlife

Yemen, 18

Zohar, 6
Zonta, Mauro, 176 n.9